Creative Capacity
Development

Creative Capacity
Development

Learning to Adapt
in Development Practice

Jenny Pearson

Kumarian Press
An Imprint of Stylus Publishing

Creative Capacity Development: Learning to Adapt in Development Practice
Published in 2011 in the United States of America by Kumarian Press,
22883 Quicksilver Drive, Sterling, VA 20166 USA.

The text of this book is set in 11/13 Garamond.

Editing and book design by Nicole Hirschman
Proofread by Beth Richards
Index by Robert Swanson

The paper used in this publication meets the minimum requirements of the American National Standard for Information Sciences—Permanence of Paper for Printed
Library Materials, ANSI Z39.48–1984

Library of Congress Cataloging-in-Publication Data

Pearson, Jenny.
Creative capacity development : learning to adapt in development practice / Jenny
    Pearson.
        p.   cm.
    Includes bibliographical references and index.
    ISBN 978-1-56549-329-2 (pbk. : alk. paper) — ISBN 978-1-56549-330-8
        (casebound : alk. paper) — ISBN 978-1-56549-416-9 (library ebook) —
        ISBN 978-1-56549-417-6 (consumer ebook)
        1. Community development—Cambodia. 2. VBNK (Organization : Cambodia)
    3. Postwar reconstruction—Cambodia. 4. Economic assistance—Cambodia.
    5. Technical assistance—Cambodia. I. Title.
        HN700.3.Z9C665   2011
        331.25'9209596—dc22
                                                                    2011002058

For Jessie, Jaimie and Isabel
And all Cambodian children
That their lives may be lived to the full, in peace

Contents

Illustrations   ix
Foreword   xi
Preface   xv
Acknowledgments   xvii
Acronyms   xix
Introduction   1
    VBNK   2
    A Sense of Purpose   5
    Overview of the Chapters   6

1   Culture and Context   9
    A Note About Cambodian History   9
    On Being a Cambodian Trainer   12
    Beliefs and Behaviors   20
    Complex Trauma and Its Implications for Capacity Development   25
    Conclusions   44

2   Serving a Sector   47
    International NGOs   48
    Cambodian NGOs   53
    Royal Government of Cambodia   63
    Donors   66
    Regional Work   67
    Private Sector   70
    Keeping Pace With the Sector: An Evolving Mission   71

3   A Learning Journey   77
    First Steps   77
    Pivotal Learning   86

Developing a Learning Practice in VBNK   89
Getting Strategic About Staff Development and Learning   96
A Story to Tell   103

4   Creativity and New Dimensions of Response   107
David Glass   108
Creative Facilitators   110
Early Innovations   112
Creative Innovations for Learning and Change   119
Magic or Monster?   132

5   Organizational Nuts and Bolts   139
Funding and Fees   139
Growth, Change and Competing Agendas   142
Teamwork   158
Localization   169

Learning From the Long Haul: Some Conclusions   179
*The Essential Starting Point for Effective Capacity Development
    Is Culture, Culture, Culture!*   179
*The Psychosocial Legacy of Complex Trauma Creates Significant
    Challenges for Effective Capacity Development*   180
*Capacity Development Is a Discipline in Its Own Right, and It Is
    Values Based*   180
Learning Is a Skill That Needs to Be Learned and Practiced   181
Individual and Organizational Learning Are Inextricably Linked   182
Creativity Builds Safe Space for Change and Has Proven Benefits   182
Creativity and Learning Support Relevance and Sustainability   183
Some Simple Ideas That Anyone Can Try   183

Appendix: Post Trauma Stress Disorder and Its Relevance in   185
    Postconflict Societies
References   191
Index   195
About the Author   205

Illustrations

Figure 3.1   Learning at CDRA.   88

Figure 3.2   The Wall. Reproduced with kind permission   95
              from Arthur Delvecchio, TA, VBNK.

Figure 5.1   Organogram 2003.   155

Foreword

Capacity development as both a process and an outcome is about people changing their attitudes, relationships, and behaviors. To do this, people need motivation, incentives, space, access to resources, confidence, support, and, in some cases, political protection. And they need to master and apply new skills. Sounds straightforward so far. But, of course, it isn't. Helping us to understand *why* it isn't and, more important, what can be done better to help people develop their capabilities is the subject of Jenny Pearson's book.

This book looks, in particular, at the implementation of practices to do with knowledge, learning, and adaptation in the context of establishing in Cambodia a new NGO called VBNK in the late 1990s. We can start with the idea of knowledge. In the world of international development, knowledge in the form of generic "best practice" solutions has traditionally been given the most emphasis. Countries or organizations or individuals in partner countries are seen to have gaps or weaknesses in what they do. They need to improve. Modern strategies and techniques in the form of transferred solutions can be put in place through training or technical assistance. Something indigenous and faulty can be replaced by something imported and functional. And such an approach can, of course, be effective. Many countries in Asia, most notably Japan in the nineteenth century and China, Taiwan, and South Korea in the twentieth century, made a point of seeking out and adopting the best international practices in a variety of fields.

But we have come to know something about the limits of this approach. In countries that lack the capability to choose a strategy and implement it, external actors can assume too much power in deciding what is faulty in a country and what isn't. Many times, they get it wrong. Imported knowledge by its very nature does not originate in the context in which it is being applied. Simply put, it may not fit and may not be relevant. And what's worse, it may not even have the potential to gain the legitimacy and acceptance that is necessary to ensure its survival as part of a country's institutions. Its adoption may, in practice, end up making things worse. Part of the challenge is thus to fit indigenous and imported knowledge together into some sort of coherent evolving pattern of capacity development.

The idea of learning is another tricky issue to get right. For many people in modern technological societies, learning is an obvious key to personal and professional growth. And the more, the better. Individual effort is the key to a better future. The risks come with *not* learning or being a slow learner. But this optimistic view is not a universal one. One of the great strengths of Jenny's book is its highlighting of the dangers and discomforts that can come with learning. In the Cambodian context, learning can be constrained as it intersects with hierarchies of power, position, age, and gender. Knowing, not learning, is valued. The legacy of psychological trauma from the Khmer Rouge period can shut down the personal will to learn at a deeply personal level. The cultural permission for people to learn can be unclear. In such a context, how can "modern" approaches to reflective practice and creativity best be promoted? Is it best to go "with" or "against" the cultural grain in such circumstances?

Finally, there lies the perennial issue of dealing with uncertainty and complexity *at the same time*. Some interventions rely on the application of planning, control, and prediction. Others are more oriented toward adaptation and incrementalism. As might be expected, both are necessary in different ways and at different times and for different reasons. All of us, for example, feel the need to have a clear direction. Larger groups and organizations need some sort of strategy to help generate some sort of collective action. And government agencies, in particular, need to operate on the basis of structure and planning. And yet we know that few predetermined efforts at capacity development survive close contact with reality. "Black swans" in the form of unexpected events overturn most early choices. The real goals and interests of participants emerge only during implementation. Conventional strategic planning falls away. Flexibility and the ability to improvise become critical.

The challenge of dealing with all these capacity yins and yangs brings us back to Jenny Pearson's book. Buried deep in the heart of every successful effort at capacity development is some sort of informal sense-making and coherence-making activity. This can come from a tacit two-person partnership, a management team, or a coalition or network made up of people from the country and those from the outside. Technical assistance, it turns out, goes both ways. The resulting collaboration can enable key actors to fit ideas and practices together, to customize, to integrate, to adapt, to make relevant, and to create space and meaning. These "connectors" and "sense-makers" link up people and opportunities. They search and innovate and encourage others to do the same. They reassure, protect, and buffer. They keep things moving forward. They act as capacity entrepreneurs. They protect the integrity of the process from other groups in the government or in external agencies who would otherwise bend it out of shape. In effect, they take elements of the indigenous and the external and create a more resilient composite that has a chance of achieving some sustainability and legitimacy.

Few of these crucial skills are taught or even openly recognized, a situation that makes this book even more important. Its key contribution is to give us an inside view—most important, that of a harried practitioner—of how this sense-making and coherence-making process actually works in real life. In many ways, it charts Jenny's personal and professional journey as she struggles herself to learn the skills of reflective practice that are needed to achieve greater effectiveness in her own organization. VBNK lives on today in Cambodia as a testament to the success of her efforts.

Peter Morgan
Washington DC, USA
November 19, 2010

Preface

In July 2008, Jenny Pearson, the founder of VBNK, retired after 11 years of service to the organization. Throughout her time as director, Jenny led VBNK and its staff on a journey of learning.

On the eve of Jenny's departure, VBNK's board and senior management recognized that we were losing not only Jenny but also a big chunk of our institutional memory. Thus, when Jenny approached us about writing a book on VBNK, we were in full support. We happily gave her permission to research the myriad documents that had accumulated in the VBNK archives over the years and also to conduct one-on-one and group interviews with both former and current VBNK staff.

The journey began in April 1997, when VBNK officially opened for business. In its first year, VBNK offered a curriculum of open access courses targeting managers of NGOs who needed core management and project management skills. By 1999, VBNK had begun to broaden its capacity to respond to increasing demands for a wider range of services, including from NGOs, from institutions and agencies from central and local government, from multilateral and bilateral donors, and from the private sector, all contributing to the social development sector in Cambodia. VBNK began to grow in response to these needs.

A partnership with the David Glass Ensemble led to the Center for Creative Development at VBNK. The work of the CCD helped shape the development of CHART (Creative Holistic Action-research for Relationship Transformation), an action learning project aiming to promote locally relevant, process-oriented, and empowering development practice within Cambodia. Other innovations were a subsequent Women's Leadership Program, tailored to women leaders in government, and a Leadership Development Program, working with mid- and senior-level NGO managers. Linking creativity to development practice is now a proven approach to helping individuals unlearn old habits and reconstruct the narratives guiding their personal and professional lives.

Embedded in VBNK's approach to creativity and learning has been an ever-deepening appreciation of the barriers to individual and organizational change and growth that the cultural context has imposed and the psychosocial legacy of the complex trauma that years of conflict have embedded in Cambodian society. Training and organizational development interventions are designed to recognize these barriers to change and to provide space for individuals and organizations to explore new ways of thinking, working, and relating to others.

Today, VBNK's program still includes training services, but there is an increased emphasis on the dual methodologies of coaching and training to deepen learning for individuals and teams and also on a holistic approach to organizational development of Cambodian NGOs. This approach has clearly demonstrated that moving beyond traditional training and organizational development interventions into processes that promote learning and its integration into everyday work practices has positive and lasting impacts.

Under Jenny's guidance, and mindful of the need to keep building its own capacity, VBNK strengthened its efforts to become a learning organization and to be more strategic in its approach to learning and development. While all VBNK staff members remember Jenny for her leadership in all of the various achievements described above, they most readily testify to how she contributed to their personal growth.

We warmly congratulate and thank Jenny for this excellent and insightful documentation of VBNK's experiences with creativity and learning in capacity development in Cambodia—with the closely intertwined threads of her personal learning journey and the experience of integrating learning into VBNK's programs and practices woven throughout the book. We believe that *Creative Capacity Development: Learning to Adapt in Development Practice* will be a valuable resource for development practitioners in Cambodia and that there is much that the global development community can learn from both Jenny's and VBNK's experiences in developing and successfully applying a learning approach to capacity development.

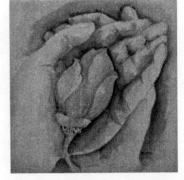

Cheryl Urashima   Graeme Storer
Chair, VBNK Board   Director, VBNK
   of Directors
October 2010

Acknowledgments

Above all, my thanks must go to the staff of VBNK, past and present, for all they contributed to VBNK's success and for all I learned during the years of working with them. It is impossible to name them all individually, but I must mention some because of their special contributions and years of loyal service. Leng Chhay, Men Maronel, Phum Thol, and Vanly Virya for being willing and able to step into the space and lead the learning. Mov Lean, Sim Noreth, Sok Sovanmealy, Som Dany, and Tan Chantha, who have traveled the road from the start, and all the other women who inspired me with their dignity, resilience, and bravery along the way. Chi Sothy, Khe Sothoeun, Mour Meng Hong, Ou Saorn, Srey Saren, Srey Vanthorn, Tem Sokchea, and Vong Thavy, who continue the good work. Finally, the long-term support team members, Chu Sokha, Eang Sarin, Hay Ngin, Men Sothearun, Ngov Sambath, Thong Kheng, Touch Chean, Sin San, and Sok Sarim, and, most especially, Chheav Navuth for years of getting me safely through Phnom Penh traffic. Expatriate colleagues through the years were fewer, but even so there were too many to mention all. I would like to say a special thank you to Conor Boyle, Sally Brooks, and Paul Masson for sharing the load, each in their own way; to Nicol Levick for all that I learned from her; to Arthur Delvecchio for knowing what it means to be an adviser; and to Nigel Goddard and Enda Moclair for making my dream project a reality.

Many others supported me and VBNK by giving their time and expertise as members of the VBNK board, and I feel fortunate to also count many of them as friends—Josephine Barbour, Roger Biggs, and David Saumweber all made an extra contribution by serving as the chair, as did Chhim Vandeth, Lim Siv Hong, Thong Beauphara, and Sharon Wilkinson by serving for the full six years allowed. I must also make special mention of Cheryl Urashima, who helped us start VBNK when she was in a different role and then, as chair of the board, oversaw the transition to my successor. She also gave me invaluable support when I was writing this book.

Very special thanks are due to Karl Schoenberg and Henk Bakker, and to all their colleagues in EED and ICCO, who worked to make VBNK's relationship with them a real partnership beyond the budget.

Among the many consultants who contributed to VBNK, I owe a special debt to Jan Willem Rosenboom, who helped us get started; to Moira O'Leary and Meas Nee for Learning for Transformation and so very much more; to David Glass, Rob Hale, and Matthew Jones for the love and creative inspiration they shared so generously; and to Leang Seckon for helping us find new ways to express who we are.

We worked with many, many different organizations and participants over the years: my gratitude goes to them all for trusting us to help them on their journeys. I also learned a great deal from the interactions I had with others in the development world, most particularly from James Taylor, his colleagues at CDRA in Cape Town, and other practitioners I met at CDRA events and also from staff and other members of the INTRAC Praxis Project Catalyst Group. It was through the Praxis Project that I first met Peter Morgan, whose own work has contributed so much to understandings of capacity development and who has encouraged and supported me throughout the writing of this book: I am especially grateful to him. I am also grateful to Professor Lawrence Haddad, and the Participation, Power and Social Change team at the Institute of Development Studies, who gave me the time and space in 2007 to start distilling and writing about my learning with VBNK.

I thank Jim Lance at Kumarian Press for his belief in the story that I have to tell and his encouraging support while I have been writing it. Others who generously gave time to reviewing parts or all of various drafts and made invaluable comments and contributions are Lucy Carter, Beth Goldring, Jane Martin, Ashley Macpherson, Ellen Minotti, and Luisa Perticucci. I am grateful to Roo Griffiths for her editing and patient Americanization of my English English.

The development community in Cambodia is a constantly changing group of Cambodians and expatriates coming and going, and a few who stay. Many people I have met during the years have helped, challenged, and inspired me with professional support and personal friendship in ways too numerous to mention. I thank them all.

Last but by no means least, I would like to thank my successor, Graeme Storer, for his considerable support in the writing of this book, for pulling off the remarkable feat of enabling me to leave fully but also stay connected in the happiest of ways, and for energizing VBNK with new commitment to the journey.

Acronyms

ACR	Australian Catholic Relief
ADB	Asian Development Bank
AIDS	Acquired Immune Deficiency Syndrome
ALC	Action Learning Cycle
ARLP	Action–Reflection–Learning–Planning
ASEAN	Association of Southeast Asian Nations
AusAID	Australian Agency for International Development
BFC	Better Factories Cambodia
CCC	Cooperation Committee for Cambodia
CCD	Center for Creative Development
CDRA	Community Development Resource Association (South Africa)
CHART	Creative Holistic Action-research for Relationship Transformation
CIDSE	*Coopération Internationale pour le Développement et la Solidarité* (International Cooperation for Development and Solidarity)
CNGO	Cambodian NGO
CNSN	Cambodian NGO Support Network
CPP	Cambodian People's Party
CWS	Church World Service
DCA	DanChurchAid
DNA	Deoxyribonucleic Acid
EED	*Evangelische Entwicklungsdienst* (Church Development Service)
ELC	Experiential Learning Cycle
EU	European Union

EZE	*Evangelische Zentralstelle für Entwicklungshilfe* (Church Center for Development Aid)
FUNCINPEC	*Front Uni National pour un Cambodge Indépendant, Neutre, Pacifique, et Coopératif* (National United Front for an Independent, Neutral, Peaceful, and Cooperative Cambodia)
HI	Handicap International
HIV	Human Immunodeficiency Virus
HR	Human Resources
ICCO	Interchurch Organisation for Development Cooperation
ILO	International Labour Organization
INGO	International NGO
INTRAC	International NGO Training and Research Centre
IO	International Organization
IPP	ICCO Partners Project
LDP	Leadership Development Program
LIP	Learning Implementation Plan
MDP	Managers Development Program
MOU	Memorandum of Understanding
NGO	Nongovernmental Organization
PDP	Proposal Development Program
PTSD	Post Trauma Stress Disorder
RGC	Royal Government of Cambodia
SWOT	Strengths, Weaknesses, Opportunities, and Threats
TA	Technical Adviser
TTM	Traditional Tibetan Medicine
UK	United Kingdom
UN	United Nations
UNDP	United Nations Development Programme
UNTAC	UN Transitional Authority in Cambodia
US	United States
USAID	US Agency for International Development
VBNK	Institute to Serve Facilitators of Development
VSO	Voluntary Service Overseas
WLP	Women's Leadership Program
WSP	Water and Sanitation Project
WTO	World Trade Organization

Introduction

This is the story of a learning journey that many individuals have traveled together. At its heart lie an organization and its staff, working to make learning and creativity their way of life, as well as my own journey as an expatriate working to support capacity development in Cambodia over 15 years. Yet, while the focus is on one particular organization, the challenges faced and the lessons learned are relevant to all development organizations and practitioners everywhere.

This is a story of a nongovernmental organization (NGO) trying to improve the quality of its program by being a learning organization and, within this, by developing individual staff capacity to support social development in a postconflict environment. It is about recognizing both individual and systemic blocks to change and being willing to experiment with and embrace creative approaches from multiple disciplines in order to be more effective in challenging intractable development problems. It is about understanding that we have to *be* the change we want to see and struggling to achieve this reality. It is about ensuring integrity by having internal practices that match public commitments on issues such as gender equality, participatory processes, and transparent governance. It is a story of successes and failures and of what has been learned from both. It is about achieving organizational sustainability through constant monitoring of the external environment and making internal adaptations to keep the program relevant. It is about recognizing and working with capacity development as an important discipline in its own right rather than treating it as an assumed by-product of other activities. Finally, it is about trying to influence the broader development sector in positive ways through ideas and example. While this last is hard to do, and almost impossible to assess, individually and collectively all development organizations should aspire to create positive impact beyond their own immediate sphere of operations. Thus, the themes in this story are issues with which all development organizations and professionals should be concerned.

Einstein said, "We can't solve problems by using the same kind of thinking we used when we created them," which seems particularly pertinent for many development challenges. In countries like Cambodia, culture comes together with experiences of war and trauma to create multiple substantive blocks to change and development. In such a context, capacity can neither flourish nor be sustainable if development methods simply uphold or repeat the conditions and processes that were instrumental in repressing potential in the first place. Nor will change happen if development practitioners continue to use the approaches, tools, and techniques that replicate past ineffectiveness. There are no easy or simple answers. Being effective within such complexity requires challenging stuck worldviews and development paradigms so that it is possible to break unhelpful patterns of response. As the French novelist André Gide said, "One does not discover new lands without consenting to lose sight of the shore for a very long time." We will find the new lands of effective capacity development practice only if we consent to let go of the comfort of control and predicted outcomes. The complex systems within which we work call for us to take creative risks and learn together in order to stimulate new ways of being, doing, and thinking, starting with ourselves as practitioners and change agents.

A central premise of this book is that people achieving their full potential is not just a matter of intellectual accomplishment but also about being physically, emotionally, and spiritually healthy. This holistic conception of capacity makes it impossible to define end results, because we cannot know how things will look when people are truly able to achieve their full potential, hence the need to let go of control and predicted outcomes. This book sets out to show how one organization risked moving beyond simplistic answers and to show the successes and challenges that emerged as it traveled the road of creativity and learning.

VBNK

The organization at the center of the story is called VBNK, an English acronym for its Khmer name that means Institute to Serve Facilitators of Development. VBNK is a not-for-profit NGO with no political or religious affiliations. It is a support organization, a very particular type of development agency that does not provide financial support to the organizations with which it works. Instead, support organizations offer a range of services designed to enhance the capacity of other organizations to deliver their own programs. Some support organizations are independent; some are membership based or network based.

A few are in Northern countries working internationally with NGO communities in both the North and the South. The vast majority are national entities working within one country or region. If Cambodia is any indication of the norm, the proportion of support organizations to implementing organizations is very small indeed, maybe less than 1%.

By its very nature, the term "support organization" implies strength, embodying the knowledge, skills, and expertise needed to support the capacity development of other organizations. This raises some unique challenges for national support organizations in developing countries because while they may provide services very similar to those of their Northern counterparts, there is one fundamental difference between them. Northern support organizations are generally able to recruit personnel who already have the qualifications and experience necessary to work effectively, whereas the majority of national support organizations need first to develop the capacity of their own staff so that they are able to facilitate the capacity development of others. This is also true for international NGOs (INGOs) with national staff implementing in-country partnership programs that provide both funding and capacity-building support to local NGOs. So, while the focus may be much sharper for a support organization, the issues are applicable to all developing country-based agencies with a capacity development mandate.

Being a support organization presents a number of interesting opportunities and challenges. The opportunities lie in being able to work with and have a positive impact on many individuals and organizations across multiple disciplines. There are always opportunities to go beyond reactive responses to requests, to be proactive in recognizing emerging trends and challenges, and to offer creative responses. Keeping the organization relevant also involves taking risks by challenging people and organizations to work with new ideas when it becomes clear that old approaches are not achieving the desired results.

The challenges are many, starting with the fact that a support organization is heavily dependent on having a good reputation in its target community and that this is only ever as good as the last satisfied customer's word. In a small community where word travels fast, there is little margin for error. Second, as a general rule, each customer needs a service only once, and the limited need for repetition creates a constant demand for something new. A third challenge is that identifying results beyond participant satisfaction and learning requires longitudinal follow-up, which needs to take into account other influential factors: in complex working environments, it is impossible to claim that any one intervention is solely responsible for behavior change or project impact. A final major challenge is that of costing. Being proactive and experimenting through creativity and learning require an investment of time and resources that market prices for the services delivered cannot sustain.

VBNK was established as a support organization in response to an identified need for NGO staff in Cambodia to acquire management skills. It has never been part of VBNK's mandate to work at a community or service delivery level, and its contributions to Cambodia's development have always been made indirectly, through services to build the capacity of staff and organizations directly engaged in social development activities. VBNK's success and sustainability are therefore dependent on three key factors:

- the quality of its relationships with the sector it serves,
- its ability to maintain constant and finely nuanced monitoring of the sector and the external environment in order to identify emerging trends and needs, and
- its ability to adapt strategically and appropriately in response to changes in the sector and environment.

As Chapter 2, "Serving a Sector," describes, VBNK started as a management training institute for the NGO sector, offering a curriculum of open access courses on core and project management skills. Very early on, clients began requesting assistance with organizational development processes, and VBNK expanded its services to meet this demand. The original focus on both predefined courses and the NGO target group had to change and expand. VBNK is now known as an institute offering creative approaches for a range of program and organizational development needs; training is just one strand in an array of facilitation, consulting, and coaching methods offered. Response to the environment also entailed extending the target group beyond the NGO community to cover a broader group of social development agencies.

VBNK is at the creative edge of capacity development practice in Cambodia, and its methods and philosophies have attracted interest and support from elsewhere. Taking a leading role in informing and influencing others requires that an organization continually push itself to integrate and practice its own innovations before it can introduce them with integrity to others. VBNK's practices have prompted others to adopt new thinking and practices, and we frequently find exciting synergies with other creative thinkers who want to do things differently. But being ahead of the curve has its challenges, most notably in terms of the ability of staff to grasp and work with new ideas, making organizational life a constantly evolving set of finely tuned balances between innovation and internal capacity. There are usually very long gaps between an inspiring new idea and the point when others have sufficient understanding to implement it competently. I was always aware that we could go only as fast as the staff could keep up, requiring unending compromise between ambitions and realities.

A Sense of Purpose

On any journey, the horizon is a moving target. As the traveler progresses, different aspects of the landscape come into view and change her or his perspective on the terrain. There is awareness that moving forward will bring something new and different into focus, but there are no certainties as to what it might be or look like. I have a social work background and, supported by Voluntary Service Overseas (VSO), I came to Cambodia from the United Kingdom in 1995 as a volunteer, full of hopes about what I might achieve in a two-year training project. I think I actually believed this might be enough time to transfer enough knowledge and skills to a group of Cambodians to make them effective NGO managers. My first encounters with Cambodian realities soon taught me that I had to think about what I was doing very differently and take it one step at a time. Yes, people were learning things in my training courses, but for many different reasons that learning didn't immediately result in them being able to take over from expatriates. Later, people seemed to assume that I, as VBNK's director, had a strong vision. This tended to surprise me because while I was always committed to the organization's vision statement, I didn't think of it as a personal vision. I think what people saw was a strong sense of purpose guiding my work. In keeping with the values and practices of my social work background, I tend to focus on individuals. The more I understood the real situation in Cambodia,[1] the more I shifted my focus away from skills building toward the people behind the position titles. I tried to find approaches that might contribute to helping Cambodians overcome the legacy of their traumatic past.

The two-pronged strategy that I adopted in my work was the result of my gaining an understanding of Cambodian culture and the psychosocial impact of complex trauma. First, there continues to be a big need for Cambodians to acquire knowledge and skills so that, whatever their role, they know what they should be doing and how to do it well. It is necessary to start with a realistic assessment of existing capabilities and potential and then accompany people step-by-step on their developmental journey. I applied this approach equally to our program and to how we managed the organization internally. The other part of the strategy was to create the time, space, and means for people to explore practices that might help them heal. In my working context, healing does not mean using medical models or offering therapy. It means exploring and drawing on the learning of multiple disciplines to find approaches and activities with proven therapeutic results. Some simple activities can be extremely effective aids for healing. For example, telling your story can provide release; learning to talk to your neighbors can start to build trust and relationships; painting can be a channel for expressing that which cannot be put into words. Over time, I came to understand the strong role that cultural factors played as blocks to progress and so broadened the approach to incorporate ways that challenged people to examine their own culture and decide for themselves which aspects of it might be inhibiting their progress.

But life was a series of checks and balances: sometimes I thought I understood things and then realized I didn't. Other times, I had a useful insight but didn't know how to translate it into meaningful action. I wanted to work in new ways, but it was necessary always to keep the work on core skills on track and also to ensure that the staff were ready to embrace a new initiative. However wonderful a creative idea may be, there is nothing to be gained from being so far ahead that others can make no connection with what you are doing.

Implementing these strategies became increasingly complex as we moved beyond skills building, because we were continually deepening our understanding of the cultural and experiential complexities that prevent skills from being put into practice and that inhibit learning and change in the broadest sense. The more I understood, the more I realized that a healing approach is much more likely than skills building to lead to positive change and that this involves working in ways that help people unlearn old habits so they can be open to new and different ideas. This can be done in many ways, ranging from gentle persuasion to constructive confrontations. As I hope to show in what follows, working creatively is a particularly effective and enjoyable way to address these deep and difficult issues.

Overview of the Chapters

The chapters that follow do not tell the story of VBNK and its learning journey chronologically. Instead, I present the themes and issues under their own headings, trying to show where there are important linkages between them. (Note that unless otherwise indicated, block quotes cite internal private documents of VBNK, 1999–2008.) Chapter 1, "Culture and Context," sets the scene for all that follows. After a very brief summary of the past 60 years of Cambodian history, I start, in the section "On Being a Cambodian Trainer," with an analysis of the cultural factors that influence staff attitudes toward their work and that create substantive hurdles in the way of trainers becoming learners and facilitators. This is followed in the section "Beliefs and Behaviors" by an exploration of the more general values and cultural issues that have surfaced in VBNK's organizational life. The concluding part of this section, "Complex Trauma and Its Implications for Capacity Development," is a summary of what I have learned from disciplines such as psychology and mental health relevant to the Cambodian postconflict context. The complex relationship between culture and the psychosocial legacies of war and trauma explains a great deal about blocks to learning and change. I show how understanding the psychosocial impact of complex trauma is an essential prerequisite to understanding the complexities of capacity development in a postconflict society. The appendix provides a brief analysis of why post trauma stress disorder is insufficient to understand postconflict societies fully, including some short examples from other countries.

Chapter 2, "Serving a Sector," provides a description of the growth and changes in the subsections of the development community in Cambodia since the early 1990s and how VBNK has supported these. The two main groups are described in "International NGOs" and "Cambodian NGOs," followed by shorter comments in "Royal Government of Cambodia," "Donors," "Regional Work," and "Private Sector." This chapter concludes in "Keeping Pace With the Sector: An Evolving Mission" with a review of how VBNK has regularly refreshed its program and mission in order to stay relevant to the changing social development sector it serves.

In Chapter 3, "A Learning Journey," I recount the steps and complexities in the long-term staff and organizational development processes that VBNK has worked with since its establishment. The section "First Steps" describes the very intense staff development program of the first few years, which, despite being comprehensive, did not result in the expected development of capacity because, we later realized, we were not addressing the right issues. In "Pivotal Learning," I describe how attending a course in South Africa gave me both the insights and the ideas I needed to start doing things differently. "Developing a Learning Practice in VBNK" describes how difficult it can be to change attitudes and develop a learning culture and that basic messages need constant repetition and reiteration in order for them to become embedded in organizational culture. This is followed by "Getting Strategic About Staff Development and Learning," in which I describe how we developed strategies to link all the key elements of our staff and organizational development into a cohesive whole that responded to our circumstances and program needs. Concluding the chapter with "A Story to Tell," I pull together my key findings on learning within VBNK's particular contextual and cultural circumstances.

Chapter 4, "Creativity and New Dimensions of Response," is where I describe the way that VBNK has worked with creative processes for both internal and program development and how this unique approach has put VBNK at the cutting edge of capacity development practice. The first parts of the chapter, "David Glass" and "Creative Facilitators," describe how we did it. I then go through "Early Innovations" and "Creative Innovations for Learning and Change" to describe the ways we used to integrate creativity into the program. Finally, in "Magic or Monster?" I analyze the benefits and pitfalls of using creative practices in the development context, concluding with a summary of the very real and proven benefits that can flow for both individuals and organizations when creative practices are used appropriately.

Chapter 5, "Organizational Nuts and Bolts," is a brief summary of some aspects of organizational life behind the story of creativity and learning, which show that the road to innovation is by no means straight and smooth. This section covers "Funding and Fees," "Growth, Change and Competing Agendas," "Teamwork," and "Localization," which is a description of why VBNK did not localize to Cambodian management, as originally intended. In the brief concluding "Learning From the Long Haul: Some Conclusions," I summarize what I believe to be the most important points about learning and creativity for capacity development and give a few pointers on how others might incorporate some simple, but effective, practices into their organizational life.

Note

1. I have been helped enormously in my understanding of Cambodians, their beliefs, and their experiences by having met some members of a Cambodian family very shortly after I arrived here and by living with three generations of that family for more than a decade now.

1

Culture and Context

A Note About Cambodian History

At the mention of Cambodia, many people respond with a comment about the Khmer Rouge regime, which lasted from April 1975 to January 1979 and is rightly known as one of the most brutal and devastating episodes of the twentieth century. What few people realize, however, is that this period was just one in a history of tumultuous upheaval caused by civil and regional wars lasting decades. It was a time of intense political chaos and change that is far too complicated to recount in detail here, so what follows is a very simple chronology of the main events since World War II.

Cambodia had been a French colony, known collectively with Laos and Vietnam as French Indochina, for nearly 150 years when King Sihanouk ascended the throne in 1941, aged only 18. The French apparently believed that this young king would be easier to control than any of the other possible choices, but they had made a mistake. King Sihanouk proved to be an astute political negotiator in the years of turmoil following World War II and the Japanese occupation of Cambodia, and, as a result of his efforts, Cambodia achieved independence in 1953. But the years before and after independence and the transition to a constitutional monarchy were marked by complex political maneuvering, which gave rise to many competing factions that were to be influential in the coming decades. A very simple summary is that various parties and factions aligned themselves in two key groupings: the communists and procommunists, who led the left-wing resistance to the French throughout the region, and those on the right, who supported the king and his anticommunist policies.

In 1955, King Sihanouk abdicated the throne to lead a national political movement *Sangkum Reastr Niyum* (People's Socialist Community). For the next 15 years, the *Sangkum Reastr Niyum* governed the country, with the now Prince Sihanouk ruling as both prime minister and head of state for more than a decade. Changes started to happen in 1966, when General Lon Nol, then a supporter of the prince, was appointed prime minister, with the prince retaining his controlling role as head of state. Sihanouk kept Cambodia out of direct engagement in the American–Vietnamese war[1] but not out of the national and international political turmoil that swirled relentlessly throughout the region during those years. Opposition to Sihanouk and his style of rule strengthened as national and regional events became ever more complex. Views about this period are sharply divided between those who think it was a golden age and those who believe it was an era of totalitarian incompetence that set the scene for the horrors that followed.

In 1970, Prime Minister Lon Nol fronted the opposition that ousted Prince Sihanouk from office while he was out of the country. Supported by governments in the region, Sihanouk rallied troops to try to reclaim his position, and the country plunged into civil war. Over the next five years, the Communist Party of Kampuchea, which the prince dubbed the Khmer Rouge, systematically gained control of both rural areas and opposition factions. By early 1975, it had the country under its control and the capital, Phnom Penh, under siege. In April, Khmer Rouge soldiers entered the city, overthrew the Lon Nol government and declared the state of Democratic Kampuchea.

It is a cruel irony that many Cambodians, tired of the years of war, initially welcomed the new regime. The horrors of what the Khmer Rouge did to Cambodia under the guise of a democratic revolution are well documented. To impose its ideology, the regime ruthlessly dismantled the state, separated families, carried out mass displacements to new locations, forced labor, and banned money. It ensured total compliance through rigid control of all food supplies, keeping most people on the edge of starvation so they had no energy for resistance. The stories of the regime's cruelty, especially to the rich and educated, are legion. No one knows for sure, but estimates are that up to 2 million people, one-quarter of the population, died as a result of starvation, brutality, and torture.

The first relief came in January 1979, when Vietnamese forces invaded in retaliation for Khmer Rouge attacks across the border. Some Cambodians who had managed to escape and regroup in Vietnam accompanied the invaders. They overthrew the Democratic Kampuchea government but did not fully defeat the Khmer Rouge, which continued to control several parts of the country. A new government was established in Phnom Penh, which declared the People's Republic of Kampuchea. Unfortunately for the population now trying to rebuild their lives and country, the West saw this government as a puppet of the Vietnamese, who had not left. Some UN agencies worked to provide humanitarian relief until 1983, but geopolitical considerations controlled even this, and no bilateral aid came from Western countries.

Again, the events and decisions of this period are far too complex to describe here, but two points are worth noting. First, incredibly, given that the world now knew what the Khmer Rouge had done, the Khmer Rouge continued to hold the Cambodia seat at the United Nations until 1991. Second, although this is known as a period of international isolation, the communist bloc countries and China were all providing support of various kinds to the different factions. But the denial of Western aid and of direct support from the United Nations meant that the country had limited external resources with which to meet its massive reconstruction challenges. Eventually, in 1989, the various combating factions started tentative negotiations with each other. The Paris Peace Accords, signed in 1991, cleared the way for the UN Transitional Authority in Cambodia (UNTAC), which oversaw the first national elections in 1993.

But Cambodia's troubles did not end with this momentous turning point. First, the Khmer Rouge did not join the political process, and it continued to wage civil war for several more years. Second, the Cambodian People's Party (CPP), which had governed throughout the 1980s, did not accept that it had lost the election to the royalist FUNCINPEC party (*Front Uni National pour un Cambodge Indépendant, Neutre, Pacifique, et Coopératif,* or the National United Front for an Independent, Neutral, Peaceful, and Cooperative Cambodia). The ensuing political standoff was resolved when King Sihanouk suggested a power-sharing arrangement between the two parties, to be headed by co-prime ministers. This uneasy coalition ran the country until 1997, when the CPP staged a coup d'état and seized power.

Many have substantive criticisms of the CPP and its government, some of which may be fully justified. Nonetheless, a great deal has been achieved since it took control in 1997. Notwithstanding the terrible poverty in which many still live, the country has begun to prosper, and basic social services are gradually coming into place. The economy is growing, and Cambodia has taken her place as a member of the Association of Southeast Asian Nations (ASEAN) and the United Nations. Some of this progress can be attributed to Prime Minister Hun Sen's successful negotiation of the surrender of the last remaining factions of the Khmer Rouge in 1998, at last bringing the war to a close. As I discuss below, complex trauma, the legacy of the Khmer Rouge regime and the war years, remains embedded in Cambodian society in multiple

ways, but in 1998, for the first time in decades, Cambodians were able to envision living in peace. As someone commented to me in 2000, "I think that
now, maybe, it is OK to hope."

On Being a Cambodian Trainer

VBNK's first facilitation of an event other than a training course was in 1998,
at the request of a Cambodian NGO (CNGO) that needed to develop a
strategic plan. We did not have time in our schedule to support their entire
planning process, so we agreed to help for two days with the facilitation of a
Strengths, Weaknesses, Opportunities, and Threats (SWOT) analysis and, if
time allowed, a visioning exercise. As the two trainers designated to facilitate
the process had no previous experience of such exercises, our preparations were
intensive, and it was agreed that I would be in the room to backstop them
whenever needed. On the appointed day, 30 of the CNGO's staff assembled in
our training room, and one of the trainers began to introduce the program. After
the formalities, he explained that he and his colleague would not be teaching
the staff anything, only leading them through a process of doing their own
analysis and decision making. The reaction was instantaneous and shocking,
both for its vehemence and for the volume of noise it generated.

   In summary, the group members believed that it would waste both their
time and their organization's money if they sat in a room at VBNK listening to
ignorant and inexperienced trainers who could not tell them the right answers.
With my support and suggestions, the trainers tried for almost two hours to
explain that they could not give the "right answers" because the process was
about the participants making their own assessments of the current status of
their organization. To no avail. Several members of the group repeatedly stated
their intention of leaving. Eventually, at the trainers' request, I intervened.
While the group members did not believe me any more than they had believed
my Cambodian colleagues, I was able, using my status as the director and a
foreigner, to persuade them to stay and try the process, on the understanding
that they need not return the next day if they did not like it. Fortunately, once
they started, the participants really enjoyed this unprecedented opportunity to
share their opinions on the state of their organization, and so they returned the
next day. VBNK has worked with that CNGO on various staff and organizational development processes many times since.

   That incident was highly instructive of the challenges in facilitating any
type of process outside the expected norms of training. It was a difficult experience for the trainers, because it was unpleasant and caused them huge loss

of face, and, unsurprisingly, it badly undermined their confidence. Once the planned process got started, they were able to facilitate very competently, but they were nervously aware that the group might once again erupt into noisy protest at any moment. Understandably, the trainers determined they would never put themselves in such a position again. I often remember what happened that day because it was the first time VBNK met such a reaction, but sadly it was far from being the last. Even now, more than a decade later, with NGO staff having been through innumerable training courses using participatory methodologies, traces of the assumptions and attitudes involved in that incident surface regularly among participants and, on occasion, among the trainers too.

Lest the analysis of trainers and their attitudes that follows appears to be entirely damning of their competence, two points need to precede it. First, this analysis is about how it was in the early days of VBNK. Second, it has to be balanced with recognition of many areas of capability and professionalism. Most of the trainers (there are exceptions everywhere) worked hard to do the best they possibly could when in the training room. They took pride in their work and wanted to use the best tools and techniques available to help them achieve good results. They always enthusiastically welcomed opportunities to learn about new content and training methodologies. Through the trainers' good work, VBNK has consistently delivered many successful training courses that have contributed to developing the skills and knowledge of staff in social development organizations. And, as I describe later, there have been many encouraging and positive changes in recent years. What I describe here is the composite of how it was at the start and the challenges that emerged when we recognized the need to change.

Cambodia is similar to many Asian cultures in holding teachers in very high esteem. As noted in the *Learning for Transformation*, a seminal research study on development practice in Cambodia (O'Leary and Meas 2001), teachers have always had high status in the social hierarchy of communities. These days, teachers are often poor because they do not earn a living wage, but attitudes have changed little, and teachers still command great respect. This respect embodies several assumptions and expectations: "Teachers are regarded as having the knowledge and the 'right' answer and it is their role to transfer the knowledge to the students" (O'Leary and Meas 2001, 62). It is the teacher, not the student, who is held responsible for the student's learning, and it is expected that the transfer of knowledge will happen through didactic, teacher-centered methodologies. In Cambodian culture, asking questions is prohibited by fear of causing people of higher status to risk losing face if they do not know the answer. Nowhere embodies this prohibition more strongly than the classroom, where students dare not question their teacher about anything. The student's task is simply to write down what the teacher has said.[2] Possibilities and probabilities are not options; all information the teacher conveys is a certainty and right. Anything and everything else is wrong. Very little outside the taught curriculum has value as learning. Teachers do not think of themselves as learners but as others think of them—as people who already know everything they need to know. In keeping with the Cambodian adage "know 10, teach 7," teachers will prevent others from achieving their level of knowledge by withholding some of what they know, thus protecting their privileged position in the community.

What I learned and struggled with during the early years of VBNK is that these cultural norms apply also to a person employed by an NGO as a trainer or in any other position with a title that conveys notions of expertise. All the expectations of trainers, both their own and those of others, are grounded in prevailing cultural attitudes toward teachers. This creates a range of very significant problems for organizations trying to develop a learning culture because, fundamentally, trainers do not believe they need to be learners in the broader sense of the word. While there are of course exceptions, in general trainers expect simply to be a conduit to pass on knowledge. No differentiation is made between subjects where the rules are fixed and can be transferred by rote learning, and working with complex social situations that call for high-level analysis, skillful decision making, and facilitation of change processes. Trainers expect, indeed are hungry for, new tools, techniques, and materials, but their expectations are of a conveyor belt approach, within which they will receive new content or rules from someone who already knows it and then they will transfer it to others in the same way. There is no perceived need to analyze, or practice the use of, learning in order that delivery be based on real understanding and practical experience.

While the challenges arising from "transfer of training"[3] are a concern worldwide, it appears that in Cambodia a range of factors, which correlate with some of the mental models Senge (2006) described, create a particularly unyielding disconnect between what is learned in training rooms and its application to workplace practices. Some of VBNK's trainers also carried management responsibilities for their teams. On more than one occasion, I observed team leaders who did an excellent job delivering training on good practices in participatory staff management using highly autocratic management within their teams. The biggest concern was that when this incongruity was pointed out, the trainer-managers did not perceive that their behavior was an unacceptable contradiction or that it compromised their integrity in the training room. They always had reasons to justify why they did not need to apply what we taught others. Contrary to Senge's supposition that once the gap between espoused theory and theory-in-use is recognized, the process of learning will begin, it was impossible to get some VBNK trainer-managers to recognize there was a problem to be addressed. This proved to be a profound block to our internal learning processes and compromised our organizational integrity.

A mental model that surfaced in the very early days of VBNK, when we were working intensively with the first group of trainers to prepare them for delivery of the first course, surfaced when the technical adviser (TA) Sally Brooks used the phrase "shades of gray." The trainers had never before heard this phrase, or anything like it, and the concept that it conveys was a mystery to them. We spent a long time explaining what it meant, and they returned to the discussion several times over the following weeks as they tried to understand and absorb its meaning. This was an interesting and instructive incident for both Sally and me, because we started to understand the depth of the trainers' belief, based on their own educational experiences, that life is constructed of information that is right or wrong. Metaphorically speaking, everything is simply white or black: gray does not and cannot exist. We came to realize that our Cambodian colleagues truly did not understand the validity of having a continuum of opinions and choices between two extremes.

The belief that, for all subjects and issues, there are only right and wrong answers is deeply ingrained in trainers and participants alike and has a major impact on training room activities. This is noted in *Learning for Transformation*: "The belief that the teacher has the right answers and the students passively accept knowledge and memorise is deeply rooted" (O'Leary and Meas 2001, 107). Repeatedly over the years, I observed how the conditioned need for the right answers required attention in training processes. Participants would always expect the trainers to tell them if their ideas were right or wrong; nothing could be left unresolved. No matter what the subject, failure to go through a detailed process of validating individual or group outputs would lead to negative evaluation of the training process. This expectation of certainties creates significant challenges in working with reflective learning practices.

A Cambodian once told me that when two Cambodians meet they instantly and automatically assess who has the higher status, and this assessment will dictate all relations between them thereafter. *Learning for Transformation* also comments on the importance of status in Cambodian life: "Everyone knows, and needs to know, their place relative to that of others" (O'Leary and Meas 2001, 48). This is another aspect of Cambodian thinking that gets carried into the training room, and it is one of Senge's "basic diseases of the hierarchy" writ large (Senge 2006, 171). It is no exaggeration to say that trainers are hypersensitive to their status relative to participants. One frequent way that this attitude manifests is in the lack of value that trainers give to participants. Why would they value them, in a social construct that holds that students are empty, waiting for the teacher to fill them with knowledge? Again, this belief and the behaviors that go with it are reflected across the entire development community:

> The exhortation to "learn from the villagers" is too often simply rhetoric as the educated practitioner cannot believe that there is anything they can learn from an "uneducated" villager—rationalising that if the villager really knew things they would not be poor! (O'Leary and Meas 2001, 93)

For an organization such as VBNK, working across multiple sectors of the NGO and development community, it is impossible to have a team of trainers with firsthand experience of all sectors. Indeed, one of the very valid criticisms leveled at VBNK down the years was that the trainers did not know how to adapt their materials to sector-specific contexts in order to make them more relevant for participants. Yet the trainers regularly had access to all the rich and varied experiences the participants brought from their fieldwork in many different sectors. In different learning cultures, trainers can draw out and listen to their participants, learn from real-life examples to deepen their knowledge, and improve their training methods and materials. Had they been able to do this, the VBNK trainers would have built up a body of field-based knowledge to enrich and improve the quality and relevance of their training. In reality, this rarely happened, unless as a direct intervention from an expatriate, because neither trainers nor participants ascribed real value to the participants' knowledge and experiences from practice. Rather than draw on what emerged from discussions in training delivery to upgrade session materials, the trainers would prefer to request more "tools."

There is a generally positive and respectful attitude toward trainers, but there are some exceptions. When participants are older and, especially, if they are more senior, trainers will feel inhibited in a number of ways and unable to challenge inappropriate contributions or behavior. Linked to the right and wrong issue noted above, this can on occasions lead to an older or more senior participant being told that an incorrect answer is right, to avoid causing loss of face. A related issue is that age and gender condition the ascription of respect, with the result that no matter how smart or qualified a young female trainer may be, she will have an extremely hard time getting any participant to take her seriously. As those born after the Khmer Rouge regime have experienced less trauma and had somewhat better education, they are showing the greatest hope in terms of potential. But attitudes toward young people represent a serious drawback to the overall capacity development agenda in Cambodia.

The issue of qualifications is also critical. A donor engaged VBNK to carry out basic management training for the secretariat of a high-profile government institution, the staff of which had been assessed as lacking even the most rudimentary knowledge of good management practices. A large formal opening ceremony for all participating staff preceded the training. From the lecture hall dais, the institution's secretary-general, the donor's representative, and I all made speeches, after which the floor was opened to questions. The first question was a direct challenge to VBNK, illuminating how the participants viewed themselves and us. "Who are you," the questioner required to know, "that you feel you are qualified to train the managers of this institute?" He went on to explain that they were all holders of senior positions in government (which was something of a stretch because, while high profile, the institute was essentially powerless and its staff were, therefore, in a political backwater) and some of them "even hold bachelor's degrees." Fortunately, I was able to respond by introducing the Cambodian trainers who would be working with them, all of whom held either master's or bachelor's degrees. Honor was satisfied, and it was accepted that VBNK was suitably qualified to give the training. The prejudice implicit in that challenge surfaces often: senior Cambodians believe there is nothing that other Cambodians can teach them. This belief is held even by those who have no qualifications or experience for their position, because the allocation of many government positions is ultimately about the dominance of political loyalties over merit.

The issue of the trainers' experience was, and remains, a significant problem. Cambodians use the analogy of frogs in wells to describe situations in which people have limited vision or perspective on an issue, and they will often apply the phrase to themselves. The years of war and international isolation resulted in the majority of Cambodians having very limited exposure to, or understanding of, the world outside their borders. An example of this is the conversation I had with our finance officer about the introduction of a salary tax. He could not apologize enough, he said, for this inexplicable initiative that his government had introduced that would clearly cause great inconvenience to everyone; he had no idea what they were thinking of. He was truly astonished when I explained that multiple forms of taxation are a fact of life in developed countries and the source of much of the development aid his country receives.

Even now, options for employment in professionally run businesses (as opposed to many small family-based market or manufacturing enterprises) or NGOs are relatively few, with the only other source of formal employment being the government. Consequently, very few people have any breadth or depth of exposure to issues and alternative concepts of life on which to draw for their work. Reading is not a common practice, and the person who will pick up a book to research something he or she needs to know is exceptional. The lack of a reading habit is also a fundamental block to good writing skills. Some people in development have had opportunities to study and/or travel overseas and consequently have both more comprehensive general perspectives and specific skills. But those with international qualifications and experience remain a small minority, and they are in high demand in the international organizations (IOs) and the donor sector or as very senior managers in NGOs. VBNK has attracted only three such people, all of whom made very valuable contributions to the organization. Thus, from the start, and even more so as VBNK's program embraced learning and creativity, it was an ongoing challenge to recruit and retain staff who had the potential to become sufficiently skillful for VBNK to be able to keep ahead of its rapidly developing target group.

As noted above, the trainers were, generally, very professional in a number of ways. Their professionalism, however, was bounded by the belief that the only necessary assessment of success is participant satisfaction, which is easily, but not necessarily accurately, assessed at the end of the training event. In terms of Kirkpatrick's classic method of evaluating training, this represents only the first of four levels of evaluation.[4] The second level, "what has been learned," can be assessed only if detailed pre- and posttraining testing mechanisms are in place, which was not possible for the majority of VBNK's work. Accurate assessment of the other two levels—"changes in workplace behavior" and the "impact of that changed behavior"—require substantive posttraining follow-up. In the early days of VBNK, when the whole community was working with relatively unsophisticated assessments of needs and ways to answer them, participant satisfaction was a "good enough" criterion by which to make crude judgments about quality and success. But as the community developed, it became apparent that simple answers were achieving very little, and everyone realized the need for deeper analysis of individual and organizational change in the Cambodian culture and context of that period. It became essential to VBNK's sustainability to be able to work in ways that demonstrably produced results beyond the level of satisfied participants. The big challenges started to surface when we tried to expand our program methodology to include the facilitation of learning, because embracing the concepts of learning required the trainers to stop seeing themselves as experts and to become learners instead. Trying to introduce this change was what led me to realize the extent, depth, and power of the cultural and contextual blocks to change and the challenges involved in trying to overcome them.

In his chapter on mental models, Senge (2006, 172) cited the work of Argyris, who has identified the trap of " 'defensive routines' that insulate our mental models from examination," resulting in "skilled incompetence," which is a way of saying that we learn to protect ourselves from the "pain and threat posed by learning situations." This resonates very strongly with my experiences in VBNK. The ingrained need for right and wrong, the disconnect between espoused theory and theory-in-use, the power of hierarchy, and the risk of losing face all conspire to preclude openness to reflection and examination of mental models. As discussed below in the section on complex trauma, much of this resistance is a common response to prolonged negative experiences. In my observations of some staff, I sometimes wondered if they, having survived such extreme traumas in life, simply don't have the energy to engage with anything that isn't absolutely essential or life threatening. Understanding a problem's roots does not, unfortunately, provide the solutions. The VBNK staff, along with the majority of our participants, were all individuals with multiple skills, including active use of "defensive routines" to resist any significant challenge to their patterns of thinking and understanding the world. Thus, the majority of VBNK trainers resisted, albeit rarely overtly, calls to work in practices grounded in different mental models. In addition, many were unable, for a variety of reasons, to analyze their own competence gaps. Repeatedly, program staff would insist that VBNK invest in further capacity development initiatives. Yet rarely during assessment processes, such as annual appraisals, would those same staff be able to articulate specific weaknesses or gaps that needed to be addressed. On the contrary, they would usually deny they had any such needs, not recognizing how this contradicted their ongoing requests for more capacity-building activities.

Once I recognized these factors were at play, I began to understand the bewildering complexity of the changes we needed to achieve and that progress first required significant unlearning to remove blocks before we could move toward the learning that would create new attitudes and competences. This led to an understanding that standard approaches to staff development were not achieving significant change and that creative practices might be more effective. I also realized that there was no map for the road we needed to travel. It was going to be a case of trial and error on the internal changes, while trying to maintain business as usual for the outside world.

Beliefs and Behaviors

Most of my daily interactions were with my Cambodian colleagues, which resulted in a very rich tapestry indeed. It was the usual complex and ever-changing story of organizational life—good days and bad days, comings and goings, successes and challenges. All of these were complicated by the fact that I was a foreigner working in a very different host culture and that we were operating in two languages. I made mistakes in how I dealt with Cambodians, and they made mistakes in how they dealt with me, but in general we got along together reasonably well. The biggest challenges came from incidents that showed the different values at work within the organization. I cannot begin to describe all the various issues that arose or the multiple ways in which we tried to ensure that VBNK was an ethical and values-based organization. What follows is a brief summary of my understanding of and VBNK's work on values and a few anecdotes that give a flavor of this complex and largely ignored aspect of organizational life and development practice.

My original understanding of organizational culture came from the work of Edgar Schein (Schein 1985), who identified three layers of culture: artifacts and creations, values, and basic assumptions. More recently, I have followed with interest any work that will help me understand how values influence development organizations and their practices. Moira O'Leary's doctoral dissertation, based on research in Cambodia, sheds much light on the vexed subject of the often pronounced difference between what people say and what they do (O'Leary 2006).[5] Many development agencies are working to change aspects of society in order to empower those who live in poverty. To do this effectively requires long and deep processes to uncover the values and basic assumptions that people hold about the world and to help them find ways to change those of their beliefs that are unhelpful to them. I have seen statements of organizational values that do not seem to me to be values at all; they are more often operating principles or a list of words like "respect," "participation," or "solidarity." I came to a working definition of "values" as "the deeply held beliefs that influence our behavior and attitudes."

We spent a lot of time in staff retreats and other events exploring which values should be part of VBNK's culture. For a long time, we didn't have a written statement of VBNK's organizational values, because I feared that once we produced one, the subject would get the "What's next?" treatment. Eventually, it was necessary to consolidate our thinking, and we produced our values statement in 2005. Thereafter, we spent a session in each learning week[6] reviewing our understanding and application of one of the values, in order to keep them fresh in everyone's mind.

Money is something that often brings different values to light. The first time we sent trainers on an overseas course, we had our first encounter with the tip of a very troublesome iceberg. We had provided the trainers with the recommended allowance for necessary expenses, plus a contingency allowance. When they returned, their expense claims included expenditure of the contingency allowance on items such as sightseeing, souvenirs, and gifts for their families. After discussion, we realized the trainers had no experience whatsoever of issues like expenses, so they had no notion that a contingency allowance was meant for emergency use and that it was inappropriate to spend the organization's money on things like personal gifts. The expenses were eventually reconciled, but only after we had worked through a lot of upset. Variations of this issue surfaced often as we strove to establish understanding and principles about proper use of the organization's money and resources. For me, it was a rude awakening to the fact that Cambodians and expatriates held some widely differing assumptions and values about organizational norms. Clearly, we needed to do something to clarify the assumptions and values that were relevant, but how to do so was not immediately obvious. Time and again, it was only when they surfaced through particular incidents that we uncovered the beliefs and attitudes underlying the behavior.

Professional and commercial interactions in Cambodia are, like other aspects of society, governed by a complex set of rules, many of which involve corruption, which is perhaps the biggest and most obvious issue bringing differing values and assumptions to the surface. A donor representative once said to me, "In X, where I last worked, the system was corrupt, but here corruption is the system." It is endemic in every part of Cambodian society, so development agencies aiming for zero tolerance can find it hard to complete even simple functions. I recall trying to convince a staff member that it didn't have to be this way. My argument was that if every Cambodian determined that, from the next day, they would refuse to make any payments to corrupt officials and shopkeepers, then those people would realize they had to operate differently, and the practice would stop. The notion of official and commercial transactions that didn't involve corruption was beyond her imagination, and her response to everything I said was, "You just don't understand, Jenny; that's the way it is and it can never change." As with other development agencies, VBNK had clear policies and procedures on the use of organizational money, but we still uncovered incidents such as falsified expense claims; someone involved in purchasing getting "commission," which of course increased the price VBNK paid for the articles; and so on. I have strong suspicions that on more than one occasion, VBNK staff used their own money to buy their way through a government process that simply wasn't going to happen without payments being made to officials. While I think we managed to keep corruption under reasonable control, I never allowed myself to assume it wasn't happening somewhere or other in the organization, and we always took swift action when it did come to light, in order to discourage others.

An exercise we did in a values session illustrated how stressful it is for NGO staff to live in these dual worlds. The role-play was of a staff member who urgently needed a passport. The first time, they talked to the official as an NGO worker, and the second time they talked to him as a private citizen. The two conversations were entirely different and produced very different outcomes: one involved money, and the other didn't. In the discussion afterward, the staff talked about how hard it was to switch between the different ways of operating as they moved backward and forward between their workplace and the rest of their lives. This problem is so deeply engrained in Cambodian culture that many people simply do not see anything wrong. There is a saying: "Corruption is the fuel to make things happen." Many Cambodians, however, like working in an organization with expatriates because it gives them the welcome protection of being able to say, "My boss is a foreigner and won't let me do this."

A different problem we had several times early on was people retaining their status as government employees. From the early 1990s, it became common practice for people to be granted leave of absence from their government jobs to join an INGO without being required to resign. I did not realize this was happening until two incidents caused VBNK significant problems. We subsequently revised our recruitment procedures and employment contracts to ensure we didn't get caught out again. In one incident, a trainer with us for about 10 months was showing good potential when he handed in his notice because he had been recalled to his government department, the training unit of a government university. A few weeks later, that training unit put out a brochure advertising its curriculum, approximately 80% of which was a straight copy of VBNK's courses. We pursued this in various ways, and eventually the training unit withdrew the courses that had been taken from VBNK. When the dust had settled, the former employee told someone that until I made a fuss about it, he simply hadn't realized there was anything wrong with what he had done.

Another incident concerned a manager. It came to light that she was still on the payroll of a ministry and that two or three times a week, when I thought she was out and about on VBNK business, she was calling into her office at the ministry. We talked this through, and she promised she would resign her position and stop her visits. About a year later, I was showing a visitor around and introduced him to the manager. Later, the visitor expressed his confusion: on the previous Saturday morning, he had been part of a team selecting government employees for a month-long training course in a Scandinavian country, all expenses paid by that government. Our manager had applied and been selected. When I tackled her about this, she truly had no idea why her actions might be considered inappropriate. Her justification for not having resigned from the ministry as promised was "It could all break down again, then the NGOs will go, and I will need that government job." More worrying was that her motivation for applying for the course had nothing to do with professional development, only that it would enable her to visit her sister, who lived in northern Germany. She saw nothing immoral in misusing aid support money intended to help build the ministry's capacity, and she thought I was unkind and unreasonable in wanting to stop her from having this opportunity. She had to go.

Petty dishonesty happens everywhere, so the guard who was routinely siphoning petrol from staff vehicles could have been working anywhere. But the guard who put acid in another's drinking water because he thought that was the way to gain respect was a different matter. Fortunately, the dissolving plastic cup alerted the intended victim that something was wrong before any harm was done. The perpetrator's logic in thinking that such a dangerous action would gain him respect has always eluded me. Another mystifying incident concerned a training team leader, one of the first team recruited in 1997, who took three days' leave, purportedly to attend a family wedding in the provinces. When she did not come in the following Monday, someone tried to call her and was told by a family member that she had gone to the United States. We later received a brief note from her saying she had enjoyed working at VBNK but felt it was time to move on, thank you and good-bye. She must have been making plans for a long time but had confided in no one at VBNK. I have never understood why she didn't tell us and resign in the normal way. A colleague commented that it was because "We just don't trust each other."

These are some of the more colorful incidents that occurred within VBNK, but they are just the tip of the iceberg. There were repeated, sometimes daily, issues to deal with in trying to imbue the organization with a culture of honesty and transparency and with the respect for everyone that is inherent in good development practice. It proved to be impossible, however, to change some attitudes in the organization, as demonstrated by experience with the first of VBNK's values: "VBNK believes that people are the main resource for Cambodia's development and that creating equitable relationships between them is a key factor in achieving positive social change." As noted above, because young people have not experienced the same debilitating traumas as did the preceding generations and are also getting a much better education than those generations, they are Cambodia's brightest hope. They generally have fresh ideas and new energy that can make a good contribution to any organization. All this was agreed in theory within VBNK, but the reality was that older staff members were unwilling to tolerate young people behaving in ways that they considered inappropriate and disrespectful. We lost several bright youngsters because they were repeatedly subjected to criticism and reprimand from their older colleagues. Nothing was ever said in public sessions, but quiet private follow-up would always let the youngsters know how they had transgressed.

Similar issues occurred in relation to male behavior toward women, an issue that sometimes brought me into conflict with male colleagues. On more than one occasion, I knew I was causing male staff to lose face through my public reactions to inappropriate behavior toward women. It was a judgment call, and I know that at least one person was very angry with me for a long time. But had I not reacted, my silence would have been taken as implicit approval, and I was not willing to be seen to condone behavior that I felt to be morally wrong. I made the choice based on my values, one of which is that women should not, in any way, be treated as inferior to men on the basis of their sex. The men came to know that it was not wise to behave disrespectfully toward women when I was around. After a man succeeded me as director, some male staff assumed that different behavior would now be acceptable, and the predominant external culture of offensive sexual humor and disregard for women's feelings and opinions surfaced within VBNK. These men got a very rude awakening when they realized that my successor is probably even more opposed to such behavior than I am.

Values are at the heart of many developmental change processes. For development practitioners, national and expatriate, this can create considerable dilemmas in finding ways to hold the balance between having respect for local culture and working to bring change where aspects of that culture contribute to poverty and injustice. Being confronted by values totally different from your own can create considerable discomfort, as can having someone challenge you about your own cultural beliefs. As mentioned above, I struggled with the way that discrimination against women in Cambodian society showed up within VBNK. On matters I considered less critical, I deferred to my colleagues. What we tried to do in VBNK, especially in the CHART project,[7] was help both colleagues and participants understand how their worldviews were constructed and that, far from being written in stone, they could challenge and discard them if they found them unhelpful.

In the complex array of social and professional rules of interaction that govern people's lives, there is a recurring theme of people unwittingly contributing to the creation of their own problems. Some beliefs are so deeply embedded that they influence people to behave as if they are true. One young female staff member was demotivated because she felt that participants saw her as a silly girl and disregarded her. In a women's empowerment session, I asked the group, "What in your own behavior contributes to the problems that you complain about?" The young woman later told me that question was an epiphany, because she realized that she was being treated like a silly girl because she was behaving like one, conforming to social norms and expectations about her as a young woman. When she walked into the training room with a different belief in herself, she found the participants treated her differently and gave her the respect that her ability deserved.

Such small incidents are but a tiny drop in the ocean of change that needs to happen within all development organizations in all cultures before justice and equality can become the norm. But no ocean would exist without all the tiny drops, so we should take heart each time we contribute one.

Complex Trauma and Its Implications for Capacity Development

The description above gives a brief introduction to some aspects of Cambodian culture that are relevant to understanding the restrictions that can occur within capacity development initiatives. Cultural factors are only a part of the picture, however: in any postconflict society, the complexity of both culture-based responses to social upheaval and the psychosocial impact of war are increased by their interaction. What follows here is a summary of my deepening understanding of the psychosocial legacy of complex war-created trauma and how this legacy combines with aspects of Cambodian culture to inhibit both individuals and society from achieving their full potential. My previous study and experiences in social work gave me a framework for analyzing all that I have seen and learned and thus guided me to look beneath superficial presentation to try to understand what was really happening. Although my understanding deepens continually, I think of what I write about here as pivotal learning, because it was only when I started to understand the complicated ways in which complex trauma and cultural factors interact to inhibit the healthy development of individuals and societies that I started to realize the need for radically different approaches.

When I arrived, Cambodia was still a country in the throes of civil war. I knew there must be historical and contemporary effects on both individuals and society, but I had little idea exactly what those effects might be. While recent history has undoubtedly influenced Cambodia at many different levels, most notably its economic development and geopolitical relationships, my work on capacity development has motivated me to learn and understand primarily at the level of individuals. I gradually came to realize that a very complex set of cultural and experiential factors was creating blocks to learning and change, and I found it invaluable to draw on other disciplines, most particularly psychology, to analyze my experiences and observations. Most of what follows is about Cambodia, but studies from other postconflict societies, especially countries of the former Yugoslavia and in Central and South America, were very helpful to my learning. Through reading about what has happened in those countries, I was better able to understand the Cambodian experience and to identify which responses and trends are unique to Cambodian culture and which are observed as universal in similar circumstances.[8]

Elements of war and sources of trauma survive, and in some cases thrive, long after the primary conflict has stopped: people have to live not only with the past but also with ongoing threats. The psychosocial effects that accrue in such circumstances, when combined with influential cultural factors, are extremely relevant to any attempts to develop capacity, because they create and maintain inhibitors of change. These multifaceted inhibitors are real and potent, yet are rarely recognized, acknowledged, or understood, because they exist at the level of an individual emotion and functioning or within unspoken rules of relationship not obvious to an outside observer. Because many development initiatives ignore such important realities, they are, if not doomed to fail, certainly doomed to underperform, and this has often been the case in Cambodia. Unfortunately, too many capacity and organizational development interventions are designed and delivered by people who make assumptions based on their own worldviews and how others present, not on the deeper realities of the culture and context.

The roots of the verb "to heal" are in the old English word *hāl*, which means "whole." Modern definitions include "to make sound or whole, to restore to health, to cause (an undesirable condition) to be overcome"[9] and "put right so that people are friendly and happy again" (Sinclair 2001). It is difficult to know why development agents working in postconflict societies do not fully recognize the need for healing. In Cambodia, it may be that the magnitude of needs for basic survival overwhelmed all other considerations. It may be that Cambodian cultural interpretations of recent history and healing are not seen as issues that have any relation to each other. It may also be that the astonishing resilience with which Cambodians have achieved so much since the end of the Khmer Rouge regime has disguised this need. Whatever the reasons, with the passage of time, the need for psychosocial healing appears to have slipped from the agenda. However, as the analysis below shows, the failure to address this need has had far-reaching consequences for the country's development.

Conceptions of Health and Illness

For one to be able to offer appropriate support after traumatic events, it is first necessary to know what the range of normal and abnormal responses might be and then to assess the responses that people are showing. Anthropology tells us a great deal about how individuals function while living in stability within their own culture. Development practitioners working in postconflict societies, however, need to know much more about different cultural responses to abnormal circumstances because, as more than one expert has noted, maintenance of normal behavior after a traumatic experience can be an unhealthy aberration.

Somatization is a syndrome that tends to have negative connotations as a disorder in Western thinking, yet this way of feeling mental or emotional experience within the body is the norm in many traditional societies. This is particularly true, as Dr. Derek Summerfield, a psychiatrist noted for his work during and after conflicts, commented on cultures such as those of Southeast Asia, where harmony is considered necessary to the well-being of the collective, and individuals are therefore constrained to suppress anything that might create a disturbance (Summerfield 1991, 163). In a paper on the psychosocial impact of war in Cambodia, Anne Harmer noted the frequent occurrence of somatization in Cambodian culture as a way to express distress (Harmer 1995, 4). The causes of the somatization do not go away but take second place to their physical manifestations—most commonly extreme fatigue, palpitations, recurrent headaches, and inexplicable body pain. There are now some Western psychological and physical disciplines that recognize forms of somatization and work with the belief that "biography is biology"; that is, that the body becomes the receptacle of memory that, particularly in cases of extreme trauma, may cause ill health.

Somatization does not preclude the individual from having other responses and may exist alongside them with equal, greater, or lesser force. For many, however, it is the physical symptoms to which they will pay the greatest attention. This has implications for approaches to both physical and emotional healing. Maria Kett observed of internally displaced people in Bosnia

> a variety of stress-related complaints including depression, "nerves" and high blood pressure, which may be treated with medications. While many of the patients acknowledged that these problems could be a result of the anxieties they encountered on a daily basis—uncertainty, insecurity, bereavement, poverty, fear, unemployment, lack of privacy, financial resources or prospects—they took the pills anyway as they made them feel "better." (Kett 2005, 210)

Many people suffer from ongoing debilitating health problems, some of which could be avoidable or treatable. For example, sleep disturbance is mentioned in many studies of refugees and survivors, both Cambodian and others, draining the ability to function effectively, not only physically and intellectually but also emotionally and spiritually. Given how much inadequate sleep can reduce individuals' ability to work at their optimum, this must be acknowledged as another block to capacity development. An NGO providing social work support in rural Cambodian communities has documented sleep disturbance as the most common presenting problem among those coming to it for help. I have not, however, been able to find any research studies conducted within Cambodia.

An individual's external presentation is framed by socially sanctioned norms. Both external presentation and internal order can lie on a continuum between healthy organization and extreme disturbance. External appearances (body language, actions, behavior, and speech) are generally a very small representation of all the complex interactions of thoughts, emotions, beliefs, and physical functioning going on internally. What a person chooses to display externally is generally dictated by social norms or sometimes by a situational imperative for safety. In many circumstances, people will, consciously or unconsciously, attempt to hide difficult or powerful feelings and thoughts in order to be seen as socially compliant and acceptable. However, the body has strong and sometimes uncontrollable links between cognitive, emotional, and physical responses to stimuli, so, for example, signs of fear might leak into external appearance, whether their owner wants them to or not. The psychosocial effects of trauma this chapter discusses are not, generally, of a nature that falls under any description of mental illness. However, if an individual is unable to resolve strong negative emotions and experiences, he or she may develop mental or emotional illness and show related signs of disturbance, provoking a range of responses from others. Some disturbance might be tolerated; other behavior will prompt reactions on a spectrum between caring support at one end and control or avoidance at the other.

In a study on the meaning of mental illness, Shikha Dixit (2005) posited that concepts of health and illness are created by, and embedded in, the broad system of meaning that any given society constructs from its knowledge base and belief system, significantly determined by notions of acceptability. He noted that in traditional cultures, ill health is often interpreted in relation to the spirit world, and mental illness is usually associated with evil forces such as malevolent spirits. Cambodians, for example, believe in multiple causes of both physical and mental illness, including Buddhist karma and the influence of evil spirits. In such circumstances, diagnostic tools based on Western constructions of meaning, common sense, and health are bound to be of limited value. One of Freud's gifts to Western societies was the language of psychoanalysis, and many terms in everyday parlance, such as "damaged" or "emotionally scarred," are used to describe the cause of unhealthy behaviors. Other cultures and languages, however, do not embrace either the concepts or the language of mental illness as defined in the West. In Cambodia, the only relevant word in common usage is *chkoo-ut* (crazy), used for people behaving in obviously strange ways.

In many cultures, the individual is not a unit of meaning in social constructs, and the norms of kinship networks may determine how people deal with their experiences and emotions. Interpretations of behavior, health, and illness should therefore be concerned with multiple factors of individual and group functioning and well-being, not just an individual's symptoms. Another danger of relying on a medical model of symptoms is that when people are constrained by cultural mores to turn their distress and disturbance inward, rather than into observable symptoms that fit a preconceived model, they might be overlooked.

Responses to anyone whose condition or behavior is outside the norm are, therefore, variable according to the belief systems of those involved. Health professionals trained in Western disciplines are most likely to assess symptoms within a medical model, whereas traditional healers will use different criteria.[10] Summerfield has studied this issue worldwide, including in Thai border camps for Cambodian refugees. His view is that many responses to trauma are adaptive according to cultural norms, and before any judgment is made about the mental or emotional health of the individual, the responses must be analyzed in that cultural context. As he commented about Cambodia,

> Local traditions and points of view give rise to psychological knowledge, meanings attached to events, and the way help and healing is sought. There is more than one true description of the world. To take one war zone, Cambodia, the taxonomies of traditional healers range across the physical, supernatural and moral realms, and are at odds with the linear causal thought of western practitioners. (Summerfield 1996, 18)

Summerfield noted the effectiveness of the traditional healers, known as *kru khmer*, who used a framework for diagnosis and treatment that was very different from Western models. He is concerned that Western psychiatric models are in danger of becoming definitive and thereby dominating other ways of knowing the world, in another form of postcolonial domination. Harmer also noted the need to understand both responses and coping mechanisms within their cultural context and the fact that the labels put on responses to extreme stress are rooted in Western concepts of health that do not necessarily have meaning in other cultures (Harmer 1995, 4).

Understanding health issues in contemporary Cambodia requires knowledge of both traditional and Western beliefs about physical and mental health and illness and about the provision of health services, which are all beyond the scope of this book. However, even the brief overview given here indicates that if health issues were studied from the perspective of complex trauma, the findings might shed considerable light on issues of general well-being and functioning.

This very brief review of the literature indicates that both healthy and unhealthy responses to trauma may be defined very differently according to the cultural context in which they occur. Analyses of health and illness that do not address cultural interpretations of the world are rarely relevant or helpful for the people concerned, and because their foundations tend to be in Western experiences and medical models, it is particularly important to avoid assumptions that currently prevalent theories about mental health and psychosocial responses to trauma are universally applicable.

A Framework for Understanding

The word "psychosocial," being a combination of the word "psychological," pertaining to the mind or mental processes, and "social," pertaining to how groups organize and interact, is concerned with the interface of the individual and the collective. A study of psychosocial functioning is, therefore, concerned with the individual, with her or his individual ability to function in relationship to and with others, and with the relational health of society as a whole, all within the framework of the national or ethnic culture by which individuals and groups make meaning of their world.

People subjected to long-term violence, repression, appropriation of resources, impunity, and other horrors through successive waves of war and conflict live in states of constant and continuing fear for their well-being and survival. In such circumstances, the negative psychosocial legacy for individuals, groups, and society is just as inevitable as the destruction of physical infrastructure and damage to institutions of state. Such was the case for Cambodians in the decades prior to 1998, but, as in other countries, the cessation of long-term conflict did not result in immediate transition to a state of peace, whereby people could feel fully safe and secure. As noted in *Learning for Transformation*, even in 2001 personal insecurity was a "recurring issue throughout the research" (O'Leary and Meas 2001, 117).

The appendix briefly reviews the condition known as post trauma stress disorder (PTSD) and some studies conducted in other postconflict societies. All are forerunners to a body of knowledge about a syndrome being referred to as "complex trauma," which is yet to be recognized by medical authorities, although many experts are lobbying that it should be. There are different definitions of complex trauma according to context, but all include two key features: repeated experiences of trauma, and trauma occurring over extended periods of time. Some also incorporate multiple types of trauma and/or escalating seriousness. Dr. Felicia Mueller, a US psychotherapist, gives an illuminating description of the multiple ways in which complex trauma can affect an individual's capacity to function:

> When the human organism is repeatedly exposed to traumatic stress, disruptions can occur in brain functions and structures, endocrinological function, immunological function, and central and autonomic nervous system arousal. These biological disruptions interact with psychological, emotional, spiritual, and cognitive processes and a variety of disturbances can result that go beyond the . . . symptoms that characterize PTSD. (Mueller n.d.)

Most sources agree that simplistic symptom-based treatment programs are ineffective because they fail to address the interactions between the multiple factors involved. Survivors of complex trauma need to experience comprehensive processes that first establish safety and then incorporate, as needed, physical care, facilitation of mourning, creation of meaning, and reconnection with others.

I have found it extremely helpful to learn that there is now this conceptual framework that embraces the whole person complexity of what people suffer in times like the Khmer Rouge regime and explains that such experiences cause damage in many ways not previously understood. Caution is needed, however, because complex trauma has been defined within Western psychiatric disciplines; as yet, little has been done to understand its relevance and helpfulness in terms of how people from other cultures interpret their condition and responses.

In Cambodia, the Royal Government of Cambodia (RGC) health system and the NGO sector now provide some mental health services, but these are far from sufficient, because there has been little acknowledgment of the extent of the need. Western observers have noted that Cambodian mental health professionals are also the survivors of trauma, and many probably still carry its unresolved negative effects. Also, because most of these professionals have been trained in Western models, diagnostic approaches have a tendency to overlook or reject trauma as a factor. It appears that many patients whose symptoms may have been caused by trauma are being diagnosed as schizophrenic. This must be a concern, given that Summerfield documented Cambodian refugees as each having suffered an average of 16 major trauma events, some of which fall under the UN classification of torture (Summerfield 1991, 161). Those who did not leave undoubtedly suffered the same or more. In addition, there can be no doubt that Cambodians' cultural interpretations of their experiences will differ from those offered in Western medical models. Yet the extent of this legacy has yet to be formally acknowledged and addressed on any meaningful scale by either government services or development initiatives.

Frozen States

Dr. Vamik Volkan, who specializes in the psychology of large-group violence and societal trauma arising from human-created events, has concluded that when societies suffer extreme experiences of trauma at the hands of "others," they experience a range of psychological results, especially if other negative realities, such as poverty, are present. These results include a shared sense of shame, humiliation, dehumanization, and guilt; a shared inability to be assertive; a shared difficulty or inability to mourn; patterns of emotional response, such as strong feelings of anger and revenge alternating with passivity and helplessness;

and unhealthy patterns of behavior and relationships, both between people and with their environment. He further noted that people have an ongoing need to overcome "the other," for fear that the other will once again overcome them. The inability to resolve powerful emotions often leads to individual antisocial behavior, such as domestic violence, rape, and the inability to care for children properly. In broader social spheres, the negative behaviors manifest in ways such as organized crime, pollution, and destruction of the environment. Volkan noted that shared psychological effects, far from diminishing over time, can become embedded in society and subsequently transferred from one generation to the next through "transgenerational transmission," creating further, albeit different, impacts on future generations (Volkan 1998).

Schein's study of the impact of Chinese brainwashing of US civilian prisoners also offers useful insights into how people may get stuck in unhelpful emotions and responses (Schein 1956). Introducing the notion of coercive persuasion, he used the analogy of people becoming "frozen" in their thinking and behavior as a result of what they have been led to believe. While this study related to a specific, deliberate process of changing people's beliefs, there are similarities with the processes of forming and reinforcing beliefs through traumatic socialization experiences. The Khmer Rouge *angkar* (organization) used large-scale brainwashing techniques to maintain control of the population. They had rules for every circumstance, including a command that people empty their heads of every thought except those the regime put there: "Do not harbor private thoughts!" (Locard 2004, 294). No one was in any doubt that dire repercussions, probably death, would follow any sign of individual thought or initiative. People who have experienced such extreme repression or trauma are often found to have the cognitive and emotional "stuckness" of Schein's frozen state. Harmer noted that some "dysfunctional behavior" appeared to originate in the self-protection and coping behaviors that people had developed in order to survive (Harmer 1995, 2). Survivor behaviors of lifesaving importance during times of danger can become immutably embedded in an individual's array of cognitive and emotional responses, impossible to let go of even when no longer needed and potentially detrimental to postdanger rehabilitation. When this is combined with unresolved negative feelings, the results can be emotionally or functionally paralyzing for the individual.

It may not be immediately obvious in everyday life that an individual or group is in a frozen state, as much may be embedded below the conscious. In the context of the generally held Western belief that repression of bad memories can create psychosocial problems, it is of concern that "many Cambodians appear to suppress memories of traumatic experiences, attempt to 'forget their past' and find it hard and painful to talk of their experience" (O'Leary and Meas 2001, 68). Even so, Leng and Pearson noted how much the wounds of the past remain resolutely a part of everyone's reality:

> The trauma left by the Khmer Rouge cannot be "let go" easily, and it became a reflective wound (easy to remember and go crazy with) that remains in the Cambodian mind and heart and cannot easily be healed. The wound blocks Cambodians from moving forward constructively. (Leng and Pearson 2006, 3)

This is one of the issues where culture and experience come together unhelpfully. The cultural need to suppress anything that might cause disharmony, combined with uncertainty about whom it might be safe to talk to, leaves many people feeling alone with their painful histories, which in turn adds to the general level of mistrust in society.

Eventually, in a variety of ways, people reach a point of equilibrium or stasis within which they can function, and society as a whole settles into patterns of functioning and interaction that become the norm. The point when this happens of course varies across individuals and groups: for some it never comes, but for the majority it happens sooner or later. The important point to note is that the appearance of stasis does not necessarily mean that past traumas have been resolved; more likely they have been consigned to an internal place where they are not overtly visible.

In countries such as Cambodia, where there has been little opportunity for anyone to deal with the past, stasis masks frozen states, memories, and emotions that make it difficult for people to function at their best.

Loss

Whatever trauma individuals have experienced, it is likely to be combined with, and exacerbated by, their experiences of losing loved ones and important possessions or opportunities in life, all of which have negative impacts to varying degrees. Innumerable survivors of the Khmer Rouge regime have no idea what happened to multiple members of their families—if, when, where, or how they died. Despite extensive documentation of mass graves throughout the country, there is no detailed information available on who lies at each site, and the expensive process of DNA identification is not viable for a poor country like Cambodia. Lack of information about the fate of relatives results in many individuals or families living with painful unanswered questions and an inability to accept that someone is probably dead. I have had many conversations with Cambodians who, even now, 30 years after the end of the Khmer Rouge regime, are still making visits to the last known whereabouts of missing family members to search for information that might provide a lead to knowing their fate. The Documentation Center of Cambodia[11] still regularly receives new requests for information to post on its website. In addition, during the Khmer Rouge regime, many lost their home, land, employment, access to education, and social status.

Volkan observed that both individuals and societies can become stuck in a state of unresolved mourning for those who have been lost, a condition he named "perennial mourning" (Volkan 2006, 24). While acknowledging that grief is always unique and individual, he noted that there are normal patterns of healing after bereavement, which allow a return to healthy functioning after cognitive and emotional accommodation of the loss. In more than one post-conflict situation, it has been noted that, especially for women, it is necessary to have possession of the body in order to confirm that a loved one is actually dead.[12] Not having the corpse, or even sight of it, creates disruption to traditional mourning rites and processes. Those stuck in perennial mourning are unable either to complete the mourning process or to let it go and move on. They are, Volkan said, "doomed to remain preoccupied with aspects of their mourning process for decades to come and even until the end of their own lives" (Volkan 2006, 21).

The results of unresolved loss show themselves in many ways. In my Cambodian family, one of the older brothers bled to death after the Khmer Rouge cut his hands off. Some years ago, a young man from a neighboring village, disabled in both hands, presented himself to the elderly mother as the reincarnation of her murdered son. Her unresolved grief, and her belief system, led her to accept him without question. For a time, she embraced this stranger as a family member, much to the consternation of her surviving children, who eventually convinced her that he was a pretender. Another example that gave me an insight into the extent of the pain that many still carry was an incident with a staff member whose life had been particularly marked by loss. From a young age, before, during, and after the Khmer Rouge regime, she had suffered more loss than anyone could be expected to bear with equanimity. When she experienced yet another personal loss during her time at VBNK, she was clearly struggling with her emotions. Her behavior began to be very erratic and a cause for concern, but she denied that anything was amiss. At one point I suggested that she have a good cry and let out some of her feelings, but she responded with, "If I start crying it will be like after Pol Pot times, and I will never stop." I noted that she said "after," rather than "during," Pol Pot times, as overt displays of grief in those days would inevitably have led to severe negative consequences. I found myself at a loss as to how to help her, because I had no point of reference to connect with her interpretations of her experience.

I have come to believe that overwhelming loss and unresolved mourning are profound elements of the collective of contemporary Cambodian society. There may be Cambodian families that survived the Khmer Rouge regime intact, but I have yet to meet anyone who did not lose some or many family members during those years. The numbers are staggering. It is not unusual for people to tell you, "I lost all 9 [or 11 or 14] members of my immediate family." Or, perhaps, "I watched my parents and then all my brothers and sisters die of starvation. I was the only one to survive. I was 12 when it ended, and I had no one." Yet, although individuals, families, and society all carry jagged, gaping chasms of unresolved loss at their very core, I have never come across any research about how these extraordinary events and losses are held or understood in contemporary Cambodian society. As noted in *Learning for Transformation*, the combination of life experiences and a culture that values face and harmony has taught Cambodians not to go deeply into their feelings (O'Leary and Meas 2001, 104), so the grief and pain are rarely, if ever, mentioned. Mental health specialists report that the usual response to any display of memory-provoked distress is "don't cry, forget it," effectively suppressing the memories and emotions behind the distress. Only during the 15-day Pchum Ben festival during September/October every year, when families by the millions flock to *wats* all over the country to remember and honor their dead, can one get any sense of the pain and anguish that are still part of their everyday reality.

Fear and Mistrust

As a result of my years of living and working with Cambodians, I have come to believe that fear remains the most powerful and prevalent emotion within Cambodian society. Other writers quoted here, such as Leng, Meas, and O'Leary, make frequent references both to its prevalence and to its relevance to many other issues. Fear, of many things both real and imagined, controls the behavior of the majority of citizens, including those who appear to have the most power and resources, as demonstrated by the large numbers of bodyguards some politicians and businesspeople employ. One of the most frequently spoken phrases in everyday communications is "*khnom acht hien*" ("I don't dare"). This phrase is used time and again to explain inaction in many different circumstances.

An ongoing process of women's empowerment workshops that I undertook with the female staff of VBNK vividly illustrated the extent to which fear exists and is a block to learning and change. Outputs and anecdotes in a range of exercises highlighted the prevalence of fear as a factor blocking change, either at home or at work, even though it was rarely expressed overtly. In a short exercise to explore this issue more deeply, the group quickly listed 28 different fears they held about their everyday lives and that were, therefore, controlling their thinking, emotions, and behavior (Pearson 2011b). The fear about the dangerous Phnom Penh traffic is unique to this city (and eminently sensible); others, like mothers' concerns for their children's health, occur everywhere. However, a number were specific to Cambodian culture and history, such as fear of being labeled a bad woman through gossip and, most notably, fear of political instability leading to war.

Fear of revenge is a powerful control mechanism within social interaction in Cambodian society. Alexander Hinton explored the trait of "disproportionate revenge" (Hinton 2005, 45) that has always been prevalent in Cambodian society, possibly because the dictates of face require a response to be more powerful than the provocation. The Khmer Rouge leadership used this concept mercilessly in propaganda to manipulate the poor rural population to take viciously violent action against the ruling elites and anyone with an education. The culture of revenge still appears everywhere, and even those who would never think of resorting to violence to settle a grudge will find other ways to be satisfied. This is particularly true of relationships between people of different status. Leng and Pearson explained that you expect people whom you have caused to lose face, especially if they are your senior, to seek revenge because you would seek revenge if they caused you to lose face (Leng and Pearson 2006, 19). For example, if your boss loses face because you show that you know something she or he doesn't know, you could expect to lose your job as a result. I lost count of the number of times VBNK staff said they could not do something, for example, disagree with me, for fear of losing their job. The fact that in more than a decade nobody ever lost their job for disagreeing with me held no sway against the expectations that I would behave as a Cambodian leader would. Discussions with colleagues also revealed that many situations will prompt a spontaneous fear that they cannot really explain, and then they feel guilty because they are inhibited from doing something.

The mistrust in contemporary Cambodia, also cited in *Learning for Transformation* and by the women's group as a block to change, is another complex issue that a range of emotional, cognitive, and historical factors have created. In the women's group, it seemed that there was a blanket assumption that no one could be trusted to any degree at all (Pearson 2011b). Lacking any criteria or means of assessing how to apply varying levels of trust to different people, the women said that the simplest solution was not to take any risks and to trust only immediate family. One causal factor is the substantial disruption and destruction of old-style communities based primarily on kinship networks, combined with the integration over time of former Khmer Rouge into mainstream society. Not knowing who people are, where they have come from, what they might have done in the past, or what their political affiliation is makes everyone fearful of engaging with each other beyond superficial norms of social niceties. As various studies note repeatedly, mistrust is endemic in society, and it is clear that the VBNK women's group is representative of the norm. A US Agency for International Development (USAID) report noted that women in focus group discussions talking about microcredit schemes "complained about a lack of trust and unwillingness to help in time of need" and also stated that they would join groups only with their immediate family members (Kumar, Baldwin, and Benjamin 2000, 7). This was thought to be one explanation as to why self-help initiatives have not been as effective in Cambodia as elsewhere. The study noted that the Khmer Rouge leaders had an obsessive level of distrust in virtually everyone, including each other, which led them to demand "nothing less than complete control of its citizens' thoughts, achieved through fear, repression, and indoctrination" (p. 3). Meanwhile, Meas noted that the legacy of the past, current levels of violence and impunity, authoritarian styles of leadership, and obvious deep and endless mistrust between Cambodia's various political factions and leaders do nothing to help the general population overcome their own mistrust, either of their leaders or of each other (Meas 2006, 3, 5). He posited that until trust is restored between different groups in society, there is little chance of significant human resource development in Cambodia. From an outsider's perspective, lack of trust among Cambodians appears to be so habitual that no one has any idea about how to begin trusting each other again.

Creating Meaning and Moving On

Cultural and social constructs, often inextricably linked to religious beliefs, exist for the purpose of allowing individuals and groups to make meaning and sense of their world and to create rules of interaction and behavior that will enable them to function together within harmonious relationships. Similarly, memory is organized according to cultural understandings of the world, which differ between societies. The study of meaning, memory, and learning tells us that the creation of meaning about current experiences is dependent on having in place an appropriate frame of reference and cognitive structure to enable the anticipation and assimilation of new experiences and changes. Such a framework is created from past experiences and social learning. The US psychiatrist Dr. Adam Blatner, noted for his work in psychodrama, wrote about the need for meaning and the complex processes by which it is constructed:

> The number sense to be considered here is in the hundreds or thousands, the number of mental images, cognitive constructs, stories, beliefs, known facts that the mind must connect with in order to generate a sufficient sense of coherence. (Blatner 2007)

Blatner went on to note that deeply disturbed feelings will arise when an individual is unable to create meaning from her or his images.

At its most extreme, the inability to make meaning according to agreed cultural frameworks leads to both disorientation of perceptions and distortion of the important mechanisms for individuals and groups to relate to each other and their culture, which results in the relationships themselves becoming distorted. Thus, when large groups are trying to make sense of abnormal experiences, the impact becomes something greater than the cumulative impact on individuals and results in phenomena such as the transgenerational transmission that Volkan identified. In Cambodia, the Khmer Rouge's assault on all aspects of Cambodian society was one of the most profound attacks on a national culture ever seen, astonishing not least because its genesis and implementation came from within. It seems that nothing was left unscathed as the Khmer Rouge dismantled or controlled multiple facets of everyday life, from family relationships, through the use of money, to religious practices and, most important, the availability of food—the very means of life itself.

When an individual is in crisis or extreme danger or living under a long-term repressive regime, the situational imperatives of survival often lead to a bypassing at the time of the need to create meaning. Changes in status, relationship, work, and so on are accommodated if they are the means of surviving. Cambodian survivors, especially the professional city dwellers who had to perform hard manual labor working the land, will speak of innumerable instances when they did things they had never imagined they would do. Everyone has a story, and in this complex area, distinctions between victim and perpetrator become blurred, which complicates any understanding of how survivors will deal with their experiences. As described in Teeda Butt Mam's story of life during the Khmer Rouge regime, "We survived by becoming like [the Khmer Rouge and the village cadre]. We stole, we cheated, we lied, we hated ourselves and each other, and we trusted no one" (Criddle and Butt Mam 1987). A former member of the Khmer Rouge, now working as a senior administrator in a major IO, once told me, "I did some terrible things in that period. I did what I had to in order to survive," the implication being, in the context of the conversation, that he had killed. The horrors of war and violent conflict thrust people repeatedly, against their will, into situations where what they do or experience is beyond the realm of anything previously done or experienced and for which they have no sense-making cognitive structures. It is possible to minimize negative consequences if the individual subsequently receives the opportunity to process the experience in ways that he or she finds meaningful, but if this does not happen, the long-term effects will be damaging.

Marc Nichanian raised the issue of sense making in relation to mourning, when reflecting on the lasting impact of the violent pogroms in Armenia in 1895 and 1915, known as "the Catastrophe":

> Let us assume that the only human response to death is mourning. But is mourning a response to senseless death? . . . Everywhere, it seems, mourning is sufficient to make sense; faced with the Catastrophe, on the contrary, *a sense is necessary so that mourning can occur.* (Nichanian 2002, 105; original emphasis)

It is hard to imagine any framework within which an individual or group can make sense of, or be reconciled to, mass murder, and this is almost certainly a factor contributing to unresolved mourning.

When Cambodian survivors emerged from the nightmare years, they had virtually nothing to help them make sense of what had happened. Even though multiple aspects of social, economic, and cultural functioning have been restored or rebuilt, nothing has helped anyone to understand how such a profoundly destructive ideology arose from within. This has made rehabilitation considerably more complex than in those societies where some components of social and cultural order remained intact. In such circumstances, individuals find other ways to deal with what happened, because the time and opportunity to make meaning of, and accommodate, their experiences never arrived. There is, for example, a state known as "dissociation," in which the mind detaches from information that it cannot handle comfortably and effectively. Another is "fragmentation," in which the mind breaks an event into smaller pieces that it cannot then reassemble into the whole, resulting in an inability to recall the full experience. Depending on their extent, these coping mechanisms may or may not affect how the individual deals with the minutiae of everyday living and social interaction when the trauma is over.

At some point in the postconflict period, despite all the residual problems, the everyday life of the general population reaches a form of stasis. Variations of the phrase "life goes on" are commonplace everywhere after difficult events: the immediate danger or crisis passes, one day follows another, the individual or family needs shelter and food and so people begin to function in patterns of behavior and relationships that become or present as normal, in the sense of being routine, purposeful in the pursuit of everyday functioning and lacking overt signs of conflict or disturbance. The reality, however, is that these patterns of behavior are almost certainly masking many residual and unresolved impacts of the trauma, and it is not possible to know the extent to which these factors distort perceptions and affect people's ability to rebuild their lives.

Implications for Capacity Development
In any postconflict country, beneficiary target groups and the national staff of development organizations are all likely to have experienced multiple negative events and conditions. In Cambodia, this included being subjected to a brutal regime that exercised total control over all aspects of daily life and denied all other ways of being in the world, multiple traumas that normal mechanisms for making meaning could not accommodate, multiple losses of loved ones and physical and social assets, severe malnutrition resulting in impaired development and damage to health, and, for some, disrupted and poor quality education. Complex trauma can cause both physical damage and cognitive and emotional legacies, any or all of which can act as internal inhibitors to prevent people from moving forward. The effects manifest both in individuals and in the collective. In such circumstances, it is not surprising that few manage to achieve their full potential and that there are many implications and consequences for capacity development initiatives.

For many people, the status quo, however bad, is preferable to risking change that could attract negative repercussions or represent the start of a slide into more troubling, difficult, and painful circumstances, summed up in the Cambodian saying, "Take the beaten path even if it is crooked." As Leng and Pearson noted, many Cambodians reject prospects of change because they believe that it is "risky, frightening and likely to lead to disaster" (Leng and Pearson 2006, 31). It is important to note that experience is not the only source of resistance: in traditional Cambodian culture, to acknowledge the need for change is to acknowledge that something is wrong or not working, which attracts loss of face (O'Leary and Meas 2001, 107). Resistance is often hidden behind smiles and words of agreement, and as many hopeful change agents, myself included, have discovered in Cambodian culture, smiles and words of agreement are no guarantee of acceptance. They simply mean, "I've heard you, and I'm going to give you the response I think you want to hear."

Many development approaches are fundamentally rooted in an assumption that cognition is all that is needed to prompt or sustain change. But, as Blatner noted, even in normal circumstances, real change comes only when an intricate web of perspectives and dimensions are addressed at the same time:

> A single formulation, insight, or even interpersonal influence is rarely sufficient to move people deeply. Generally, there needs to be a host of reinforcing experiences, often involving a range of modalities. (Blatner 2007)

A helpful insight on the seeming inability to change comes from Volkan's observations, noted above, about passivity, a feature of Cambodian society often cited by those frustrated with the slow pace of change being achieved by development projects. My own interpretation is that it is not so much passivity as a type of paralysis caused by fear, although they may look the same. Paulo Freire described similar behavior traits as "fatalism in the guise of docility" (Freire 1970, 48), which he believed to be the legacy of history and experience rather than inherent personal or national traits. Freire challenged beliefs that God created people's circumstances and argued that the majority of the oppressed simply do not understand that humans create the order of things that oppress them.

In Cambodia, fatalism is deeply embedded in the prevailing Buddhist belief system of karma. I have heard many variations of "We must have been bad in past lives for this to have happened to us." While Freire's arguments may well have validity for the Cambodian context, Meas offered a more pragmatic explanation of what lies beneath the seeming passivity of Cambodian people (Meas 2006, 7). In his opinion, mistrust between people and their leaders prevents the creation of any sense of safety, so people simply follow, as to do otherwise risks repercussions.

Meas went on to discuss how this plays out in the concept of participation, so beloved of development theorists and practitioners alike. In his view, the combination of culture and recent history has allowed the powerful to appropriate participation to fit their needs, which do not include empowering others. People participate in processes to show that they support authority and will do what is expected of them by a local leader (Meas 2006, 4). However participatory things may look on the surface, such activities do not involve empowerment. Development interventions therefore have to overcome multiple inhibiting factors, arising from Cambodia's age-old social hierarchy coupled with extreme negative experiences of power. Trust and safe spaces need to be established before people may feel safe to explore change.

An example of experience being a block to change is VBNK's long-term work to use self-reflection and peer feedback as tools for learning from practice. Despite extensive time and support spent helping older staff understand the concepts, many of them found it difficult to put this into practice. Some would actually cite not being able to get past their memories of self-criticism sessions during the Khmer Rouge regime, after which the "confessions" of wrongdoing would invariably lead to death. People mostly appeared simply to be stuck and unable to engage meaningfully in reflective self-analysis without repeated practice of the techniques involved, and for some not even then. This was not unique to VBNK staff. The *Learning for Transformation* researchers paid a great deal of attention to whether reflective practices were being used to support learning, and overall they found that they were not.

> There is extreme reluctance on the part of some staff to "dare" to speak up or reveal the problems they are experiencing in their work. This can be understood from the perspective that in former times people learned that silence and not drawing attention to oneself was the way to stay alive. While not now life threatening the thought of losing face, or even losing their job, is enough for staff to keep quiet and to hide or not disclose problems. Importantly, change is perceived to come from the top—not from the initiative of ordinary staff persons. (O'Leary and Meas 2001, 86)

Thus, cultural issues combine with experience to create resistance that is deeply embedded and hard to overcome. One manager, frustrated in her efforts to make open and honest feedback the norm in her team, told me that after making a comment to a staff member, he responded with "If this was Pol Pot times, your feedback would have me killed." Interestingly, the staff member was not old enough to have participated in self-criticism sessions, but the manager was and so the response proved to be a very effective way of deflecting and undermining her attempt to be honest with him.

Cambodians lived through, and continue to experience, trauma and disturbance from many different sources. In none of the aid or development programs undertaken since the Paris Peace Accords in 1991 has any large-scale, systematic, or comprehensive attempt been made to address the negative psychosocial impact of Cambodia's past in order to begin the process of national healing. Consequently the foundations needed for substantive learning, change, and development are not in place. Leng and Pearson expressed the relevance of this:

> The experiences . . . have very strong influences on Cambodians' ability to learn and change. Most of the lessons seem to prevent Cambodians from daring to do something in the future and do not help and support Cambodians moving forward constructively. Cambodians felt manipulated by several regimes, and, as a result, a culture of trauma, fear, distrust, hidden feelings, hopelessness, following and not challenging was created. (Leng and Pearson 2006, 5)

The question that still needs an answer is, "Why is the need for physical reconstruction so readily accepted in all sectors and societies, while the need to heal emotional wounds is barely acknowledged and rarely addressed?"

Conclusions

In the sections above about Cambodian trainers and their beliefs and behaviors, I described how some aspects of culture militate against learning and change. I then provided some analysis of the psychosocial impact of war and trauma on individuals and societies. Four key themes summarize the ways in which these issues of culture and context work together to create blocks to learning and change.

The first is the extent to which cultural beliefs underpin all understanding of, and responses to, trauma and the fact that it is inappropriate to assume that Western models of analysis, rehabilitation, and treatment are relevant to all cultures, because they are not.

The second theme concerns the making of meaning. If people and groups who have been through extraordinary events are unable to make meaning of their experiences, their unresolved memories and feelings will result in distorted perceptions and relationships that impact negatively on their general functioning.

The third theme is the knowledge we now have that in postconflict societies, impact occurs not only at the individual level but also, more importantly and more extensively, at the societal level, with major implications for how the society functions after the conflict.

The final theme, most pertinent for those working in any way to facilitate the development of capacity, is that complex trauma creates profound and lasting effects that inhibit both individuals and groups from embracing creativity, learning, and change.

By linking analysis of culture with that of postconflict context, I have tried to provide a unique insight into the complexities that we must take into account when thinking about interventions to promote change. These represent major challenges to any outsider working in and with populations that have been through tumultuously damaging times, such as those experienced by Cambodians. The first challenge is to understand the culture and how different concepts might be interpreted within it. The second challenge is to understand that beneath apparently normal behaviors, there may be reduced physical capacity and/or unresolved emotional and cognitive legacies, creating any number of repercussions in relation to how the individual functions. The third challenge is that what appears as resistance may not be deliberate or conscious so much as an inability to be, think, or do differently or to respond positively to people, change initiatives, or anything perceived as a risk. Last, it is important to recognize that behaviors that appear to be negative or unhelpful may not be individual pathology but could be better understood in terms of large-group responses to traumatic and unresolved experiences.

Human beings, individually and collectively, cannot be fully understood within simplistic models and frameworks; real understanding can come only through embracing all the complexities of human systems. The potential for capacity exists within all individuals and organizations, but attempts to develop this capacity will be successful only if they take as much account as possible of the environmental and systemic factors relevant to the presenting need. Failure to take account of such complexities, especially the inhibitors of change, invariably results in limited or short-term change, if any. Interventions therefore need to be subtly and sophisticatedly nuanced to multiple aspects of cultural and contextual relevance if they are to have any chance of producing sustainable benefit. There are no simple solutions.

Notes

1. This is the name by which the Vietnamese war is known in Southeast Asia.

2. This situation is changing, and there are now many successful initiatives to introduce student-centered pedagogies into all levels of the Cambodian education system.

3. "Transfer of training" is the term used in corporate and government training sectors for the theory and practice of learning acquired in one setting, such as a training course, being

integrated into practical usage in another setting, most usually the workplace. Many institutions are now using this theory as the basis for evaluation of the effectiveness of training. A very informative discussion of this subject is Taylor (1997).

4. Donald Kirkpatrick was professor emeritus at the University of Wisconsin. He first published his ideas about evaluation of training in 1959, in a series of articles in the *Journal of American Society of Training Directors*. He has subsequently written other significant works about training and evaluation. See www.kirkpatrickpartners.com.

5. This thesis was also published by VBNK as a series of four booklets in English and Khmer. See www.vbnk.org.

6. See "Developing a Learning Practice in VBNK" in Chapter 3 for a description of VBNK's learning weeks.

7. This was a four-year action research project that VBNK launched in 2003, which is described in "Creative Innovations for Learning and Change" in Chapter 4. The acronym stands for Creative Holistic Action-research for Relationship Transformation.

8. The appendix gives a brief summary of some relevant and interesting studies.

9. See the Merriam-Webster online dictionary: www.merriam-webster.com/dictionary/heal.

10. A particularly powerful example of different medical belief systems is the story of Lia, a girl born to a Laotian Hmong refugee family in the United States. The narrative starts when Lia was three months old and had an epileptic seizure shortly after her sister had slammed the front door of the apartment. Her family had no doubt that the noise of the slamming door had "profoundly frightened" her soul, which had then fled her body and become lost. They recognized her bodily symptoms as "qaug dab peg which means 'the spirit catches you and you fall down.'" While the medical seriousness of epilepsy is recognized in Hmong culture, the condition is not understood within any scientific explanation of irregular electrical activity in the brain. The Hmong hold primarily to their spiritual interpretation of the condition, and epileptics are regarded as specially blessed and often become shamans. Lia had many more seizures, and the story of how her parents, family, and community and the US medical system wrestled with each other's understanding, beliefs, and practices is painful and enlightening in equal measure. In the ensuing years, despite great care and concern from both her family and the medical system, Lia's condition became increasingly severe and resulted in profound and lasting damage to her functioning. Sadly, each side continues to blame the other for her deterioration (Fadiman 1997).

11. The Documentation Center of Cambodia is an NGO that was established to record and preserve the history of the Khmer Rouge regime for future generations and to compile and organize information that can serve as potential evidence in a legal accounting for the crimes of the Khmer Rouge. See www.dccam.org.

12. Kett noted that in Bosnia, women were unable to mourn their loved ones until they received positive DNA identification of the bodies. There were negative effects on the development of other children in families where mothers were stuck because they had not been able to complete the mourning process and move on with their lives. South Africa's Truth and Reconciliation Commission was taken by surprise when women testified that the inability to claim the body (or even body parts) of loved ones and perform traditional funeral rites was a breach of their human rights. To fulfill its stated purpose of contributing to the nation's healing, the commission undertook to find and return the remains of more than 50 people, even though this activity was outside its original mandate and budget.

2

Serving a Sector

In the first chapter, I described some aspects of Cambodia's culture and postconflict context that are relevant to capacity development. The other important part of the background to VBNK's story relates to the growth and change of the social development sector itself in response to Cambodia's needs.

This chapter gives a perspective on the organizations and institutions that have contributed to the country's reconstruction and rehabilitation since the fall of the Khmer Rouge regime. Some aspects of the social development sector are unique to each country; others may be applicable to all developing countries. Thus, some of this description is unique to Cambodia, but much of it could be applied to the way that organizations operate in any developing country. While it may well be the case that many organizations have developed their country strategies and operations in order to be fully sensitive to local culture and context, I know of no study that has analyzed or documented this process in action. The description I provide here is of the different groups of organizations and institutions with which VBNK has worked as I have observed them through VBNK's service delivery interactions with them. I then recount VBNK's processes of adapting to keep pace with the changes in the sector, reflected in progressive amendments to the mission statement.

I make no claim that what follows is a definitive analysis of a sector. VBNK is usually asked to engage with individual or organizational challenges, weaknesses, and needs, and these aspects are not the whole picture of the sector. An organization staffed by fully competent personnel would have little need of VBNK, apart from occasional facilitation of a retreat or planning event. Most commonly, VBNK has worked with individuals and organizations when there has been a need to improve performance or learn something new. The work might be a reactive response after problems have occurred or a proactive intervention to help learn from past experience and develop a way forward. That what follows is biased toward those needs is in no way intended to detract from the strengths and accomplishments of many individuals and organizations in the different groups, only that to focus on those issues would not be relevant to VBNK's story.

Another important point of introduction entails a brief comment about the much bigger and ongoing capacity development discourse that began more than two decades ago, when the RGC first allowed INGOs to train its staff. The findings of two studies on technical assistance in Cambodia (Godfrey et al. 2000; Land and Morgan 2008) are not encouraging, because they show that donor practices have resulted in the same limited progress that is endemic throughout the aid industry. Currently, the RGC and its development partners are actively engaged in initiatives stemming from the Paris Declaration and the Accra Agenda for Action to enhance aid effectiveness and, within this, capacity development. Despite the emphasis in the Accra Agenda for Action on the contribution of civil society, aid effectiveness initiatives have yet to result in any obvious impact within the NGO community. Not since the early 1990s has anyone undertaken comprehensive research into where NGOs fit within the broader capacity development agenda, either as providers or as recipients, or into the overall contribution that NGOs are making to Cambodia's development.

The role and contribution of INGOs in Cambodia is well documented for the period from 1979 to the early 1990s. Thereafter, apart from technical and sector-focused studies, the general commentary stops, and all subsequent focus is on CNGOs and the development of civil society. Given the numbers, the scope of the activities of the INGOs, and the amount of money the INGOs bring into the country each year, this appears to be a serious omission in analysis and understanding of an important contribution to the country's development. None of the statements NGOs periodically make about their work and the money they bring into the country comprises a balanced and objective appraisal of both the positive and the negative impacts that the ever-expanding NGO community creates. Understanding the role and effectiveness of the NGOs, especially with regard to capacity development, is recognized as important, yet the necessary data and analysis do not exist. To explore the full relevance and complexity of this subject requires much deeper discussion, beyond the focus of this book.

International NGOs

It is appropriate to start with a brief summary of the history of the INGOs in Cambodia, because they were active from 1979, more than a decade before any national organizations came into existence.

INGOs were quick to provide some of the emergency relief needed to alleviate the desperate humanitarian crisis after the fall of the Khmer Rouge regime. Most INGO contributions were made through consortia, the largest led by Oxfam United Kingdom, another supported by US church groups, and a third supported by Catholic agencies. A few INGOs chose to act independently, and by 1981, 13 were active in country. From 1982 onward, geopolitical maneuverings resulted in the United Nations and most Western countries holding Cambodia in isolation. The INGOs working inside Cambodia during these years were acting in defiance of Western international policy, which had, among other things, effectively stopped the flow of bilateral funding. One way in which the Cambodian government sought to gain control of external interventions during this period was by formalizing its relationships with the INGOs. Everything INGOs did had to be through the central administration, in a role that has been described as an "attempt to fill the void created by the virtual absence of multilateral and bilateral donors, other than Eastern bloc countries, working on large-scale projects" (Bennett and Benson 1995, 172). Expatriates were forbidden to train or give technical assistance directly to Cambodians and were allowed to live in two hotels in Phnom Penh only.

Up to 50 INGOs were active during the 1980s, working with Cambodian refugees in the camps on the Thai–Cambodian border. The story of the refugees is also long and complex, beyond the scope of this work. In brief, many hundreds of thousands of Cambodians fled the country throughout the 1970s and 1980s. In the camps, INGOs worked under the overall supervision of the United Nations, meeting basic humanitarian needs and helping equip the refugees for a new life in the future. For some, this meant resettlement to a third country; for others, it was training in various skills in anticipation of eventual return to Cambodia. Some established INGOs started their Cambodia programs in the camps; several newer ones now working in the country started as border camp projects. Another important development in this period was the establishment in 1986 of the NGO Forum on Kampuchea. This forum, initially made up of 20 European, Australian, and US organizations, began the process of lobbying for an end to the international isolation and for the establishment of development assistance for Cambodia.

In 1989, some political factions began taking steps toward a peaceful solution for the country, which opened up the political space for an inflow of aid that continues to this day. Given the highly complex political situation and the fact that many government institutions had yet to be established or to achieve full capacity, many donors chose to channel their aid through INGOs. This was not a comfortable period for the INGOs, as they were effectively being used politically to bypass the government. However, the INGOs began to be able to hire Cambodian staff, work directly with government personnel, and start work in the provinces, albeit in limited ways. The early 1990s saw what has been described as "a plethora of new NGOs" (Bennett and Benson 1995, 173) arriving in country in anticipation of a substantial increase in the volume of aid. To facilitate the incoming agencies, 25 INGOs founded an umbrella body, the Cooperation Committee for Cambodia (CCC), in 1990. The CCC was never intended to be a coordinating body, only a facility for sharing essential information and for liaison between the RGC and INGOs. The CCC is still active as a membership organization for INGOs and CNGOs today.

Somewhere along the line, the government's strict control in the 1980s got lost, and from the early 1990s any organization could come in and set up a program. While the number of INGOs has continued to increase ever since, it is hard to know how many were or are operating in the country at any given time. There is now a standard Memorandum of Understanding (MOU) process for INGOs to register with the Ministry of Foreign Affairs. To fulfill registration requirements, the INGO needs an MOU with a different ministry, for example, Health or Rural Development, which specifies the contribution it is making to the development of the country under the auspices of that ministry. The CCC has monitored data from the Ministry of Foreign Affairs, which in 1999 estimated that there were more than 200 INGOs in country and which in 2010 had MOUs with 337 organizations.[1] However, there are no restrictions on expatriates buying a business visa, and an unknown number of organizations have chosen this route to facilitate the presence of their expatriate personnel in country, making it impossible to know exactly how many are actually there.

Since 1979, INGOs have worked on just about every humanitarian and social need that exists in Cambodia. An increasing number have changed from sector-based programming to integrated community development approaches, although many still retain sectoral specialisms, such as health, education, agriculture, water and sanitation, child welfare, and many more. In addition, there has always been a group of INGOs concerned with democracy, human rights, and advocacy on issues such as the environment. There are many faith-based INGOs, mostly but not exclusively Christian, some of which proselytize (many do not).

Programmatically, the majority of INGOs have been motivated by the need to find effective mechanisms to alleviate poverty and its attendant ills and to facilitate social change by empowering communities. They have differing views about working with government. Some, especially those in the health sector and those using a community development approach, are active in developing good relationships in order to work cooperatively with both central and local authorities. Others take exactly the opposite view and actively avoid or bypass Cambodian authorities, which they are able to do in the current legal vacuum. Since 2002, many have been engaged in supporting the development of commune councils as part of their community-level projects.

My orientation to Cambodian development in January 1995 was through the group of seven INGOs that had initiated the project I was to manage. Six of the seven had significant similarities, in that they were all nonproselytizing Christian organizations that had been active through the 1980s, some from the very first days of emergency relief in 1979. Political changes had allowed them all to move into community-level activities, although some were still supporting central facilities. Three also had funds and projects to support CNGOs. Without exception, this group described their Cambodia program as atypical, because in other countries their strategy was to support local civil society organizations, including churches, and their operations were therefore smaller and did not involve implementation. The seventh organization, Pact, had arrived in the early 1990s, with funding from USAID to implement a community outreach project, which was a mechanism for supporting a broad range of initiatives and the development of civil society. All seven are still operational in Cambodia, but most now have significantly different programs.

In the mid-1990s, most INGO projects had expatriate management, because local staff had yet to acquire the skills and experience for this level of responsibility. Much internal capacity building was underway to prepare Cambodians eventually to take over management positions from expatriates, and this was the rationale for my training project. Over time, such processes have achieved considerable success, and these days it is unusual to meet an expatriate project manager. Most INGOs still have expatriate country representatives, but only in a few very large organizations do expatriates hold other management positions: most are advisers or coordinators. Another long-term trend has been the localization of projects or whole organizations as CNGOs.

Despite the fact that INGOs are usually in a position to provide better salaries and benefits than CNGOs, they can still struggle to find staff with the right level of knowledge, skills, and experience to implement programs and run the organization effectively. This is particularly true at entry level, where applicants may be young graduates with very little relevant experience. It is also true at the most senior levels, where strong capacity for analysis and strategic thinking is not yet a common feature. Furthermore, possibly because they recognize the demands and stresses that go with senior management, many competent people appear to prefer to stay in middle management rather than step up to higher levels of responsibility. Organizations that do have highly competent senior managers try very hard to keep them.

INGOs used VBNK services in different ways. A few made strategic decisions to partner with VBNK for all their Cambodian staff capacity development needs or for their localization processes. Through relationships that deepened over the years, VBNK was able to support some very substantive changes in these organizations. It can be said with confidence that, for this group, VBNK has contributed significantly to the progressive "Cambodian-ization" of the management and also to the successful localization of several organizations. Many other INGOs have used VBNK consistently, albeit with less strategic intent, as their primary training provider and/or to facilitate their internal organizational development processes. However, on more than one occasion, it was disconcerting when a good relationship and long-term work between VBNK and an INGO came to an abrupt halt with the departure of one country representative and the arrival of another, the newcomer apparently deciding to stop implementation of the predecessor's capacity development strategies.

Other organizations sent staff on courses on an occasional and as-needed basis, commissioned customized in-house training, had VBNK facilitate some of their own internal activities, and/or supported training and organizational development processes for their CNGO partners. A different form of engagement occurred when VBNK was contracted to support the capacity development component of project implementation. This was particularly the case in decentralization projects, because VBNK had developed considerable relevant expertise when it was engaged to help develop the original training for commune councilors before the first elections in 2002. Some large INGOs have never used VBNK, because corporate resources cover their capacity development needs internally.

One example illustrates the mutual benefits that can accrue through long-term partnerships. Church World Service (CWS) has been working in Cambodia since the early 1980s, and its current program is one of integrated community development, peace building, and emergency relief. CWS was both one of the organizations that supported VBNK's establishment in 1997 and its first customer. Since then, both organizations have come a long way on their journeys of organizational learning. Their different missions and programs mean that they work in very different ways, but both are committed to the search for answers to the intractable problems of poverty and social injustice in Cambodia. The synergy of shared purpose has resonated through the years and kept the two organizations moving forward together.

CWS found in VBNK a source of new ideas and supportive facilitation to help it learn and change. CWS staff participated in two rounds of the CHART project and in a Leadership Development Program (LDP). They actively embraced opportunities to work with creative practices in their organizational development processes. They also participated in different initiatives, such as the Development Café discussion forum and the Intergenerational Dialogue Conference. In CWS, VBNK found an organization willing and able to work with new ideas, both in community-level implementation and in internal processes. Feedback from practice helped VBNK refine and develop both the content and the implementation of the relevant initiatives. The partnership was also supported in early years through CWS staff serving on the VBNK board, including its country director serving as chair during 2001–2002. While the relationship with CWS stands out because of its consistency and longitude, it is by no means unique in terms of the quality of VBNK's relationships with some INGOs.[2]

While only a minority of INGOs could be described as well resourced, as a group INGOs are generally better placed than most CNGOs to support staff capacity development and organizational development processes. On this basis, they are likely to continue to be one of the core groups that VBNK serves for the foreseeable future.

Cambodian NGOs

The first fully Cambodian NGO was established in 1991 to work with women in an area on the outskirts of Phnom Penh.[3] Many others, initially known as local initiative groups (Bennett and Benson 1995, 179), quickly followed in Phnom Penh and other parts of the country. Responding to urgent humanitarian needs was a common motivating factor when Cambodia was still in the throes of civil war, necessitating emergency relief and assistance, with a pressing and ongoing need for anything that contributed to the alleviation of poverty or the provision of basic services. A number of new organizations created in advance of the first national elections in 1993 were active in preparing the population, through widespread voter education programs on democracy and human rights, for the momentous day when many would vote for the first time in their life.

Organizational origins were varied. Some were founded by individuals who had never left or by returnees from the border camps, where they had received skills training from INGOs. Others were started by returning diasporas, sometimes as offshoots of Cambodian associations in other countries, mostly the United States. A few were directly founded by INGOs, donors, or institutions. The earliest known report specifically about CNGOs was written in 1993 for an INGO, a summary of which in 1996 noted a key finding: "When the NGO sector began in Cambodia, local groups were characterized by high hopes, high aspirations and motivation, but, with some exceptions, little knowledge about development in the NGO sense of the word" (CNSN [Cambodian NGO Support Network] 1996a, 1). I think that today, few would describe hopes, aspirations, or motivation as high, and in some cases, less positive characteristics have replaced them. It could also be argued that knowledge about development is still far from widespread.

At the time of my arrival in January 1995, many CNGOs had been established, and the INGOs in my project were working with many of them. No definitive numbers were available, but various support organizations had each documented at least 100 CNGOs, with limited crossover of their lists because the INGOs were working in different sectors and geographic areas. Some CNGOs were then already large, well resourced and well organized and implementing substantive programs. At the other end of the scale might be the small community groups that came together to do something whenever they managed to get some resources. Some commentators felt that the development of the sector had been donor driven (CNSN 1996b, 1), because donors were actively looking for groups that could be helpful in implementing their own programs. Others disputed this assumption, noting, "Most CNGOs still have no reliable outside funding at all, but work on a semi-voluntary basis with whatever resources they and the communities they work with can put together" (CNSN 1996c, 1).

A number of bilateral donors felt that the development of civil society organizations was an essential element in the country's reconstruction and made funds available for that purpose. While sector-based funding tended to go directly from donors to CNGOs, support for other target groups was channeled through intermediary INGOs. For example, at that time USAID was directly funding health and education organizations, but it channeled its support to the human rights and democracy sector through The Asia Foundation and to more generic community and social development organizations through Pact. These intermediary organizations provided both grant and technical support to multiple CNGOs for many years. Some INGOs felt strongly that all INGOs should step back and let the local organizations find their vision, voice, and solutions to problems. At the same time, they and others were noting that they were overwhelmed with requests for funding and other types of support.

The rapid evolution of the sector in the early 1990s meant that CNGOs were able to help people in many different ways. For example, health organizations were able to fill some gaps in service provision, and in the mid-1990s, when HIV/AIDS began to spread, CNGOs joined the response and made an invaluable contribution to Cambodia's success in containing the epidemic. Similarly, other organizations supported agricultural development, education initiatives, women's rights, credit and savings programs—the list is endless. In the early days, anyone who could articulate a good idea as the basis for a project would most likely find a donor willing to support it. A few organizations were implementing programs that fell under a generic community development approach, but in general the concept of integrated community development became widespread only during the late 1990s. The burgeoning CNGO community was also providing some much-needed paid employment for many people.

However, in the mid-1990s, INGOs with partner support programs started to express concerns about many aspects of CNGOs and how they worked. A group of organizations supporting CNGOs, which came to be known as the Cambodian NGO Support Network (CNSN), organized a partnership workshop in July 1996. The papers produced for and after that conference provide a very rich source of information about the state of CNGOs at that time.

A common observation was that CNGOs were "very much influenced by the examples of INGOs" and that, consequently, they adopted organizational structures and norms about which they had little understanding (CNSN 1996c, 1). This included concern about the development agenda, in that Cambodian organizations were adopting foreign ideas about development that they did not fully understand. They lacked both confidence in their own ideas and critical analytical skills to adapt and apply imported concepts to the Cambodian context. This either was coupled with or led to failure to value and work with traditional knowledge and customs, and to involve communities in decision making. Frequently cited concerns were that staff did not know enough about their target communities and their needs, there was insufficient involvement of communities in the identification of priority needs and possible solutions, and community workers did not have sufficient knowledge and expertise to make appropriate responses to needs. The two schools of thought about the causes of these problems were either that workers from rural communities had very limited education or experience to guide them or that workers from urban areas had no knowledge of, or respect for, villagers. It is likely that both were true. Overall, widespread results included flawed project design and poor implementation practices. However, no one was offering any fundamentally different approaches.

Donors and support partners also began to worry about the instances of corruption, misuse of organizational resources, autocratic management, and nepotism that were coming to light. This sometimes happened where one, often charismatic, person had founded the organization without any governance or accountability structures. A report prepared for Novib (Oxfam Netherlands) stated, "Strong leadership is a significant advantage for the successful establishment of a new local NGO. . . . However, strong leadership in the Cambodian context seems to exclude a participatory approach and accountability" (CNSN 1996d, 1). In addition, it seemed that many CNGOs were focused on organizational trappings and benefits, such as air-conditioned offices, phones (then a rare and valuable commodity), and four-wheel drive vehicles. At least one commentator felt that the INGO and donor communities had only themselves to blame for this problem, because of their own, sometimes ostentatious, use of such resources (CNSN 1996c, 1). Another concern, albeit not so common, was the belief in some CNGOs that the organization existed to keep staff in paid employment rather than to implement a program.

Some organizations were struggling from a lack of resources, because of both donor practices and the paucity of what communities could raise for themselves. A final area of concern noted at the time was that all attention was on the implementation of projects and programs. A more balanced approach, incorporating organizational development, was needed if the CNGOs were to survive.

These issues can be summarized as concern that organizations and their staff did not have the knowledge, skills, or attitude necessary for their work to result in sustainable benefits for their target communities. Donors that had been so keen to give money just a few years before now wanted to introduce initiatives to strengthen the organizations and to discuss monitoring, evaluation, impact, accountability, transparency, governance, and such like. Many of these concepts were entirely new, with no resonance in either traditional Cambodian culture or people's recent experiences. The result was confusion, sometimes to the point of mystification, coupled with stress and anxiety as the CNGOs began to realize that the already tenuous flow of funding and other support was now in question. The challenges of integrating some key development and governance concepts into the culture of the sector continue to this day.

Support partnerships have always been a critical factor in the development of CNGOs and, in some cases, in their very existence. Reports and documentation from the workshop in July 1996 describe the newly emerging CNGOs with no development experience on which to draw and the international actors, some with long histories and existing programs of their own in Cambodia, some new arrivals with a range of different agenda. Despite needs on one side and good intentions on the other, a particularly difficult and complex set of issues had emerged in the partnerships between the two groups. Programs for CNGO support were, for the most part, still responding to emerging needs and thus were somewhat unstructured and lacking in clear criteria. The reports discuss what was happening in the partnerships, highlighting how much everyone was trying to find their way to effective working practices in this uncharted territory. It is not surprising that these circumstances led everyone involved to experience significant difficulties.

The CNSN continued to operate for some years and in 2001 commissioned a study of the work done to support the CNGO community. The study findings were that little progress had been made in five years. The main need identified was to strengthen CNGOs through development of leadership and good management practices, with particular emphasis on accountability and improving analytical and problem-solving skills. The study commented on the complexities and challenges in the partnerships:

> Support Agencies are also having difficulty keeping up with the varied and changing needs of Cambodian Non-governmental Organisations. Staff are expected to provide support on a huge array of issues and skills, and it is impossible to address everything at an appropriate level. There is also a lack of baseline information from which to assess impact and progress. . . . The main partnership themes that have come out of this report are the need to define a common set of values for Non-governmental Organisational work in Cambodia, to be aware of the power differential between Support Agencies and Non-governmental Organisations, to encourage good leadership, and for improved educational opportunities in development. (Richardson 2001, 1)

The staff teams of support agencies are an interesting factor in this scenario. Most INGOs had appointed Cambodian staff teams to implement their partnership activities. The knowledge and competencies needed for this role are wide ranging, across technical, organizational, financial, and personal skill sets. The reality was, of course, that INGO staff originally were often not much more skillful and knowledgeable than those they were trying to support. It was often the case that the supporter was just one step ahead of the supported. Yet INGO staff held enormous power in these relationships, a factor that, in the highly nuanced structures of Cambodian society, was not lost on either side. While the majority of INGO partner support officers have striven to do this work to the best of their ability, it remains a reality that many lack the full range of skills needed to do it well. Lack of self-confidence can tend to result in a heavy control orientation, thereby reducing the flexibility and creativity that might prove to be more supportive of achievement and capacity development. I surmise that if CNGOs were asked how they have experienced the complicated combination of support and control within these relationships, most would say they have experienced more control than support. Sadly, there have also been cases where support officers have abused their power over local partners.

In summary, the CNGO scenario was complex at the time of VBNK's establishment in 1997, and it still is. The number of CNGOs continues to grow, with support from many different international agencies. The latest estimate is that there are about 1,500 registered with the Ministry of Interior, but, as with INGOs, there is no way of knowing how many more exist outside the registration system. From the early days, CNGOs have made a valuable contribution, initially responding to humanitarian emergencies and providing basic social services. The sector was then, and remains, unregulated, and it has a complicated relationship with the RGC. All the achievements and the growth in numbers notwithstanding, many CNGOs still have substantive problems to overcome in terms of their operational and organizational weaknesses.

Important lessons can be drawn from reviewing the early history of CNGOs:

- The rapid growth of the CNGO community is owed in large part to the availability of financial and other support. It is unlikely that it would have grown in the same way or had the same characteristics if there had been less money or fewer support partners.
- Much of the support offered was given without, or before, accurate assessment of relevant capacity. The result frequently was extremely unrealistic expectations on both sides.
- Issues such as the values, practice principles, and other assessment criteria that support partners employ to assess the capacity and performance of local organizations need to be introduced

before contracts and implementation. Trying to apply these concepts retrospectively causes multiple problems for everyone concerned.

- Long-term strategies and commitments to support capacity development in local organizations would result in much more effective and sustainable capacity than does the more common practice of ad hoc interventions linked to short-term projects.

Many INGOs have had support for local partners as part of their program strategy since the 1990s. Some, but not all, appear to have learned and adapted, but it is disconcerting to see the frequency with which recommendations based on these lessons continue to appear in reports and evaluations. The indications are that there is still a long way to go before partnership practices achieve optimum effectiveness.

CNGOs were half of VBNK's original target group, so there were expectations that VBNK would be able to provide solutions to some of the problems. Having assessed the full range of needs, it was easy to identify those that fit VBNK's mission, namely, management, and those that were best left to others, such as sector-based technical skills, English language skills, and basic office, bookkeeping, or computing skills. The initial approach was to offer short, practical training courses on organizational and project management. Many CNGOs did not have any core funding that covered a budget for staff development. It was therefore helpful when Pact established a Scholarship Fund to which CNGOs could apply for course fees and for the travel and accommodation costs incurred by provincial participants coming to Phnom Penh for training. DanChurchAid (DCA) subsequently took over and supported the Scholarship Fund for several years, until strategic changes in its Cambodia program caused it to withdraw its support. Even though the Scholarship Fund was very successful in enabling hundreds of CNGO managers and staff to attend training, it took a good while to find other donors willing to support it.[4]

VBNK's support to CNGOs expanded over time to include customized training and many different forms of organizational development interventions. Often, donors paid for these activities, sometimes for work with only one organization, at other times for groups of their CNGO partners. The biggest such project was commissioned by the Interchurch Organisation for Development Cooperation (ICCO) for 18 of its CNGO partners. The work took place in three phases, over four years, 2005–2008. Within the Cambodian development sector, the ICCO Partners Project (IPP) was highly innovative in using an organizational learning model and creative practices as its approach to organizational capacity development (Pearson 2011a). The success of the project demonstrated how far some of the CNGO community and VBNK had come since 1997.

There have been many other successes, and many individuals and organizations are today more competent as a result of the services and support they received from VBNK and other sources. But overall, the CNGO community still displays some of the intractable weaknesses that emerged at the start, as follows.

Individual Management Skills

To some extent, CNGOs are the entry level for the entire development sector, continually losing good staff to organizations that offer the prospects of advancement, higher status, and better salaries and benefits. Therefore, CNGOs frequently take on new staff, who need capacity development in core management skills such as staff management, report writing, budget control, and so on, in addition to any technical skills they might need.

Organizational Capacity

To survive, organizations need the capacity to analyze both their broad environment and specific problems in their target community and then to conceptualize, formulate, and implement effective responses. Internal capacity is characterized by having an appropriate structure and necessary systems in place, and learning for long-term sustainability. Donors often express the view that many CNGOs are stuck in a repetitive pattern of doing what once brought them success, unable to recognize the changes in their environment and target groups. In short, they neither think nor act strategically. I once asked the director of a CNGO how the staff identified needs to inform and guide their annual activity planning. The response was, "We don't plan based on needs; we plan based on what we can do." Another problem is that even organizations with a strong mission can be seriously affected by chasing money to keep the organization afloat. This was never more obvious than in the early and mid-2000s, when several bilateral and multilateral donors initiated multimillion dollar projects in response to the HIV/AIDS epidemic. Organizations with no previous experience of health or health-related issues applied for, and got, funds to implement HIV/AIDS-based projects.

Leadership and the "Shining Star Syndrome"

The strong leadership mentioned in the Novib report cited above often manifests in what I call the "shining star syndrome." It continues to occur in CNGOs, although I understand that it is far from unique to Cambodia. The shining star is the founding director, a person with a vision and the energy and some capacity to make things happen. These people started an NGO to make their vision a reality. Very often, but not always, they are good people with a deep commitment to helping their fellow Cambodians. In situations such as Cambodia in the early and mid-1990s, such people attract a great deal of funding and other support, because a charismatic and articulate national with a viable idea is manna from heaven for donors looking for implementing partners. Unfortunately, many of the shining stars do not have the management capacity to match their vision. They also prefer to remain the only star in their particular firmament and are unwilling to delegate power or authority for fear of staff getting some of the limelight or control. There might be a nominal hierarchy, but everyone understands that the director makes all the decisions and controls everything in the autocratic style commonly found elsewhere in Cambodian society. This style does not sit well with development practices such as participation, teamwork, staff capacity development, and so on or with Cambodians who have experienced these practices in other organizations.

One of the evaluation findings at the end of the IPP was that the attitude of leadership was the most critical factor in determining organizational readiness to embrace learning and change. The management practices of shining stars have resulted in many instances of negative impact on the sustainability of their organizations. First, such directors do very little, if anything, to build the capacity of staff or the organization. Even those who do manage to get training find it virtually impossible to implement any changes as a result of what they have learned. Second, because the director controls everything important, few systems and procedures exist beyond a process of submitting all decisions to him or her. On some occasions, when a founder moves on, his or her successors have found that they inherited what is effectively an empty shell. The third major issue is resistance to governance. Some shining stars do have boards, often made up of their friends, but they are rarely active.

Early on, the founders of Cambodian human rights and democracy organizations were feted by the donors interested in that sector. Unfortunately, some in that group saw nothing amiss in preaching democracy and human rights in public fora while practicing total autocracy within their own organization. I recall, for example, a staff member in a human rights organization being sacked for asking for a contract of employment, a fundamental right under Cambodian Labor Law. Within this group, there have been some instances of ugly conflict when boards have attempted to exercise their responsibilities, at least one of which has resulted in the demise of the organization. Differences between stated values and values actually practiced have done considerable harm both to individual organizations and to the reputation of their more ethical colleagues in the same sector.

Good Governance

Governance,[5] with increasing emphasis on having a governing board, has been a growing concern of most donors since the mid-1990s. The first initiative I am aware of on this subject was when Pact commissioned research into traditional governance mechanisms in Cambodian society, such as pagoda committees. Despite external demands for good governance, there are only a few examples of consistent good practice in the CNGO sector. Lack of transparency and accountability is rooted in several interrelated factors, such as cultural expectations of the behavior of leaders, prevailing attitudes toward information as a source of both power and danger, and the ever-present fear of losing face. The fear of losing funding support compounds all of these many times over. These factors contributed early on to patterns of hiding failure and weaknesses, which have been almost impossible to break. While weaknesses and failures are usually readily apparent to any knowledgeable observer, this does not influence CNGOs to adopt more open and honest communication. There is a naive belief that if something is not openly discussed, it is not known to others.

Regrettably, there have been instances where board members have acted inappropriately and caused very difficult conflicts. These cases have added strength to the inherent reluctance to establish boards. An example was Ponleu Khmer, which in the mid-1990s was the leading CNGO association, governed by a board elected by the member organizations. As it was providing a range of services to support the development of both individual organizations and the CNGO community generally, it had attracted significant funding. An unscrupulous individual got himself and some friends elected to the board, whereupon they set about trying to get control of the association's bank accounts. The conflict was extremely unpleasant and included the board locking all managers and staff out of the office. Ultimately, as a result of staff action, all funds were returned to the donors. The association did not survive, and although some staff subsequently started a new organization with a related mission, no similar association has been formed since.

References to CNGOs in recent works on other subjects reiterate that many of the problems noted in the early 1990s are now firmly embedded in the sector. For example, a recent study on civil society–parliamentarian interactions noted that while NGOs have made a contribution in service delivery and policy advocacy, they are financially dependent and lack grassroots authentication of their role, resulting in "upward accountability and submissiveness" (Ou, Pide, and Sedara 2010, 159). The report went on to note that NGOs are operating in political space that is allowed by the state, but that space is maintained largely through the pressure of international agencies. As a number of donors have now begun to be more supportive of government, they are offering less support to NGOs, which raises questions about the maintenance of operating space in future.

To summarize, the CNGO community has grown and developed since 1991. Some organizations have achieved much, through strong programs and sound organizational practices. Some have transformed over time into something quite different from their origins. For various reasons, a number have either just withered away or self-destructed in spectacular conflicts. Corruption and nepotism are endemic in Cambodian society today, and it would be naive to think that they do not exist in CNGOs (or INGOs), although many do their best to guard against these unhelpful practices. New organizations appear to be springing up all the time: some have inbuilt expertise because they are staffed by people with good experience from elsewhere, but others create a disconcerting sense of déjà vu, because they appear to be founded on little more than hope and unrealistic expectations, especially about funding. There are some big CNGOs with which VBNK has never worked, probably because they didn't feel the need for what VBNK could offer or because they had partners who provided all necessary support. The majority, however, remain in need of long-term capacity development support for multiple aspects of their functioning.

Royal Government of Cambodia

Relationships between the RGC and NGOs vary greatly, from highly effective and productive cooperation in some areas to open hostility in others. Many NGOs working with the authorities at central, provincial, and district levels report good relationships and harmonious cooperation, within which the authorities facilitate NGO activities. NGOs need permission and support to do their work, and for their part the authorities appreciate that NGOs can make positive contributions to their constituencies, through both resources and expertise. On the other hand, Cambodia's active and vocal human rights sector frequently criticizes the RGC in public fora, with the result that many government staff, particularly in central ministries, have concerns about working with NGOs. A general lack of understanding about what NGOs are and how they work, coupled sometimes with envy of the relatively high salaries that NGO workers earn, can add to negative feelings. Such factors can create significant hurdles for organizations like VBNK in trying to establish the relationships needed to work effectively.

In the first instance, administrative necessity motivated VBNK to include RGC staff in the target group. To be eligible for registration within government systems, VBNK needed to have an MOU with a ministry, under which we needed to be contributing to that ministry's work. Discussions with the Ministry of Education, Youth and Sports did not get us very far, because we worked with adults rather than children and young people. One of our board members had a contact in the Training and Research Department at the Ministry of Rural Development and made an introduction. Once established, the connection with the ministry proved to be fruitful on both sides. VBNK agreed to provide training each year for ministry staff on subjects such as project management. The ministry was happy with this arrangement, as it contributed to developing staff capacity beyond the parameters imposed by project-based funding. In return, the ministry gave VBNK the administrative support needed for registration and visa requirements. In the early years, when the Ministry of Rural Development was the only ministry with which VBNK worked, there were few government staff on courses.

As in many developing countries, a fundamental challenge to capacity development initiatives in RGC institutions is that salaries are low, so many staff need other ways to earn their living, which can reduce both their attendance at work and their motivation when there. Developments in the RGC and NGO sectors have happened differently and at different paces, and many NGO staff have experienced capacity development activities that have introduced them to new concepts and ways of working, far beyond anything that the majority of government staff have experienced. The differences influence attitudes in ways that have occasionally created difficulties for VBNK in implementing activities.

One of VBNK's more challenging experiences with a ministry highlights some of the issues. A UN agency sponsored VBNK to support a ministry that had identified the need to formulate a ministry-wide strategy for a particular issue. As no one in the ministry had any experience of strategy development, it was necessary to give training on the concepts before starting facilitation of analysis and formulation of the plan. It took one of VBNK's most mature and senior trainers the whole first morning of the schedule to convince the participants that training delivered in a participatory methodology would be beneficial for them. All the participants' previous experiences, and therefore their expectations, were of lecture-style training. They regarded anything else as evidence that the trainers didn't know enough about the subject to train properly and therefore thought the training was a waste of their time. The participants' attendance record at that training was probably the worst of any VBNK event ever, creating significant content continuity difficulties for the trainers. After the training, we jointly scheduled a workshop to start the strategy development process. This was deemed an important event for the ministry, requiring a large opening ceremony. The senior ministry official presiding over the ceremony arrived 40 minutes late and took three phone calls during his speech. Not an auspicious start, but worse was to come as, after the ceremony, all participants bar three announced that they were leaving for the day to attend a ceremony at the minister's home. The process got underway the next day and in due course produced a strategy, but it was not a happy experience for VBNK.

Other work has been much more positive and mutually beneficial. The legislation that introduced the commune council structure of local governance in 2002 brought about a radical change for VBNK's target group. This legislation both opened the space for and required multiple actors—donors, INGOS, and CNGOs—to work together with central government to support the new local governance structure. VBNK was approached to get involved in a number of the projects formulated in anticipation of the election of the first cohort of commune councilors in February 2002. This included being asked to work with the international decentralization expert, who was tasked with developing the basic training courses for the councilors. These requests were all significantly outside VBNK's experience, and the management team considered very carefully how to respond, including holding discussions with people and organizations inside and outside government about how the development of the commune councils was likely to unfold. Eventually we decided that we should get involved, but as this work was outside our mission, we consulted the board before going ahead. The board felt that the decision to work outside the mission was justified by the significance of commune councils for Cambodia's development. They welcomed our decision on the grounds that good quality training would be needed for the councilors and for those who would work with them. VBNK has never been a major player in the decentralization sector, but it has consistently made a contribution through different donor projects that work with multiple stakeholder groups in support of the decentralization process. Sometimes the work has been direct training to councilors and project staff working with them, but most frequently it has been in a training of trainer role, working with the staff of other agencies.

Another important initiative with government personnel was the Women's Leadership Program (WLP), described in the "Early Innovations" section in Chapter 4. Other work, on a smaller scale, occurred regularly when donors contracted VBNK to train or facilitate groups within specific ministries. More recently, VBNK has been engaged to work with the RGC on some initiatives concerned with the aid effectiveness agenda. A key government institute has recognized that VBNK can offer effective support in relation to a range of needs and that using this local organization rather than always depending on international providers is also in keeping with the commitments made in the Accra Agenda for Action.

Donors

The word "donor" covers many different types of organizations and institutions, all of which are represented in Cambodia. The RGC's development partners fall into two groups. The first comprises the multilateral IOs: the UN group, the World Bank, the Asian Development Bank (ADB), and the European Union (EU). The second important group is made up of bilateral development agencies, of which there are currently more than 20. While most of their support to Cambodia involves working with the RGC, some IO and bilateral programs also work directly with NGOs. In addition, some embassies give small grants for CNGO activities.

Another group of donors are those with foundation status. None of the big US foundations, such as Ford or Kellogg, has programs in Cambodia, although the Gates Foundation has channeled some money into HIV/AIDS work. There are, however, many smaller foundations disbursing funds generated by their own corporate investment portfolios or fund-raising activities. The next group comprises those donors that have NGO status, or something similar, in their own Northern country. For example, several European protestant church-based development organizations, such as Christian Aid (United Kingdom), *Evangelische Entwicklungsdienst* (Church Development Service [EED], Germany), ICCO (the Netherlands), and DCA (Demark), all have long-term programs in Cambodia. All of these organizations receive funding from their national government and other sources, including churches. Finally, INGOs such as Oxfam and CWS have both direct implementation and partner support programs, so they are simultaneously both recipient and donor. There are also a very small number of CNGOs in this group. The majority of donors supporting CNGOs are in these last groups: foundations, development organizations, and INGOs.

VBNK has done little direct work within the large community of IOs, multilateral and bilateral donors active in Cambodia, apart from occasional facilitation of consultation processes with the NGO community, country team retreats, and other similar events. Although VBNK has neither the capacity nor the inclination to bid directly for any large donor project, INGOs and large for-profit consulting agencies often make approaches when preparing their expressions of interest or their proposals. External entities need to show that they have local expertise, and having an organization such as VBNK listed as a potential implementing partner is a mechanism by which to meet this need. Few benefits have ever flowed in VBNK's direction from these contacts. We learned through painful experience that such agencies usually see a local partner as little more than a provider of logistics support. During my tenure, we never encountered an agency that demonstrated real respect for local culture and context, concern to build good relationships, or inclination to work in ways that also built VBNK's capacity. We experienced such agencies as extractive and concerned only with their own agenda, which they can be ruthless in achieving. On more than one occasion, I pulled out of negotiations on the basis that difficult, and sometimes just plain unpleasant, behavior and attitudes during preliminary discussions did not augur well for a successful implementing partnership.

Working with INGOs already established in country was generally of a much more constructive and cooperative nature. VBNK was engaged as the training or capacity development partner on some big projects that other agencies implemented. In such cases, our role would often be to lead the capacity development element of the project, working in close cooperation with those responsible for the other components. Sometimes this was at a central level, perhaps providing training of trainer inputs for those who would work at provincial levels. At other times, VBNK teams were actively involved in provincial activities, for example, working to build the capacity of local NGOs that were receiving funding support to work with commune councils.

Regional Work

Regional work has never been a major feature of VBNK's workload, but it has nevertheless provided some interesting opportunities. The requests were often for me to do consultancies for INGOs, contact having been made through their Cambodia office. The work tended to be evaluation or some type of organizational development activity, usually one-off interventions rather than long-term processes. During one strategic planning exercise, we gave considerable thought to whether VBNK should try to become a regional resource. Given the extent of the need in Cambodia, we decided to continue with the practice of deciding on each request on a case-by-case basis. Several times I accepted a consultancy on the condition that one of VBNK's Cambodian staff would accompany and work with me, at VBNK's expense, as a capacity development exercise.

The big exception to this overall scenario was the work that VBNK did in Tibet. An expatriate staff member of Handicap International (HI), who had previously worked in Cambodia, had gone to Tibet to set up the organization's program there. Having had staff on VBNK's Managers Development Program (MDP), she felt that similar training would be of benefit to Tibetan staff, not only in HI but also in other INGOs. She had explored the options and been unable to find any relevant training facilities in either Tibet or mainland China, so she wrote to me to ask if VBNK could help. I thought about this request for about a nanosecond before I hit the reply button to say yes, figuring that we could work out the details later. The details took quite a lot of working out, for a variety of reasons, but everything fell into place, and in 2002 we did our first training in Lhasa. The relationships developed during that visit resulted in VBNK returning every year for the next five years.

At the Tibet end, nine INGOs collaborated to support VBNK to come and deliver the program. Between them, they nominated 25 participants and apportioned the costs accordingly. Given the time and expense involved in traveling, it was decided to deliver the program in two three-week blocks rather than in six single weeks as in Cambodia. Getting the plans in place involved more than simply selecting participants and working out a budget. The organizers had to find all the core requirements for delivery, such as a suitable training venue and a large supply of flip chart paper, then in short supply in Tibet. In addition, all of our materials needed to be translated in advance into both Tibetan and Chinese. Applications had to be submitted to the authorities to get permits for the VBNK staff to deliver training in Lhasa. At the VBNK end, we needed to select trainers who not only knew the program content but also were proficient in English and then prepare them to work through translators. We also needed to locate a lot of warm clothing, as Cambodians generally feel that anything below 25°C is cold, and the team would be in Lhasa in February, when temperatures rarely reach 10°C during the day and might often be colder than −10°C at night. We made the decision that VBNK would cover the cost of an expatriate going with the staff to support them. I hoped it could be me, but my workload did not permit it for the first training, and one of my colleagues went instead. I was able to go for the second round later in the year.

The success of the first three weeks was such that one of the organizations supporting the process asked us to deliver it again for their partners. We agreed, assuming that the partners were more NGOs or perhaps community-based organizations. When we went back in October 2002, it was to deliver the final three modules of the first program and the first three modules of the second. It was something of a surprise on arrival to discover that the second group was made up of managers of factories producing traditional Tibetan medicine (TTM). At that time, China was working toward World Trade Organization (WTO) membership, and one initiative was to ensure that all medical production complied with international Good Manufacturing Practice standards. Giving factory managers some introduction to Western management theory was seen as a helpful part of that process. Once we got over the surprise, we worked out how to adjust our materials to their context as best we could, given that we had no knowledge of their work. Again, this program, completed during 2003, was considered such a success that VBNK was asked to give this group more training, on subjects such as quality management and marketing.

Later, after the completion of various training programs, two NGOs asked us to do some organizational development work. The most interesting challenge of all came when we were asked to lead and facilitate a participatory process to develop a training of trainers on microbusiness enterprise for TTM practitioners in villages. If it sounds complicated, it's because it was. In the room, we had staff of an NGO and teachers from their TTM vocational training school, plus six nomads from the project areas on the Northern Plateau. The nomads were needed to help us all understand the realities of local business practices, because in nomad areas barter and exchange are far more common than money transactions. We achieved our purpose, and the following week the VBNK trainers backstopped the teachers as they delivered the training to 30 pupils from the school. VBNK teams traveled to Lhasa on eight different occasions between 2002 and 2007 to deliver training for both NGOs and the TTM sector. I was fortunate to be part of the team on six of those occasions.

The challenges of this work cannot be underestimated, but they are in direct proportion to the rewards. The participants and trainers between them had three different first languages—Tibetan, Chinese, and Khmer—yet the delivery language had to be English. It required two full-time interpreters to manage the workload, even though all the core materials were translated in advance. We needed always to be alert to the fact that because the organizations' operating environment was very different from that in Cambodia, our materials needed adaptation to make them relevant. Working across cultures in such circumstances inevitably produces its own set of challenges, and we all had to work hard to ensure the relevance and shared understanding of even the most basic ideas. Dealing with the altitude and the cold were constant background factors to be managed, and several of us got sick at different times. Communication with home was at times almost impossible, resulting in people feeling very cut off from their families.

For all of the VBNK teams who worked in Tibet, it was an exercise in mutual capacity building. The Cambodians were invited there as experts, with something of value to share with others, and this was a great confidence booster in and of itself. Working in English and across cultures developed their communication and training skills to new levels. Exposure to a different culture and way of life broadened their horizons and understanding of the world, which gave them new insights into their own culture. Everyone worked very hard to do the best possible job, however they might have been experiencing the challenges. At a personal level, the reactions were very mixed. For some of the Cambodians, it was all stimulating, challenging, and enjoyable, and they gained a great deal from it. They took every available opportunity to explore what they could of Tibet and its culture, religion, language, and food. On a Saturday sightseeing trip outside the city, one colleague commented, "I will only ever have one day like this in my whole life. I want to remember every moment." We nearly lost the same person in the Potala Palace because he was so engrossed in everything there that he got separated from the group. For others, it seemed to be too much to cope with. At the extreme was one person who never left her hotel room, apart from when we went to work. She refused to eat anywhere other than a small and uncomfortable little Chinese restaurant near the hotel. She came on the team visit to the Potala Palace only at my insistence and never showed any interest in going anywhere else. I found it very sad that she was so closed to the opportunities that this travel offered her. For me, not only did I get to meet and work with some wonderful people but also I was able to see some of the most iconic buildings and beautiful places in the world. Working in Tibet was a privilege beyond my wildest dreams.

Private Sector

From the late 1990s onward, hundreds of garment sector factories were established in Cambodia, with two major results. First, the industry joined tourism as one of today's pillars of the Cambodian economy. Second, the factories created a new employment sector, primarily for young women from rural areas who flocked to Phnom Penh and some provincial towns to take up the newly available jobs. Two interesting outcomes from these developments were the creation of many workers' representation associations (unions) and a complex mixture of benefits and negative consequences for the young women working in the factories. Both issues resonated with VBNK because of its work on empowerment and women's issues.

After joint negotiations with the RGC and industry representatives, the International Labour Organization (ILO) established a project called Better Factories Cambodia (BFC), with the primary purpose of improving working conditions in garment factories through independent monitoring, training, technical advice, and information dissemination. As VBNK had already worked on other ILO projects, such as microenterprise development for women, the staff at ILO approached us to partner with them on one of the BFC training components, called Remediation. The training program comprised seven modules on subjects such as workplace health and safety and effective communications. Each participating factory had to send equal numbers of managers and workers' representatives. The program was considered successful and ran for several years. Through this introduction to the garment sector, VBNK was later engaged to do more work with the ILO and with other agencies interested in supporting and developing the industry.

An initiative in the World Bank's Water and Sanitation Project (WSP) is another example of private enterprise that is important for social development. Although the award-winning Phnom Penh Water Supply Authority has achieved a great deal in providing the city with safe drinking water, there is only minimal provision of this essential utility in the rest of the country. Most people are dependent on harvesting rainwater in the wet season and on private providers in the dry season. Recognizing that it will be many years before this situation can change, the WSP is working with private providers both to improve the quality of their supply through technical advice and to strengthen themselves as businesses so they can extend the scope of their service provision. VBNK is contracted to provide financial and management training to these entrepreneurs.

VBNK also worked on a number of occasions with microfinance institutes. Several were originally credit programs of NGOs and had converted to business status in accordance with legislation introduced to regulate the Cambodian banking sector. As many retained the socioeconomic development aims and values they had held as NGOs, it was appropriate for VBNK to continue working with them.

Keeping Pace With the Sector: An Evolving Mission

For several years, the INGO and CNGO communities were VBNK's primary target group; even though the focus gradually expanded, NGOs remain the core of VBNK's work, as shown by figures produced at the end of 2009. Since 1997, 35% of participants have come from CNGOs, 31% have been the Cambodian staff of INGOs, 10% have come from the RGC, and the remaining 24% have come from other agencies, such as commune councils, the demining sector, and IOs (Pearson 2010). The strategic inclusion of other types of organizations came as a result of continuously monitoring and responding to emerging needs and opportunities in the external environment and was reflected in progressive adaptation of the mission statement.

As mentioned elsewhere, VBNK has never suffered from a shortage of requests for its services. The findings of the 2001 evaluation summarize the situation then, which is still accurate in many respects today.

> VBNK's management, staff, and systems are under considerable pressure created by
> - *A rapidly and constantly developing market into which it is offering services.* The target VBNK is aiming for is constantly moving. VBNK's customers like what they get, but as they get more experienced, they want more "advanced" services from VBNK. What customers want is constantly evolving. *VBNK cannot stand still without losing touch with what its customers want or without falling behind the current "leading edge" position it has in the market it is helping to create.*
> - *A sense of endless opportunity and need for the kinds of services VBNK is offering and wanting to offer.* There is a real danger of being overwhelmed and overstretched by an endless amount of "good" work to do . . . VBNK . . . must revisit and create its own "strategic self-discipline and limits" to survive and thrive. It must learn to say "no" and be clear and strategic about why it is saying "yes" and "no"!

Having so many opportunities that they constitute a threat has been a constant theme in VBNK's life, and preventing mission drift and overcommitment has always required careful decision making.

The first amendment to the mission statement in 2000 did not make any change to the target group but expanded what VBNK offered to include consulting, facilitation, research, and publications, as well as training. Three years later, however, the development sector looked very different, mostly because of the new commune councils. As noted above, multiple stakeholders in the country's development now needed to work together in ways that had previously been neither necessary nor possible. The Strategic Plan 2003–2005 noted,

> Overall, the network of relationships and the level of shared work between all the players working in Cambodia's social development sector are growing all the time, and it is no longer easy always to make clear cut distinctions between NGOs and the other types of organizations involved.

In addition, the plan noted how VBNK's knowledge and understanding of the country's development challenges were deepening:

> Through its commitment to being a learning organization, VBNK has come to have a much more comprehensive understanding of social development in Cambodia. This has led VBNK to see its role and responsibilities differently now and . . . to revise the vision statement. The new version articulates the impact that VBNK hopes that its work can have on Cambodia's overall social development rather than focusing only on an intermediary target group.

These factors resulted in a significant change in the organization's mission, including expansion of the target group to embrace all social development organizations, although the primary mechanism for working with customers was still described as management services. At that time, the working definition of social development organizations included NGOs, six RGC ministries—Health; Women's Affairs and Veterans;[6] Social Affairs, Labour, Vocational Training, and Youth Rehabilitation;[7] Ministry of Education, Youth and Sport; Rural Development; and Agriculture, Forestry and Fisheries—and all the IOs and donors working with them on relevant projects. The need to decide about requests from the private sector emerged in later years, and, as described above, we accepted those with a clear link to social development.

The final significant adaptation to reflect new external and internal realities came with the Strategic Plan 2006–2009, when VBNK decided that it should include its commitment to creativity and drop the word "management" from the mission statement. By that time, a range of important activities, such as the CHART project and the work being done by the Center for Creative Development (CCD), were outside any definition of the word "management." Those activities, and many other pieces of work that customers commissioned, focused on the personal and professional development of practitioners and multiple aspects of organizational development, not simply management practices. By then, it was more appropriate to state the mission in terms of creativity, learning, and social change:

> VBNK's mission is to be a centre of learning, working creatively with the Cambodian social development sector in order to generate and share innovative practice, knowledge and wisdom that will contribute to positive social change.

At this point, a staff member made an interesting observation. She noted that we could change VBNK's original Khmer name to better reflect the new focus without having to change the English abbreviation. The name was officially changed in 2006 from the Khmer for Institute to Train Managers in Development to that for Institute to Serve Facilitators of Development.

The progressive changes to the mission did not cause VBNK to abandon its original roots and expertise in management training. Instead, in recognition of emerging and expanding needs and trends, the program was progressively adapted to offer a more comprehensive range of responses that include, but are not constrained by, the need for management effectiveness. Keeping abreast of all the different changes within the development sector needs the constant attention of VBNK's leadership. Reading reports and the papers is helpful to a certain extent, but the old adage that what matters is "not what you know but who you know" is particularly apt in this community, and it is necessary, formally and informally, to maintain multiple relationships. So much of what I have learned has come from personal connections and relationships with colleagues in other organizations. A number of people have, like me, been here for a long time, and their knowledge is both broad and deep, so when I need well-informed guidance about any particular issue, I know whom to ask. In the IO and INGO community, there is high senior personnel turnover, making it necessary to keep renewing relationships within those agencies in order to stay connected. Much depends on networking, the responsibility for which often fell to me as director, although I delegated whenever I could. Sometimes this involved attending events and functions that, while rarely directly useful, did serve the purpose of keeping VBNK's profile in view. Mandated to do so by VBNK's board, some senior Cambodian staff and I had the privilege of serving on several CNGO boards, and we found this a very effective way to keep in touch with what was going on in the CNGO community.

The description offered here has touched only on the aspects of the development sector that have been relevant to VBNK and its work. There are so many different agencies working in a highly complex web of mandates and relationships that it would be impossible to describe it all in detail. It is not even possible to articulate all the differing capacity development needs. Because of this complexity, no one agency can hope to work with, or influence, the sector in its entirety.

To make a contribution, VBNK had to be clear about what it was trying to do and with whom. By reflecting on and learning from its work, VBNK realized that its original purpose of providing management training was useful to many, but it was not enough to make any real difference to the country's development. As national-level developments and the relationships between agencies changed with time, so VBNK needed to expand both its range of services and its target group in order to stay relevant. Over and above supporting the sector with requested services, it took a lead by also introducing creative new practices that challenged people to think and work in new ways. This is a big undertaking for a small organization. VBNK cannot claim to have turned the whole sector around to embrace new ways of working, but it can unquestionably claim that it has influenced multiple organizations and individuals in many different ways. The fruits of these small seeds of change are still growing on the vine, and their impact will be known only in the fullness of time.

Notes

1. Data provided by the CCC.

2. This summary is adapted from a case study in Pearson (2010).

3. At the time of writing, there is still no NGO law in Cambodia. Several drafts have been drawn up and circulated in the past 15 years. All have invariably met with an outcry from human rights organizations, which have always tended to drown out other voices wanting a dialogue with the government about how best to regulate the sector. Thus, no agreement has ever been reached, and the latest draft appears to be in abeyance. CNGOs are required to register with the Ministry of Interior, under the same rules and in the same department as associations and political parties, but this is not mandatory. The process is relatively simple, in that any organization wishing to register must have an MOU with another ministry in order to verify that its work is concerned with development issues rather than business or politics. Other criteria are largely administrative, for example, local authority confirmation of the organization's address, existence of statutes or bylaws, and details of the founders and current director. Given that registration is not mandatory, many organizations exist and work outside of this framework. It is also estimated that many of the organizations registered with the Ministry of Interior are no longer active.

4. The Scholarship Fund is currently supported by the Australian Agency for International Development (AusAID) and ANZ Royal Bank of Cambodia.

5. In its analysis of good governance, the Asian Development Bank (ADB) identified accountability, transparency, participation, and predictability as the four key interrelated elements necessary to sustain efforts and ensure results. See www.adb.org/Governance.

6. Now Ministry of Women's Affairs.

7. Now Ministry of Social Affairs, Veterans and Youth Rehabilitation.

3

A Learning Journey

First Steps

Everyone who helped establish VBNK always fully understood that only a multiskilled training team could meet the management training needs of the NGO target group. As there was no pool of experienced management trainers from which to recruit, it was also understood that VBNK would need to build that team itself. Our budget reflected this need, with generous allowances for staff development and consultants to support the work.

In the first round of recruitment, we hired six trainers.[1] Three had good participatory training experience but not in management, two had a teaching background, and one, with a degree in a technical subject,[2] had no relevant experience but impressed us as having suitable potential. No one who applied had any management experience, a feature of recruitment that was to echo through the years. At that time, it was simply because very few Cambodians had held management positions. Only two of the six were women: we had hoped to recruit an equal number of men and women, but then, as in subsequent rounds of recruitment, few women with appropriate experience or potential applied. This has also always been the case for skills-based positions on the support side of the organization.

Thus, the first staff development challenge was that VBNK had a team of management trainers with no experience of management. They started on August 18, 1997, and immediately went through a two-week orientation program on subjects relevant to Cambodia's development and the NGO sector at that time. We then conducted intensive assessments of each individual's skills and knowledge as a foundation for planning his or her development programs. Training skills were only half of the equation, the other half being the content of the courses that VBNK would offer, starting with the courses developed in my earlier project. The first step was a training of trainers exercise, in which the TA and I delivered the two-week General Introduction to Management course, with the trainers as participants. The first VBNK training was delivered shortly afterward to a group of local NGO partners of CWS in Kampong Thom province, with each trainer taking the lead on different sessions. The TA was there throughout the delivery to observe and give backup support, and this enabled her to refine the assessment of each trainer's strengths, weaknesses, and development needs.

It is worth noting at this point a fundamental difference in the expectations of expatriates and Cambodians as trainers. Although single-handed delivery is not the best training practice, for a variety of reasons, there was then an expectation that expatriates single-handedly deliver short courses, working with another trainer only—but not necessarily—for longer courses or with a large participant group. In contrast, Cambodian trainers expected to work in teams of at least three, with a documenter or administration assistant in support. Much later, we managed to reduce this to two, without a documenter. So preparations included deciding how to divide the work among the team and how they would support each other during delivery.

As part of the initial assessment exercise, we had developed a personal development planning process, which each trainer and her or his supervisor jointly reviewed and revised every six months. As an appraisal process it was intense—but so were our needs, and it worked well. In addition to work targets, each trainer had to identify personal development objectives to be achieved in the forthcoming six-month period. Over the first year, the TA, with occasional inputs from me, concentrated on developing the trainers' training skills and their knowledge of our core courses. An important initiative during 1998 was a series of exposure visits to other organizations, designed to counteract some of the gaps in the trainers' management experience. These visits were to rural projects or to shadow operational managers in order to get firsthand insights into the roles, responsibilities, and challenges that our participants faced in their daily working lives.

Our first initiative specifically to work with learning approaches was in mid-1998, when an external consultant did a workshop to introduce the team to the experiential learning cycle (ELC). A substantive part of the training was about how to structure session plans so that they followed the cycle. The TA was present throughout the workshop, and she reported back that the concept had created a lot of confusion, and the team was obviously not clear about how to apply the approach. The consultant was a very experienced trainer of trainers, with whom I had worked before, so I was fairly sure that the problem lay with the trainers' understanding rather than with the quality of the training.

We decided we should persevere with introducing the model as the standard approach to session plans, but it soon became obvious that the trainers really did not have a sufficient grasp of the concept to use it appropriately. Many of the session plans developed in the name of ELC were little more than an illogical jumble of activities. Alternatively, people did what they had always done and just labeled the steps inaccurately as elements of the ELC. The TA and I soon realized that it was inappropriate to say that the trainers were using experiential methodologies. We reverted to the types of session plans for which the trainers had expertise, but references to the ELC occurred occasionally for some years. It was several years before we were able to embrace an ELC methodology with enough understanding to use it competently.

Other organizational events, such as annual retreats and the annual follow-up studies, also provided capacity development opportunities. The trainers were urged to use the follow-up studies as opportunities to learn from participants' work experiences and to get insights into the relationship between training and practice. The establishment of the management team, and other organizational processes, offered opportunities for some program and support staff to develop management skills. Another strand of opportunity, available to all Cambodian staff, was an annual allowance for external training of their choice, in their own time. In the early days, the vast majority opted to use this allowance for English language study.

An important strand of staff development activities that started in 1998 involved sending staff to external training, for example, on a locally run gender and development course. After any external training or experience, each trainer was required to give a presentation or "echo training session" to the others. The budget had an allowance for training in the region, and the first overseas experience was in July 1998. Two trainers went to one of the leading management universities in the region for a one-month course on project management. Overall, the external exposure had many benefits and could be considered successful in that the trainers learned useful things both from the course and from studying with a multinational group in another country. But the experience also highlighted many instructive issues.

First, we were confronted by the fact that the trainers' English was not of a high enough standard for the study. They all had good levels of functional English, and at VBNK we would take time to explore translations and meanings in order to ensure that everyone understood fully what foreigners were talking about. We assumed, rightly, that no such luxury would be allowed on a course at an academic institute where the participant group had multiple first languages. Even though we had arranged a crash course in English for academic purposes as part of their preparations, on their return the trainers spoke of working long into the night in order to keep up with the course reading. The second issue was the overall relevance of the content, which, it transpired, was targeted at the staff of large donor institutions managing big infrastructure projects. What the trainers learned was not particularly applicable and transferable to our target group working on NGO projects. The third major issue, about expenses, is described in "Beliefs and Behaviors" in Chapter 1.

Staff development activities were paralleled by the development of courses to be offered to our customers, because what we had when we started VBNK did not include all the important subjects necessary. The major initiative in 1998 was a suite of five courses on different aspects of project management, developed by our first consultant, Jan Willem Rosenboom, who was with us for six months. In addition, I developed new courses to be offered as modules in the MDP, described in Chapter 4. As each course was developed, the trainers needed intense orientation to the content and methods to be used, as well as support in their delivery.

It became apparent that we did not have sufficient capacity to accommodate all the necessary staff and course development activities alongside delivery of the planned training schedule for 1998. Our planning had been too ambitious, and we needed to adjust to the realities of our capacity. Fortunately, the board was supportive and understood that we needed to cancel some advertised courses in order to focus on development activities and to give priority to quality rather than quantity. This was not the only time we needed to pull back from our plans to ensure that we were ready and able to work at a reasonable standard. Being at the very edge of our capacity to deliver proved to be another feature of VBNK life that echoed through the years.

Staff and course development activities in the first year were, therefore, both concentrated in nature and broad in scope. The TA and I spent a great deal of time reflecting on everything we did to assess its relevance and usefulness and to work out appropriate ways forward. As we worked on these processes, we began to see that some of our greatest challenges lay in the realm of culture and context rather than in skills and knowledge. In November 1998, I wrote some notes in preparation for a meeting with David Glass (see Chapter 4), which I reproduce in part here (see boxed text), not only because they were instrumental in taking our staff development activities into new areas but also because they show my emerging understanding about these important issues. Back then, I knew that culture and context were important, but it was only with time that I came to understand just how profoundly and powerfully they create intractable blocks to learning and change.

Participation versus power: We teach participation, which everyone agrees with in the training, but I suspect many make no behavior change at all on return to the workplace. Reasons: historical structure of society, reinforced by events of the past 30 years, current political structure of society giving role model of power not participation.

Communication: Interpersonal communication is heavily blocked. Information is power anywhere, but here the relationships between information, communication, power, and *security* are powerfully interlocked in a very complex way, again because of recent history.

The security of formula: The right and wrong answer, black and white interpretations of life, deeply rooted rigidity in approach to many aspects of functioning. Shades of gray and flexibility are alien territory and worrying to the point of being impossible.

Risk taking: Being creative = taking risks. Making decisions = taking risks. Taking initiatives = taking risks. Taking risks = at best possible loss of face, at worst confronting the experience of your risk costing life, maybe not yours but that of someone dear to you. Result = paralysis.

Fear: Whatever their surface veneer and behavior might portray, the majority of Cambodians' motivation in life is fear. Most people are still operating from a VERY BIG fear for their fundamental security (life).

Control: Must be total or nonexistent. There can be no engaging with uncertainties, if you cannot control completely you must disassociate yourself from what is happening. Thus training is OK because in training sessions you "control" participants and process, but facilitation is very difficult because you cannot intervene to control, even if the group is going off target, and especially if group members are older than the facilitator. As a trainer you must "know" all the answers.

Problem solving, conflict resolution, and negotiating: No concept of win-win. Negotiating means standing your ground and stating your own position repeatedly. No concept of giving, of compromise, or of working toward the common ground in the middle. No letting go of your own position—fear of what you might lose if you do.

Critical thinking and analysis: Lack of critical thinking and analytical skills is probably cited as a problem for Cambodian managers more than any other issue. This is clearly linked to educational experiences, but also probably owes a lot to some of the issues above.

Management by fear of gossip: For women particularly, the cultural pressures to conform to a strict code of "acceptable" behavior are very strong. Within this code, it is completely unacceptable for a woman to be strong or assertive. If she should cross the invisible line into unacceptable behavior, the punishment will be gossip—a powerful malicious factor in Cambodian life. It is therefore essential to most women managers to stay within the boundaries of being nice to everyone so as not to attract attention and comment.

It is impossible to say "no."

In 1999, after identifying some of these constraints and through discussions with David Glass, we began to recognize how strongly Cambodian social hierarchies and experiences of extreme repression had resulted in people developing mechanisms of rigid self-control to inhibit any ideas or behaviors, for fear of attracting negative attention. Such patterns and rules of self-control must be challenged and let go before new learning can be embraced, so David did two one-week workshops with the program team designed to surface and challenge some basic beliefs and worldviews. The workshops covered relational skills such as intra- and interpersonal communication, risk taking and control, trust, and team building. The exercises David used in the workshops were based on theater practices and emotional intelligence: many are still in use in VBNK today. David devised several sessions that focused specifically on trying to release natural creativity and initiative from internally imposed constraints. Those exercises gave the staff the greatest discomfort, indicating that the process was touching on something deeply important. It was in their responses that I gained my first insights into the complex relationships between learning and unlearning. I learned that the rigid, self-imposed controls that people use to ensure everything they do is risk free become embedded beneath consciousness and are thus profound blocks to unlearning, because they allow no space or entry points for new learning. It was in these workshops, therefore, that I first started to understand that creativity could be an important component of capacity development practices.

Staff assessments of the workshops were universally positive. They found the overall experience extremely helpful, even though many of the individual exercises had been very challenging. They also expressed the view that all Cambodians should have the opportunity to engage in similar experiences. It was at their suggestion that the support staff were invited to attend future workshops with David, an option enthusiastically taken up.

The first serious complication in the flow of capacity-building processes arose in 1999, when we expanded the training team to try to meet the increasing demand for our services. We recruited several new trainers and put them through a comprehensive orientation program. This was not enough, however, to get their skills and knowledge on VBNK courses to the same level as that of the first group, which was now working in two teams. The strategy we used was to pair the new trainers with original team members for delivery of existing courses, as well as having the TA and consultants work with them on their specific capacity needs. Needless to say, we had to repeat this process every time we recruited more trainers.

As one of the objectives for Phase 1 was "to develop a core group of Cambodian management trainers," the evaluation conducted in April 1999 paid particular attention to this aspect of VBNK's achievements in the start-up years. The findings on that objective were as follows:

> Most of the trainers . . . display a strong commitment to their work . . . VBNK has provided extensive training to develop the capacity of the trainers. They have good skills to facilitate training and generally are competent to present the course material. The trainers' lack of management practice means they have a limited personal experience to draw on. This can become an issue when training more advanced managers and new course content. Further exposure to practical management situations through field trips and job shadowing will help to develop the trainers' understanding. The trainers can also broaden their knowledge through reading and/or through pursuing higher education.

The evaluators found that the trainers had minimal ability to conduct needs assessments and design new courses because of limited exposure to either the concepts or the practices. It was vital to rectify this omission if the trainers were to take over these tasks from expatriates in the foreseeable future, as planned in the original proposal. A weakness in external networking capacity was also noted, together with a recommendation for filling that gap.

The evaluators did not recommend any fundamental change in our overall approach to staff development, only that we extend it to cover additional skills and knowledge gaps. Thus, as VBNK and its program grew, the practices that had been established in 1997 and 1998 continued. The TA's work focused exclusively on staff and course development, and I allocated as much time as I could to those activities. Each year, we sent trainers on external courses both in Cambodia and around the region, but, having learned from our first experience, we were subsequently more careful with both the choice of courses and how we prepared the trainers for attendance. We instituted monthly half-day training sessions for all staff, which were often used for those who had attended external courses to share what they had learned with their colleagues. We continued to use external consultants to help with course development, but with mixed results. Unlike our first consultant, some that we hired didn't have sufficient local knowledge to adapt their technical inputs on content fully to the local context.

In the proposal for the first funding round, we had made a very particular point about the need to address gender issues:

> Ensuring the participation of women in all levels of NGOs is a difficult task in Cambodia. Traditionally, women's sphere of influence is often limited to the household, and deference is deeply ingrained. In addition, far fewer women than men have access to education, especially at the higher levels. Recruiting and developing women as managers is therefore an extremely important challenge facing all organizations.
>
> The challenge extends beyond developing women's skills as men's attitudes and behavior towards women in the workplace need much attention. Gender awareness must therefore be integrated into any training. Management training, due to its implicit treatment of power differences, especially must be designed to include gender as a key issue.

Addressing this commitment became a priority once we had some of the basics in place. Internally, we did a series of workshops for the training team, linking gender, values, and ethics. This work led to the development of policies that the board adopted in 2000. The section "Early Innovations" in Chapter 4 describes the training program we designed to support women's development.

A helpful external change came with the establishment of some commercial universities in Phnom Penh, several of which twinned with reputable international institutions to offer bachelor's- and master's-level degrees in part-time study programs. This offered an opportunity to overcome the VBNK trainers' lack of appropriate qualifications for their work. We decided to extend the level of allowances to enable individuals to pursue the studies of their choice, providing these were relevant to VBNK's work. One of VBNK's team leaders was among the first cohort of Cambodians ever to receive an MBA in Cambodia, graduating in 2002. Over the next few years, virtually all staff pursued bachelor's- or master's-level study programs.

In 2001, we recognized that the generic English language study programs that staff were attending externally were not meeting organizational needs. We had a consultant conduct a detailed training needs assessment of all staff and design an in-house program for three levels—beginners, intermediate, and advanced. Despite extensive prior consultation about timings for the lessons, attendance quickly slackened off to just a very few dedicated learners, and eventually we had to cancel the program altogether because it was not cost-effective. When exploring the reasons for this, the staff cited timing problems to justify their nonattendance, but I always suspected that the real issue was that they did not value the internal teaching because it would not lead to a certificate at the end.

In summary, this description shows that VBNK staff development activities in the early years were comprehensive. They represented a very significant investment of both human and financial resources. While our staff development strategy was never formalized into a written document, it was nevertheless sophisticated in both its breadth and its depth. We worked constantly to analyze needs for training skills, content knowledge, and personal development; then, as we better understood the needs, we created our own responses or took advantage of any helpful opportunities that came along. While this approach was generally successful in terms of equipping the teams to deliver training courses, we always knew that the trainers' lack of management and sector experience created some significant weaknesses in our capacity. Another important factor was that we were now being asked to do work that required new skill sets, most particularly facilitation of organization development interventions. What we did in the early years, although more extensive than many organizations might undertake, was nevertheless a standard approach based on a skills-building conception of capacity development.

We had tentatively started working with the idea of being a learning organization, but we had yet to find a model that worked well for our circumstances and needs. David Glass, in one of his workshops, had given us our first, very brief, introduction to the idea of creativity. But it was becoming clear that all the different initiatives were not leading to the learning and change that might have been expected. I thought that after three years, our efforts should have resulted in some significant shifts, for example, in people's analytical skills and ability to grasp new concepts, but progress was extremely limited. Nor was there any real improvement in terms of efficiency and effectiveness in the core program delivery: it was all pretty much as it had been at the beginning. This mirrored the feedback I was receiving from our target community, where people were also frustrated by the slow pace of capacity development.

There was a dawning realization that although we thought we were providing all the right solutions, we were obviously missing something important. There had to be a reason why all these inputs had as much lasting impact as water thrown on sand. We realized we had been providing all the right answers but maybe to the wrong questions. Logic led us to conclude that somehow we had been traveling the wrong road. So the next challenge was to work out how to get onto the right one.

Pivotal Learning

When we asked ourselves in 2000, "What will make our staff development practices more effective?" I really didn't have an answer. My understanding of the issues of culture and context was deepening in direct proportion to my growing frustration that nothing we tried seemed to be making any significant difference. By then, I had been in Cambodia for five years, first developing and delivering training courses myself, then, as director of VBNK, trying to establish a viable training organization. One of the drawbacks of running a local organization in a developing country, as opposed to working for an international agency, is that you are on your own: there is no regional or head office team of advisers or trainers tasked with keeping the local entity up to date with new concepts and tools. I had become, by dint of my position, one of the people in the community to whom others came for ideas and solutions, but I hadn't had a single day of training or any other form of professional input for myself. There didn't seem to be anyone else in Cambodia looking at the challenges from my particular perspective. There wasn't a bookshop, Internet access was expensive and unreliable, and I hadn't found any relevant contacts outside Cambodia. Very little of the available literature on capacity development or organizational learning focused on NGOs or Southeast Asian cultures, and this is still largely the case today. The resources and models that I did find were conceptually far too sophisticated to be relevant to our context and needs. It was another subject where it was necessary to adapt methods and materials to make them workable. The result of these combined factors was professional isolation and stagnation. I felt that if I was to lead VBNK in a change process, I needed to be refreshed with some external inputs and new ideas. The board understood the problem and said that if I could find an appropriate course, it would approve the time and budget needed for me to attend.

I had previously heard something of the work of the Community Development Resource Association (CDRA) in Cape Town and had read some of its publications. Shortly after my discussion with the board, I saw that CDRA was advertising a new six-week program, Facilitating Development From the Inside Out. The significant commitment of time and money that my attendance entailed paid off in multiple ways, in that the course was both a major turning point in my professional and personal development and the start of CDRA becoming one of the most important long-term influences on VBNK's organizational development and learning. I was fortunate that two other people who were working in Cambodia attended the same program, because that helped us all relate what we were learning to the Cambodian context. It was also very helpful, on my return to Cambodia, to be able to talk to them about the challenges of trying to use this learning in concrete ways that would benefit VBNK.

Because it was eventually pivotal in helping me become both a different person and a different sort of practitioner, I think it is valuable to share something of what I experienced in the CDRA program. Figure 3.1 is a very brief summary that I produced to share with VBNK and others on my return.

A strong feature of the program lay in its development of the habit of journaling about our various reflections and learning. At one point I noted, "I don't yet know where this process will take me, but I am very glad to be started on it." I can see now the different themes and threads that have developed from what I found important at the time.

In summary, what I gained from the course was, first, a much-needed sense of perspective on the wholeness and complexity of development. This filled a big knowledge gap because, having come to development as a volunteer, I had never undertaken a study program on development issues. I was particularly impressed by CDRA's focus on the need to identify and understand preexisting organic development processes as essential preparation for intervening in others' lives and systems. It was here that I was first introduced to living systems theory as a way of understanding organizations, which has stood me in very good stead for many work assignments since.

Second, there was a great deal of fruitful learning in exploring the development paradigms within which we define our practice. This included working on an understanding of self as the principle development "tool" at our disposal. We explored many subjects in this theme, most notably principles of good developmental practice, the nature of developmental relationships and power, transformation and change, facilitation skills, and defining our core process, that is, the approach, tools, and techniques that we use. A constant thread throughout these discussions was exploration of our beliefs and values and how they inform our assumptions about, and understanding of, development.

The third area of particular interest can best be described as whole person learning. This calls for recognizing that individuals are not only intellectual but also spiritual, emotional, and physical beings and underlines the need to work with them in ways that are cognizant of all their dimensions. This resonated strongly with aspects of my social work training and thus was not new to me, but it was a timely reminder and reinforcement that VBNK needed to do more in this respect, given its location in a postconflict society where the negative impacts of trauma were widespread.

Finally, and most important, I learned a lot about myself, and I didn't always like what I saw in the mirror during the CDRA process. I realized, for

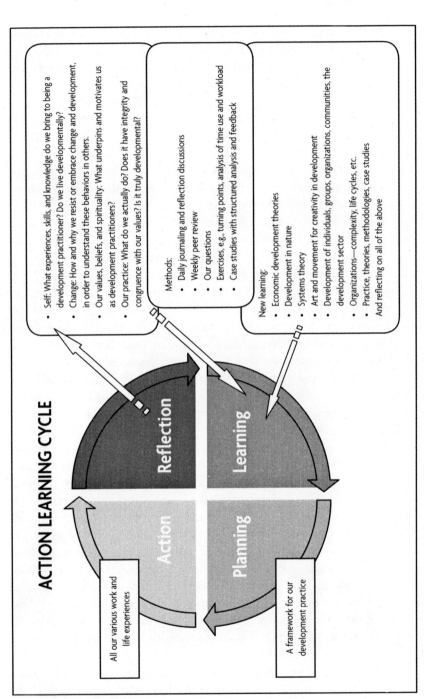

ACTION LEARNING CYCLE

Reflection

- Self: What experiences, skills, and knowledge do we bring to being a development practitioner? Do we live developmentally?
- Change: How and why we resist or embrace change and development, in order to understand these behaviors in others.
- Our values, beliefs, and spirituality: What underpins and motivates us as development practitioners?
- Our practice: What do we actually do? Does it have integrity and congruence with our values? Is it truly developmental?

Methods:
- Daily journaling and reflection discussions
- Weekly peer review
- Our questions
- Exercises, e.g., turning points, analysis of time use and workload
- Case studies with structured analysis and feedback

Learning

New learning:
- Economic development theories
- Development in nature
- Systems theory
- Art and movement for creativity in development
- Development of individuals, groups, organizations, communities, the development sector
- Organizations—complexity, life cycles, etc.
- Practice, theories, methodologies, case studies
  And reflecting on all of the above

Action

All our various work and life experiences

Planning

A framework for our development practice

Figure 3.1 Learning at CDRA.

example, that I had become highly task driven, despite my fundamental belief that people and process are more important than product. I also recognized that one of the mechanisms I had developed to cope with the complexity and challenges of my situation was to cast myself as the "heroic victim," someone nobly struggling against all the odds in a fundamentally hostile environment. I know that this can be a useful defense mechanism for people in difficult circumstances, but when I recognized it in myself, I knew immediately that it was not helpful for me or those around me.

I found the CDRA experience in its entirety both inspirational and transformative. Having arrived in Cape Town tired, driven, and full of angry frustration, I left six weeks later energized and in an entirely different, positive frame of mind, with lots of ideas about how to go forward. The time for new learning and reflection, combined with honest feedback and some thoughtful challenges, gave me insight into my work and the approach I was using, resulting in a more balanced perspective of what was good and what needed to change. I knew that I needed to slow down, reevaluate my priorities and approach, clarify my motivating values, and then bring those changes to the way I worked with my Cambodian colleagues.

It all seemed wonderful, except that when I got back to Cambodia, nothing there had changed in my absence: reintegration proved to be very difficult. I felt I was a different person in a number of ways, and I wanted to be a different practitioner, but an unchanged VBNK and workload did not offer any obvious space or opportunity for me to work differently. This is a very telling point, because I was, after all, the director, and it would be reasonable to assume that I had power to make all sorts of things happen. I did, indeed, have the power to make many things happen. But I knew that I could not control whether others were ready to embrace substantive change. Life and my social work practice have taught me the age-old lesson that we cannot change other people or even make them want to change themselves. All we can do is be and work in ways that we hope will facilitate the emergence of curiosity and the willingness to do things differently. I had absorbed what CDRA offered because I was ready for it. I have participated in other CDRA events in the intervening years and have always returned refreshed and energized by new learning and inspired with new ideas.

Developing a Learning Practice in VBNK

When I returned from CDRA, my challenge was to disseminate what I had learned and gained there in ways that would be meaningful and beneficial for others in VBNK. Some ideas were easy to introduce: for example, the CDRA program had included work with artistic media such as painting and poetry. These were a good fit with our new interest in creativity and produced enjoyable outcomes. A week of the CDRA program had been led by Dirk Marais, at that time leader of Vision Quest Africa. Dirk and a colleague came in 2002 to facilitate their two-module Strategic Life Management program for the majority of VBNK staff, and it was a great success. In later years, VBNK staff attended CDRA courses with highly beneficial results.

On the surface, it seemed that all was going well, and by the time we were developing the Strategic Plan 2003–2005, learning was central in everyone's thinking, as demonstrated by the revised mission statement, which started with "VBNK's mission is to be a centre of learning for the organizations and individuals working for Cambodia's social development." A strategic objective stated VBNK's intention to be engaged in "a two-way learning process with its participants and customer organizations, its internal functioning, and its external environment." These strong stated commitments might, understandably, lead to the assumption that VBNK actively welcomed learning and change. In reality, the statements were little more than rhetoric, behind which the blocks to learning still reigned supreme.

Having been introduced to the Action Learning Cycle (ALC)[3] at CDRA, I felt it would be a good tool to start using in VBNK. While in one respect the ALC was an instant success, and it remains VBNK's primary learning methodology both for internal practices and for work with other organizations, its introduction in VBNK provides an informative example of how difficult it is to achieve deep and sustainable changes in thinking and practice.

The ALC has a simple structure that can be applied to multiple types and levels of activity, and it can, therefore, be thought of as anything from a basic tool to a way of life. At CDRA, our reflections had explored some deep and sophisticated questions, especially about values, resulting in both conceptual and practical learning. Within VBNK, the process needed substantial explanation and simplification before it was understood well enough to be used. We had to start with very basic questions such as "What did we do?" "What went well and not so well?" "What can we learn from this?" and "What should we do differently next time?" I linked the ALC to our previous discussions about becoming a learning organization and stressed the need for learning to become embedded in the organizational culture as our way of life. While no one disagreed overtly with what I was saying, events subsequently showed that it was viewed only as another tool. The ALC was most definitely not embraced as a new way of life that required changes to the way we did things.

I had thought that the ALC could be used in several ways: for trainers and facilitators to review their daily activities with participants, for assessment at the end of courses and interventions, and for the whole organization in major activities like the annual retreat. When I inquired, although I must admit that initially my inquiries were not very deep, I was told that the teams were using the ALC and finding it helpful. After a while, I began to hear comments that can be summarized as "We've done that, what's next?" which prompted me to inquire more deeply about how the program staff were using the ALC and with what results. The findings were disconcerting. Yes, the ALC was in active use, but it was superficial use that did not result in discernable change, because no efforts were being made to follow up on any learning emerging from the reflections. It had become a tick box exercise, like an administration task to be completed after activities.

I encouraged the Cambodian managers to become active in helping teams to use the ALC more effectively to improve the quality of their work. While this idea was apparently welcomed, it did not come to fruition: everyone cited busyness as the reason for not routinely making time available for thorough reflections on what they had done. By now, VBNK had started new units and the CHART project, and because of the problems arising from the expansion, discussed in "Growth, Change and Competing Agendas" in Chapter 5, we were putting effort into fostering "cross-unit learning" as a way to keep the program connected and coherent. Unit plans for 2003 all specified time for reflection on their own activities, linked to processes to learn from, and with, other units. With the benefit of hindsight, it later transpired that the ALC and cross-unit learning were, in some respects, in competition with each other, resulting in a lack of focus and neither being done very well. Learning activities in 2003 did not therefore generate any significant changes. I was coming to the conclusion that the biggest challenge to VBNK being a learning organization was resistance to change.

The ALC works to best effect if those using it have the ability to formulate questions that will deepen discussion, and this is one of the biggest challenges in the Cambodian context. As a result of both cultural norms and repressive experiences, Cambodians are not comfortable with exploratory questions. Whereas expatriates think of questions, particularly "Why?" as a learning tool, Cambodians experience them as negative and accusatorial and respond accordingly. As mentioned elsewhere, children are not expected to ask questions of their elders, and thus in many households children's questions will be met with an angry response, until they learn to stop asking them. I recall several discussions with one senior Cambodian colleague who was frustrated with his inability to formulate questions during discussions. He said that as a child whenever he asked a question, his mother would be angry with him, so he simply stopped asking. He had buried his curiosity so deep at an early age that he had no idea where to find it again now that he needed it as an adult. Over time, through effort and practice, this colleague did manage to develop high-level questioning skills, but many others never manage it.

As no one had come up with a better idea for developing a learning practice, there didn't seem to be anything to gain from trying something new. I had by then realized the necessity of grounding one initiative before moving on to the next and that to make progress we probably needed to make time and space in organizational life for learning activities. I suggested that we periodically stop all external activities in order to work through the ALC properly. Plans for 2004 specified that everyone would take part in four "reflection weeks," and the language shifted from cross-unit learning to organization-wide learning.

Being an experiment, and also because they represented a break from the usual busyness of organizational life and program delivery, the first reflection weeks were viewed with a mixture of excitement and curiosity. They were very enjoyable, as we emphasized the use of creative processes and presentations to draw out and illustrate learning. We also merged the in-house training agenda into the reflection weeks, so they included a range of specific staff development inputs. The blanket stoppage of activities meant that everyone attended all sessions and participated in the same activities at the same time. A sense of purpose and engagement replaced the previous piecemeal feeling about VBNK's learning practices. It seemed that at last we were getting somewhere with drawing out learning from our experience and using it to improve future activities. Given time to work through the ALC systematically, the program teams could identify clear learning points in their work. Administration and finance staff also joined reflection week activities and found them helpful, especially as they had time to reflect on issues of mutual concern with the program teams. Having more time for the in-house training activities improved the quality and effectiveness of different initiatives.

The success of the experiment was such that we repeated it in 2005, reinforcing the purpose by changing the name to "learning weeks." At first, the novelty of the learning weeks ensured the planning and good facilitation they needed to be effective and to justify the amount of person resources we put into them. However, a review early in 2006 showed that despite the importance and the success to date of learning weeks, we had let the core purpose of them slip, and their focus had been lost. An example was that a number of administration tasks regularly found their way into the schedule. There were also times when it seemed that the fun aspects of creativity had taken precedence over purpose. That activities were being planned and implemented in an ad hoc manner was both a cause and a result of the lost focus. As we planned to increase their frequency from quarterly to bimonthly, including the annual retreat, the management team recognized that it had to get the learning weeks back on track by reinforcing the purpose and improving the planning. We did this by specifying core themes and issues to be worked on during the year and structuring the use of time accordingly. A unit manager took the lead with the help of a staff-nominated steering group, which eventually was able to take over both planning and facilitating activities, a significant and important shift in the ownership of the process. Nevertheless, maintaining the organizational space for learning often called for holding the line in the face of considerable pressure to schedule external activities during learning weeks, sometimes from customers, sometimes from VBNK managers juggling busy workloads.

After about three years of learning weeks, we realized that we had made a very significant error in our process. Each event was structured around the same sequence of "What have we done?" "What went well and what went not so well?" and "What can we do next time to improve?" What we had never thought to ask at the start of the sequence was "How did you implement the learning and planned changes identified last time and with what results?" For years, those of us supervising the process had worked on the assumption that it was enough to identify learning and ways to implement it and then to start the sequence afresh next time around. We had consistently been failing to close the learning loop. This was both an important insight into the ALC and how to use it to best effect and another example of flawed assumptions guiding actions. Once the gap in the sequence was pointed out, it seemed so obvious, yet it had never before occurred to any of us. After making the relevant adjustments, there was an immediate improvement in the quality of reflection, learning, and action, because that simple step introduced the previously missing element of accountability.

This brief summary of VBNK's work to make the ALC its primary learning practice is a good example of the fact that it takes years of concentrated effort to move an idea from initiation, through implementation, to meaningful integration in organizational culture. It also explains why our original attempt to work with the ELC training methodology had failed. In 1998, no one was ready for it, because at that point the trainers' understanding of learning was based on an entirely different conception than the one on which the model is based, and we had done no work on exploring that fundamental understanding and the beliefs that went with it. The brick in the VBNK learning wall (see Figure 3.2; see discussion later in the chapter), "Get each new idea grounded before moving on," represents our learning from introducing the ALC. In Cambodia, grounding a new idea can take longer than in other cultures and circumstances, because of the deep-rooted resistance factors and blocks to change. One-off activities and inputs are rarely sufficient, and an activity or process may need to be repeated many times before it is understood fully and applied appropriately. Grounding needs more than a cursory follow-up or on-the-job checkup: it calls for frequent repetition to deepen the quality of practice, ongoing discussion of successes and challenges to facilitate deeper understanding, and the use of accountability mechanisms to motivate persistence. It is also important to keep focused so that creative processes are the means, not the end purpose, of the exercise.

Another example that illustrates the challenges of developing capacity is the initiative in 2001 to start training the trainers to develop new courses. The team was keen to learn this skill, and the first sessions, on doing needs assessments and using findings to define the aim and objectives of a course, went well. We identified two possible courses that we might develop, and so we split into two groups, each with an expatriate TA to support it. Having agreed on the aim and objectives for each course, the groups then needed to find relevant materials and resources to inform the detailed design. They gathered information on their subjects from various sources: our library had some relevant books, some trainers downloaded materials from the newly available Internet, and others brought in what they had been given in external study programs. The process then ran into difficulties that we were never able to overcome.

Faced with a mass of information, the teams had no idea how to go about selecting material appropriate for their needs and then adapting it for relevance to the Cambodian culture and context in which it would be used. Lack of analytical skills is a repetitive theme throughout the NGO sector and elsewhere in Cambodia, because very few people have been educated in ways to develop that capability. Someone I know who has been working in the Cambodian education system for a long time asserted, "The basics just aren't there," because most people had an education that failed to stimulate key intellectual development processes during their formative years. Ways of thinking that are easy to acquire in childhood can prove almost impossible to attain in later life. I have since heard of analytical skills training programs that have been successful in other countries, but at that time I knew of none.

What our course development process needed was a careful analytical assessment of all the assembled materials to help make the first selection of those

The Wall: blocks to learning

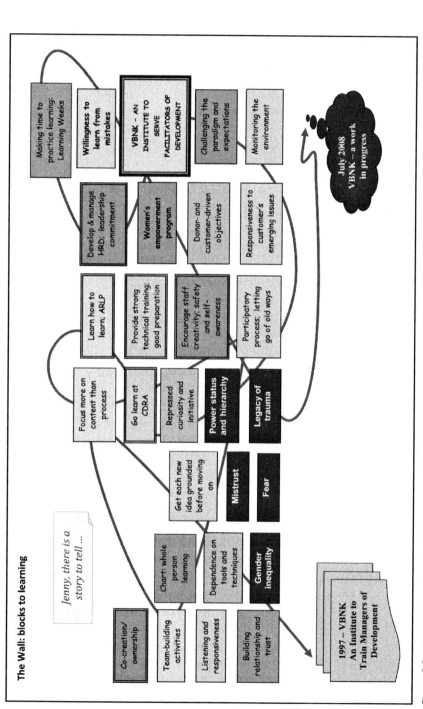

Jenny, there is a story to tell ...

Making time to practice learning: Learning Weeks

Willingness to learn from mistakes

VBNK – AN INSTITUTE TO SERVE FACILITATORS OF DEVELOPMENT

Challenging the paradigm and expectations

Monitoring the environment

Develop & manage HRD: leadership commitment

Women's empowerment program

Donor- and customer-driven objectives

Responsiveness to customer's emerging issues

July 2008
VBNK – a work in progress

Learn how to learn: ARLP

Provide strong technical training: good preparation

Encourage staff creativity, safety and self-awareness

Participatory process: letting go of old ways

Focus more on content than process

Go learn at CDRA

Repressed curiosity and initiative

Power status and hierarchy

Legacy of trauma

Get each new idea grounded before moving on

Mistrust

Fear

Chart: whole person learning

Dependence on tools and techniques

Gender inequality

Co-creation/ownership

Team-building activities

Listening and responsiveness

Building relationship and trust

1997 – VBNK
An Institute to Train Managers of Development

Figure 3.2   The Wall. Reproduced with kind permission from Arthur Delvecchio, TA, VBNK.

that might be relevant and useful to achieving the course aim and objectives. Despite several discussions and suggested ways to move forward, the teams were unable to make progress. When we took stock, we realized the extent of the challenge and that any attempt to develop the necessary analytical skills called for far more expertise and time than we had available. I learned a great deal from this initiative about what it was realistic to expect and possible to achieve. One of my assumptions had been that the expatriate TAs would be able to offer effective leadership and support for this process, but it turned out that they could not. The task of developing new courses reverted to selected expatriates until several years later, when senior and more experienced Cambodians, some of whom had studied at a master's level overseas, were able to take the lead on designing new courses.

Getting Strategic About Staff Development and Learning

When VBNK started, the first TA and I made sure that all staff development activities were tightly tied to the needs assessments and objectives of personal development planning. After she left, and during the period when we expanded the program team, we had a series of different short-term TAs and consultants. During those years, I continued the habit of both initiating internal activities and engaging with any opportunity that looked potentially interesting and informative for staff and their development. The result was a loss of focus through too many different activities and initiatives that, despite being interesting and informative in their own right, together amounted to an unconnected and incoherent jumble. The 2001 evaluation raised some very pertinent points about the relationship between VBNK's programmatic development and sustainability and the development of staff capacity.

> *The new services VBNK is already moving into require a much greater level of personal and professional competence and maturity . . .* increased customizing of training involves contracting, needs assessment, proposal development, program design, and the higher levels of facilitation needed for Organization Development consulting.
>
> *In any context, it can take five to ten years to develop these skill levels, and they have as much to do with the development of the person (self-awareness, emotional maturity, conceptual thinking ability, etc.) as "technical skills."* While there are good "basic" training delivery skills well established in VBNK, these "more advanced" levels of personal and professional competence are just beginning to develop.

In the next stage of VBNK's development . . . the emphasis must shift to the deeper personal development of its key staff. This is something that cannot be forced—it can be invited, enabled, and supported.

This analysis helped us to recognize that we had created some of our own problems through the ad hoc nature of our initiatives and that we needed some help to get more systematic about what we were doing. We planned to have a human resources (HR) adviser for a two-year period, starting in mid-2003, with the purpose of helping

> VBNK consolidate its staff development activities through the formulation of a Staff Development Policy, including relevant tools that will ensure consistency of purpose and implementation of all staff development activities . . . to work with all VBNK managers to ensure that they have the appropriate understanding and capacity to implement and sustain it themselves.

Nicol Levick was, like me, a United Kingdom–qualified social worker who had been working in Cambodia for some time already. She made no claim to being an HR specialist, but she fulfilled several of the core criteria for the position and was additionally engaged in a relevant distance learning study program.

It was through the HR adviser's approach and work that several of us in VBNK came to recognize how inextricably staff development activities are linked to organizational strategy and change management. She also helped us understand that what we needed was not a staff development policy but an HR development strategy. However, this understanding did not come easily. The HR adviser was in post during a time (described later) when there was conflict between strong competing factions in the organization. Having an advisory rather than operational role meant that she often struggled to get others to hear and value her perspective. In particular, she often seemed to be at odds with the rhythm and timing of VBNK's organizational life, in that most operational managers were, of necessity, concerned with task, delivery, and deadlines, whereas she was pressing for the space for reflective, sometimes indeterminate, developmental processes.

I still have the mind-map of VBNK's staff development activities that the HR adviser produced just after she arrived. Those activities had never before been set out in such a visual way, and the picture presented was surprising then and remains so now. It was too much and too busy. Even though we had known our efforts were uncoordinated, we hadn't realized that so many apparently unconnected activities resulted in the whole being fragmented, unguided, and lacking in purpose. After completing a detailed analysis of existing capacities, needs, and management practices, the HR adviser developed a draft strategy, presented as an emerging work in progress to help VBNK identify the best possible ways forward. It stressed the need to purposefully link everything done in the name of HR development to organizational strategy and to underpin it with clearly stated values. It included a list of 14 core interventions, some of which were a continuation of activities and systems already in place, whereas others were new ideas for consideration. The HR adviser noted, for example, that the building was not conducive to communication and informal connections between staff and suggested that it was important to rethink how we were using the space. It took the management team a good while to work through all the ideas and activities in the draft, which was also shared with the board for feedback. The strategy was reviewed and refined several months later and thereafter became the guiding framework for staff development activities.

In keeping with good staff management practices, the strategy emphasized line managers' responsibility for the professional development of their staff as an important aspect of their management performance. The HR adviser developed a learning needs assessment tool on 12 basic competencies, such as delegating, motivating, communicating, and dealing with conflict. The results showed interesting similarities in the managers' levels of skill and confidence across the different competencies. Most were very comfortable with directing and were generally informal but responsive in their approach to staff unless there were serious problems and as a group felt least confident about helping staff plan and prioritize their work. The assessment highlighted an important issue about the feedback culture within some teams and the challenges of giving constructive criticism. Of particular concern was that the managers all struggled with both the concepts and any practice of staff development beyond checking for mistakes. Some commented that even simple actions like saying "thank you" or "well done" did not resonate in Cambodian culture or were not used in order to avoid accusations of favoritism.

Having come from similar professional backgrounds, the HR adviser and I were both familiar with the concept of supervision as practiced in social work. I had been in the habit of having monthly meetings with all my direct supervisees for years, but only one other manager had taken up the practice. The HR adviser and I felt this approach could usefully be adapted to provide a helpful tool for line managers, so we devised a system of regular meetings between managers and their staff that we called "development supervision" and described as

> a planned regular (monthly) meeting between a staff member and their line manager to take time out to discuss together how best the staff member can do their work and how the line manager can support the staff member to do their work.

We specified five purposes, namely, to monitor work and relationships, to evaluate the quality of performance and identify strengths and weaknesses, to facilitate learning and change, to support, and to plan. We linked development supervision directly to the annual performance appraisal scheme. We introduced the concepts and methods of practice to the managers in a two-day workshop, which the HR adviser actively followed up in several ways.

When reviewing progress with the managers several months later, we found varying degrees of take-up and success. Although the majority had done one or two sessions with each supervisee, no one had achieved the suggested regular monthly meetings, and some staff had not yet had any sessions. Clearly, development supervision had not been assimilated as a necessary or helpful component of staff management. Various challenges and difficulties were aired and discussed, including busyness and the reluctance of some staff to engage with the process, despite a very specific initiative to "market" it to them before it started. It was necessary to return to the basics of the concept and practice on several occasions in subsequent years to keep the initiative on track and help managers find ways around the problems. At one point, it seemed the whole scheme was about to collapse, so we conducted a substantial review in a learning week to reinforce to everyone that it was an important element in VBNK's approach to being a learning organization. Development supervision is now a feature of VBNK's management practices. I know that the senior managers value it for a number of reasons, but I think that it remains a challenge for some middle managers. I have also heard from my successor that it is still necessary to regularly spend time revisiting the purpose and practice of development supervision to ensure that it is conducted appropriately.

The challenges of getting the development supervision scheme in place highlighted some factors about how Cambodians view themselves and others as managers. Two commonly found behavior patterns are in direct opposition to each other. The first relates to people saying they enjoy good supervisory relationships, although it is rare to find any characterized by openness and honesty on both sides. It is not only staff who do not want to mention any weaknesses or problems. Some VBNK managers have been very reluctant to say anything that might disturb the harmony of their "good relationship" with staff, which inevitably means that communication stays at a very superficial level. I recall one staff member who was consistently underperforming. As I had discussed this with her line manager more than once, I was surprised when he requested an upgrade for her on the salary scale. I refused because there was no way to justify an upgrade. The staff member concerned was shocked to the point of tears when told about my decision. It transpired that she really had no idea that her work was not considered up to standard, because the manager had consistently praised her. When she realized that she needed to do better, she set about it with determination and went on to become a highly competent and valued member of the team. I find it difficult to understand how a relationship can be described as good if the notion of honesty is so threatening, but I know that my perception is rooted in a different cultural context.

At the opposite end of the spectrum are the managers who blame first and ask questions later. Criticism and blame, together with a paucity of thanks and praise, are all strong features of Cambodian social interaction, and they can result in line management relationships barren of any positive motivation. On the other side, staff blame managers and VBNK for not having done enough to support them or build their capacity. Accusations can fly in both directions, as staff and managers deflect any feedback with allegations of unfair criticism and other perceived injustices. I had a problem with one manager, who was very bright and had great potential but still had a lot to learn. In previous employment, the only feedback he ever received was fulsome praise, but his pattern was to be very critical of others, and, unusual for a Cambodian, that included being openly critical of me. However, he was always resentful whenever I commented on ways that his own work could or should be improved. It caused considerable tensions in our working relationship until one day he said, "I used to think you were criticizing me just for the sake of it, but now I realize that you just want us all to do our best." I don't know what changed his understanding, but the shift was invaluable: thereafter he was open to, and actively sought, feedback, which in turn resulted in great strides in his professional development.

Giving negative feedback in constructive ways is challenging in many cultures: it is not only Cambodians who struggle to handle this well. However, cultural factors can exacerbate the challenges and make people reluctant to try. Mature senior managers are more likely to be able to deal constructively with difficult issues while maintaining harmonious working relationships. Middle managers, however, may not yet have enough experience to be confident about holding others to account without damaging their working relationships. In Cambodian culture, notions of staff development do not fit anywhere in the autocratic behavior of traditional Cambodian leaders and managers and so are not the norm. I have also observed that many Cambodian managers think of themselves as the person to be developed, without embracing their responsibility to support the development of others.

I am aware that this discussion might, at first sight, look like a drift away from the focus on learning. I would argue, however, that being open, honest, and clear about what is or isn't good enough performance is an essential element of effective line management practice, which in turn is essential for developing and nurturing learning and creativity within individuals and organizations. It is a challenge for national managers to work in this way when it is not the cultural norm.

The work on the HR development strategy proved to be an important stage in VBNK's learning journey. Reviewing progress at the end of the HR adviser's contract early in 2005, we could identify significant achievements on several elements of the strategy. It was later expanded to become an HR management strategy, in order to incorporate other relevant issues, such as recruitment and retention strategies, career development, and succession planning, and it has been reviewed and revised regularly ever since.

One of the main outcomes of the work on the HR development strategy was that we learned a lot more about learning in the Cambodian context, which has some very significant differences to the concept of learning in a Western context. My introduction to the 2004 annual report, called *Learning to Learn, Continued*, summarized progress to date as follows (VBNK 2005):

I do feel that I am closer to understanding the depth and complexities of the challenges that learning presents . . . learning as a way of life still eludes us, both in the sense of recognizing every day and activity as richly full of learning opportunities and in being able to distil trends, issues, and themes from the myriad information out there in our environment.

It may seem strange to talk of resistance to learning when surrounded by colleagues who study all hours of the day and night in order to acquire academic qualifications and who are always happy to go to a workshop that leads to another certificate. Yet most people who work so hard to get their degrees and certificates rarely achieve significant integration of their new knowledge into their everyday work practices. The Bachelor of Business Administration curriculum somehow doesn't translate into more effective management practice in the office, nor does the Master of Development Management create greater impact in project implementation, and so on.

Over the years, VBNK has tried a number of approaches to learning. . . . This work has led to some changes and improvements in how we work, but it has not achieved the desired culture change. With some exceptions, most notably the work being done in the CHART project, our intention to be in a learning dialogue with the development sector has yet to become a reality. So we have to ask ourselves why we are still stuck with some attitudes and practices that prevent us from moving into a new way of life.

The work we did at that time helped to start shifting perceptions of learning away from a concept of formal study in order to do something toward one valuable in its own right. Our first approach, both internally and for customers, focused primarily on technical skills, but gradually we moved toward more facilitative and creative learning approaches. In 2006, I noted that VBNK's working definition of learning was "the process of acquiring knowledge from a variety of sources and experiences and using that knowledge in a way that results in positive change. It is a way of life, not an add-on activity" (Leng and Pearson 2006, 29). At that time, VBNK was using the HR development strategy, the CHART project, and creative practice as its three key approaches to support organizational learning. I can liken it only to having spent years trying to find better ways to turn the treadmill only to discover that installing a pump is a much better way to draw water.

It was significant that as a result of all this work, some senior Cambodian managers developed a deep understanding about learning and became the change champions within the organization. Thereafter, learning started to be a Cambodian issue, not just something that expatriates kept pushing, and this represented an exciting, positive, and perceptible shift in organizational leadership. Cambodian managers are able to take the issues forward much more effectively than expatriates because their understanding of the blocks and challenges comes from their own experiences:

Cambodians are capable of learning, especially from their experience. Resistance to change is one of their most significant lessons, learned from their past extremely fearful experience. They adapted to the changing regimes and learned to survive. However, until someone can assure them that they will not return to their trauma, they can be stuck, and new learning cannot take place. (Leng and Pearson 2006, 26)

Cambodian managers also know how to challenge and prompt new thinking in ways that are acceptable. The story is far from over, and even now some of my former colleagues feel frustrated that progress is slow. But I knew that we were making real progress on the day that I heard a Cambodian manager expressing his frustrations about his colleagues' resistance or inability to engage with learning practices and change.

A Story to Tell

In this section, I set out some of the important themes in the ongoing and long-term process of VBNK's journey toward being a learning organization. That the journey started early on is evidenced by the Strategic Plan 2000–2002, which talked about continuing to be a learning organization and included related goals and objectives for "cross-organization learning." Some of the comments about organizational learning made in the 2000 annual report still hold true today for VBNK and all development organizations.

It is a simple fact that we must be able to learn if we are to be effective in training and advising others. . . . Without reflection and learning how will any of us ever be able to assess whether or not what we are doing is truly effective, or find ways to improve our practice? Everywhere in the sector the needs and demands on time and resources are such that a task orientation predominates and little time or value is given to reflection or learning processes. Yet interventions into other peoples' lives and development should demand careful thought and planning based on learning from what has gone before, and other sources.

While I went on to note that achieving this aim would not be an easy task, I had little idea then just how profound the challenges were or how much I myself had to learn before I would be able to offer effective leadership on this fundamental aspect of VBNK's development.

The original staff development activities had resulted in small gains but not in the results that we might have expected from such a level of input. Eventually, I came to realize that my Cambodian colleagues and I had a profoundly different understanding of learning. The things we had been doing would have worked in an English organization, and even though we adapted materials and activities to the Cambodian context, they didn't work because they didn't fit with the Cambodian approach to learning. At the same time, many people in the sector were beginning to express concerns about the limited beneficial impact of fieldwork, and they were looking for new ideas to help them tackle intractable problems. VBNK was getting an increased number of requests for activities other than training, such as for facilitation of change processes. Effective facilitation calls for high-level skills, some of which are neither easy to learn nor easy to practice in Cambodian culture. It was becoming clear that VBNK's sustainability would depend on its own ability to learn and change and then to facilitate others in their learning and change processes.

I knew that I had to deepen my understanding about learning within Cambodian culture and about the multiple factors that prevent the utilization of knowledge, skills, and opportunities for positive change. This required asking a set of questions very different from those questions that arise from a focus on skills building. Instead I had to explore questions like "How is learning defined?" "Which types of learning are valued within this culture?" "How is learning acquired and from whom?" "How is it used?" "What are the blocks that prevent learning from leading to change?" "What might be helpful in overcoming the blocks?" and "How can people unlearn fears and inhibitions in order to be open to something new?" This was the period when I realized that I also had to change and adopt a different learning style if I was to be effective in leading VBNK's organizational learning and staff development.

Nevertheless, some of my early analysis was accurate and is still pertinent today. Unfortunately, my understanding then was not yet deep enough to lead me toward more effective responses. In July 2008, VBNK jointly hosted a workshop on transformative learning with the Analyzing Development Issues project team of the CCC. VBNK decided to present itself as a case study. It did so by making a "wall" of the blocks to learning, of the things we had done to try to overcome the blocks, and of the things that we felt remained deeply rooted, intractable challenges. When I left shortly afterward, one of the TAs, Arthur Delvecchio, recreated the wall diagram, with the comment "Jenny, there is a story to tell . . ." With his permission, it is reproduced in this chapter (Figure 3.2) because I think it gives such a helpful visual representation of all the complex issues with which we were grappling.

Some people are able to draw learning from their activities without taking specific time for reflection and/or applying learning tools, but that sophisticated capability is most usually developed through high-quality education from an early age. Few Cambodians have had educational experiences that support the development of such abilities, and so in the VBNK context, both time and tools were needed to facilitate learning. Until we periodically stopped all our external delivery activities in order to have time for structured learning practices, our reflections were superficial and mechanistic and did not lead to any obvious learning and change. Even then, we made some mistakes in how we did it, and the process is still under regular review. The need to earn a substantive proportion of the budget from fees for services created constant tensions between delivery schedules and learning activities. The HR adviser coined the phrase "learning versus earning" to encapsulate the management challenges this caused.

I learned how important it is for senior management to make, and visibly demonstrate, a commitment to learning practices. Many times, VBNK was riding high on success, with demand for services constantly greater than we could meet. It would have been all too easy to rest on our laurels and think that we could let go the search for improvement. But I saw other small training NGOs that started in the mid-1990s fold because the customers stopped coming. Whether it was because they didn't realize the need to change or because they didn't know how to was never clear, but they didn't upgrade their curricula, and ultimately that omission led to their demise. The sector we were serving was developing, and we needed to keep ahead if we were to stay relevant. As the director, I had to show my commitment through active engagement in relevant activities and by ensuring that all necessary resources, including time, were available.

Reflecting with the wisdom of hindsight, I can identify my most important learning on these issues:

- Organizational learning is strategic and must be reinforced at that level. Visible senior management commitment is essential to establish and maintain the structures, mandates, and resources for what needs to happen operationally.
- Organizational learning and staff development are inextricably linked in multiple complex ways, and it is necessary to work with both simultaneously.
- The capacity for both individuals and organizations to learn is dependent on multiple factors, including being able to overcome blocks to learning. Recognizing these blocks requires a profound understanding of the cultural and contextual factors that produces them.

- Blocks to learning are not skills gaps and cannot be approached as such. Creative practices often prove to be an effective tool for dismantling blocks, stimulating new ideas, and promoting the acceptance of change.

Of these, I think the last two are the most important, although I had been working in Cambodia for at least seven years before I began fully to understand them. It would have been good to know in the early days some of the things that I know now, but it was only by working through many different initiatives, successful and otherwise, that the wisdom came. This summary is a succinct distillation of processes that lasted for years and that are continuing even now.

Notes

1. Of this original group of six, two are still at VBNK as highly valued members of the program team, three have senior positions in other agencies in the social development sector, and one emigrated to the United States.

2. Like many Cambodians of his age, he had been sent to one of the Soviet bloc countries during the 1980s to study and get qualifications in technical subjects such as mechanics and engineering.

3. The Action Learning Cycle has four steps: review of Actions (activities) undertaken; Reflection on the successes, challenges, and issues arising from the actions; identification of Learning that can be drawn from the reflections; and Planning to use the learning in the next round of actions. This process is also often referred to as the Action–Reflection–Learning–Planning (ARLP) cycle.

4

Creativity and New Dimensions of Response

Although it was central to my work at VBNK for nearly 10 years, for a long time I was unable to articulate succinctly what we were doing when we used words like "creativity," "creative process," and "creative practice." It was only when I had the benefit of distance and time away from the work after I left that I could define it to my own satisfaction. In the VBNK context, I think that creativity, creative process, or creative practice is "anything that breaks habitual patterns of reaction to stimuli and moves people into new dimensions of response." This definition can be meaningful for all dimensions of a person—intellectual, emotional, spiritual, or physical. It recognizes a point of change between past and future, it recognizes the "stuckness" that can keep people trapped, and, last, it holds implicit the notion of opening up or out. I had been formulating and working with this definition intuitively for years.

Our work with creativity was in many respects a journey into the unknown, prompting many questions. Some questions were so big, it was more important to hold them than to push for answers. For me, two of the most important questions remain: "How can we use creativity to make safe space for change?" and "What are the most effective creative practices for helping people confront and overcome their innermost fears and inhibitions?" Given the complexity of the challenges, there can be no simple and straightforward answers to these questions. It is crucial to reconsider them and answer them differently every time according to the context and the culture.

As with other aspects of VBNK's history, creativity didn't become part of the story in neat sequential steps: many different activities overlapped in time. For clarity, what follows is not a chronological account but a recounting of each of the most important threads in the story in their own right. Starting with how David Glass introduced creativity to VBNK, I go on to talk about the innovations we introduced in the program in order to offer others new ideas and experiences that we hoped they would find stimulating and helpful.

David Glass

The story of VBNK's work with creativity, creative process, and creative practice starts in the organization's relationship with David Glass and his colleagues in the David Glass Ensemble. David is a theater director from the United Kingdom who has worked extensively in developing countries, primarily with children, using processes drawn from theater to enable individuals to find creative expression and outlets for their feelings. I met David in late 1998, when he was in Cambodia with The Lost Child Project.[1] During our first conversation, I could see that David had a deep, intuitive understanding of the impact of trauma on Cambodians. I heard about the work he was doing with street children and thought that some of it would also be beneficial for adults. As preparation for a follow-up meeting to discuss possible collaboration, I prepared some notes (reproduced in the section "First Steps" in Chapter 3) on possible areas of work. Whenever I have gone back to those notes, it reminds me that for many little has changed and that those issues remain among the most obstinate blocks to learning and change. After further discussions, we all saw that there was mutual benefit in developing a relationship between VBNK and the ensemble. VBNK would have access to David, who was a multitalented actor, director, and consultant, and others in the ensemble, who were skilled in facilitation of performance-based projects. David felt a relationship with VBNK would give them some grounding in the development sector.

David talked about working with people in a way that is therapeutic without being therapy. I felt instinctively that it was an appropriate approach for the Cambodian context but did not anticipate that anything David did with the staff would be related directly to the program of management training. Instead, I felt that his contribution would help staff to improve their communication skills and to be less rigidly self-controlled and, therefore, more open and flexible in their thinking and receptiveness to new ideas. We agreed that whenever other work brought David to the region, he would also come to Phnom Penh to work with VBNK. The subject of creativity was touched on lightly during the first two workshops, and it seemed something that could be useful to explore more deeply, to help foster initiative, open-mindedness, and flexibility. Many people's initial response to the word "creativity" is an association with art and painting, followed very quickly by an assertion that they can't do it. It was much the same with the VBNK staff: we needed to reassure them that they would not be asked to do anything that would expose them to loss of face because they lacked artistic talent. When David asked what he should focus on for the third workshop, I suggested that he go deeper into creativity.

We agreed that he would follow a five-step cycle used in theater for creating performance to see how it could be applied in the development context. This was to be spread over two workshops in 2000 and fully documented so that it could be written up as a manual. The steps in the creative cycle are (1) Preparation, (2) Creative Origination, (3) Creative Organization, (4) Presentation, and (5) Reflection and Renewal. The structure of the workshops emphasized the importance of understanding not only each step but also how all the steps relate to each other in a creative cycle. This entailed looking in detail at many different ideas and concepts, some of which, like the relationship between creativity and nature, the staff could easily understand. However, people used to thinking in very rigid patterns find some ideas difficult to grasp. For example, a statement such as "the goal will move during the process" can be confusing. Holding multiple components in balance, as in "the focus is not only on the result but also on qualities as they emerge," also proved challenging. Nevertheless, this work helped people change their ideas of creativity. They began to see that creativity is all around us and a factor in many aspects of everyday life and work, for example, in how we cook and dress or how we solve problems at work. Eventually, between the two organizations, we developed the manual into a book, which VBNK published as *Creative Practice: A Guide to Creativity in Development* (Glass 2003).

David's work had a significant influence on VBNK staff, both personally and professionally. One of the most frequently mentioned benefits was stress reduction, which was interesting because David rarely did anything specific on stress management. I assumed that it was because engaging in creative activities can be both fun and totally absorbing, thereby providing refreshing, if temporary, respite from everyday worries.

Increasingly, we started to use creative exercises in our internal communications. For example, during internal workshops, small groups used role-play, body sculpts, songs, pictures, or other visual methods to present their outputs to the plenary group. These methods were both fun and frequently more informative than standard flip chart list presentations. It was obvious that, with time and practice, many staff were finding that creative means of self-expression enabled them to say things they might not dare say in conventional ways. Some also discovered they had real talent for art and poetry. The experiences with David did not, however, lead to any immediate or significant changes in workplace performance, beyond improvements in the quality of visual aids.

In response to their growing awareness and understanding, the staff requested that we take more time to experiment with creative media, so we started a series of monthly Saturday morning creativity workshops. These were entirely voluntary, but a surprising number of staff turned up each time. We used the sessions to experience different forms of creative self-expression, many of which were completely new to the staff. I will never forget the first painting session, for example. When everyone was seated at a table with brush and paints and blank paper, I asked who had done any painting before. Just three hands went up in a room of more than 30 people. Imagine a childhood in which no one ever sat you down with paper and paints and let you experiment with color and form and making a big mess. Another astonishing revelation came when we were discussing mixing primary colors to make other colors. Someone said that his family business in the provinces was making traditional Khmer floor tiles. For this, they bought red, yellow, and green dyes, but neither he nor anyone in his family knew that if you mixed yellow and red you got orange or that green came from yellow and blue. The intensity with which everyone set about filling their blank sheets of paper was fascinating to watch. Other sessions were spent on activities like dance, music, poetry, acting, and forum theater. In addition, events such as the annual retreat always included a creative activity session, such as painting the highlights of the year on a roll of paper the length of the meeting room.

Creative Facilitators

Every time that David or any of his colleagues in the ensemble, most particularly Matthew Jones and Rob Hale,[2] came to visit, we felt their presence infusing everyday life in VBNK with a surge of creative energy. I particularly enjoyed not only the different exercises they conducted but also the stimulating and thought-provoking conversations that always flowed when they were around. I don't know what VBNK might have become without their inputs, but I do know that I owe many of my ideas to the stimulation and guidance they offered. There is no doubt in my mind that David and his colleagues contributed a great deal toward VBNK's evolution into the creative learning organization that it is today. It was also because of them that I dared to bring in some other creative facilitators to work with us in different ways.

Leang Seckon is an acknowledged leader of the small group of artists at the forefront of contemporary Cambodian art. Using paint and collage,

Seckon creates exciting visual and metaphorical depictions of stories from Cambodian myths, history, and religion and his own life. His work explores and expresses the essence of being Cambodian. Apart from being very talented, he is also a warm, gentle, and engaging person. I thought it would be interesting to have Seckon spend some time with the staff of VBNK as an "artist in residence," and he also found the idea interesting. While I did not have any specific goals for and expectations of the project, I thought that an interactive dialogue with an artist could lead to new perspectives for us individually and enable us as a group to acknowledge what in VBNK's culture makes it unique. I hoped that the opportunity to work with an artist would help us all find new ways to express ourselves and develop our individual and collective creativity. As neither Seckon nor I had any idea about how to make an artist in residence project work in practice, we engaged the support of an expatriate art curator and writer who lives in Cambodia and specializes in modern Southeast Asian art. She designed the project and managed its implementation, freeing Seckon to focus on creativity and me to participate.

Seckon's studio in VBNK was the CCD room, which had no chairs, tables, or whiteboards, only mats and cushions on the floor and attractive decorations. It was very soon a magnet to which everyone was drawn. After a first introductory workshop with all staff, we worked in small groups, under Seckon's guidance, to create self-portraits, focusing on self as a person in development, learning from life's experiences. I know that every Cambodian has a story, many of which are extremely sad and painful. I knew some of the VBNK staff stories in detail. Nevertheless, I was still taken aback by the powerful ways in which some of my colleagues expressed themselves in art. The appalling experiences through which the older staff had lived showed up time and again in the paintings. Several painted the ground on which they stood red to represent the blood-impregnated land after the Khmer Rouge slaughter of their families and communities. Many included guns and tanks and other symbols of war and conflict. It was a highly informative message about everything that Cambodians still hold within them. Few of the pieces were beautiful, but that didn't matter. What mattered was the experience of self-expression and creation and the meaning that the pieces held for their creators. It is not possible to accurately measure either the short- or the long-term impact of such an exercise; nevertheless, I have no doubt that it was a good thing for us to do. It was confirmed as being worthwhile many times over in the reflections that the staff shared after their art sessions, emphasizing how much they appreciated and had benefited from the opportunity to tell their story in this medium. All participating staff members chose one of their pieces to be framed and hung in the common areas of the office, and they are all still there to remind everyone of the time spent with Seckon.

Other creative facilitators helped with more specific purpose. One such was Wendy Erd, a writer now specializing in community storytelling through film. Wendy did some excellent workshops helping VBNK staff develop their writing skills. Some workshops were for all staff, to give them ideas and exercises for writing as a creative form of self-expression. Others were for those staff members who had writing responsibilities in their work. For both groups, Wendy focused on making the connection between an idea and the page rather than English and grammar. For many people (in any culture), the thought of writing creates anxiety, because they fear getting something wrong. That anxiety gives self-censorship mechanisms full power to block any idea getting from its source to the page. Wendy's approach was to give people ways of writing that bypassed self-censorship to let their ideas flow without judgment about their worth. Some of the processes that she introduced, such as journaling and speed-writes, are still in regular use in VBNK activities.

Peter Kaufmann works with what he calls "creative communication," which is a simple phrase to describe some very complex ideas. His approach draws on experiential and reflective exercises from multiple disciplines to explore understanding of self, intra- and interpersonal expression, and relationships. The first major piece of work that Peter did with VBNK was to help explore our organizational values during an annual staff retreat, especially looking at how power relations play out in organizational life. The exercise that stands out in my memory is the "inner voice" role-play method to explore incidents or scenarios in everyday life. This method has different variations, and the one Peter introduced to VBNK involves the "audience" responding with their idea of what any of the role-play characters might be thinking and feeling but not saying. They then join the role-play, verbalizing the thought or feeling so that the inner voice is heard externally. Having experienced the power of this exercise for themselves, the program staff later adapted and used it many times in their own facilitation processes. Peter also contributed much to the CHART project, by leading the facilitation of modules and working with the project team to develop their facilitation skills.

Early Innovations

The original program of providing open access and customized training, and organization development consultancy, built VBNK's solid reputation as a service provider. Because of its work with creativity and learning practices,

VBNK is probably best known now for its innovations and for introducing other organizations to new ideas and approaches through its work with them. But VBNK was innovating from the start, even when the program was focused entirely on training. Innovation inevitably has an element of risk, and failure can result in reluctance to try again. Fortunately, VBNK's first experiments with different approaches to training were successful, and this success created the confidence for all subsequent pioneering of new ideas. I describe here VBNK's two original innovations, modular programs and the Women's Leadership Program (WLP).

The Managers Development Program

The six-module MDP was designed in 1998, before any academic study programs were available in country, to give NGO managers access to something more than random and unconnected training on different subjects. The MDP lasted for 18 months, with each module approximately three months apart. The modules were Being an Effective Manager, Staff Management, Organizational Structure and Policy, Problem Solving, Report Writing, and Financial Management. Offering a series of linked courses was then a significant innovation in and of itself, and the program had two further elements that made it unique. First, any organization sending staff to the MDP had to nominate a training mentor to support the participants in the application of learning between modules. The second innovation was to have the participants write a Learning Implementation Plan (LIP) at the end of each module to specify how they were going to apply the learning they had just gained. While in practice neither of these features proved universally robust, in the vast majority of cases they were instrumental in contributing to the successful integration of learning from the training into everyday work practices. I now know that what we developed then was in line with current thinking on best practice in the body of academic and practitioner knowledge on "transfer of training" or "transfer of learning." But in those days we hadn't heard of it and instead worked it out for ourselves.

In INGOs, the training mentor was often an expatriate manager or adviser; in CNGOs, it was sometimes an adviser or senior Cambodian. But CNGO directors usually needed to ask someone outside their organization to mentor them. In later years, graduates of earlier programs took on the mentoring role for other participants from their organizations. Prior to the commencement of each program, VBNK held a workshop for nominated mentors to explain the program content and process and to explore the commitments and expectations arising from their role. After each module, a summary of the content and copies of the LIPs were sent to the mentors so that they knew what the participants had worked on and committed to implementing after the training. The mentors were asked to submit a brief commentary on progress before the start of the next module. On the first day of the next module, all participants had to make a presentation on how they had done with implementation of their LIP. As no one ever wants to stand up in front of a group and lose face by saying that they haven't done what they were supposed to do, this proved to be a very effective motivator in terms of getting people to think about their new learning and ideas and how to apply them in practice.

There were some potential pitfalls in both aspects of this approach, which were largely beyond VBNK's control. A great deal depended on who had been nominated as training mentor and how seriously they took on the responsibilities of supporting participants. If they were not interested and engaged, all VBNK could do about it was offer some gentle reminders. Sometimes, people were interested and supportive but were not close enough to the participant's working realities to offer helpful guidance. It was also the case that the mentoring process inevitably got lost if the mentor left during the period of the program; we never found an incoming post holder interested or able to pick up this responsibility. A criticism that people in the participants' organizations often raised was that the LIPs were unrealistic and not specific and that the VBNK trainers should do more to ensure relevance when they were developed at the end of each module. Again, this was something that VBNK did not have the ability to address. It was impossible for the trainers to have sufficient knowledge of every participant's work in order to be able to offer a critical analysis of the relevance and workability of the LIP. We encouraged mentors to attend the last afternoon of each module to work with their staff on the LIPs, but few ever took up the invitation.

There were, however, some outstanding examples of success. One INGO working on a long-term localization plan decided to use VBNK's programs as part of its strategic approach to building the capacity of all Cambodian managers. Starting with the four most senior people on the first MDP, they subsequently put all of their senior and middle managers through this and VBNK's other modular programs over the next few years. One expatriate adviser was designated training mentor to all the participants, and she took the role very seriously. Between each module, she organized both group and individual coaching sessions for the participants and actively supported them to implement their learning. Over time, she came to know the course content extremely well, so she had a unique depth of knowledge with which to support the participants.

That organization stands out for breadth and depth of its approach to developing the capacity of its Cambodian managers through VBNK's modular programs. In due course, the organization nationalized all of its management positions, up to and including the directorship, although for other reasons it has remained an INGO. Another INGO, one of the leaders in the demining sector, commissioned two rounds of the MDP for all its senior and middle managers, alongside some basic management training for the minefield supervisors. This represented a huge commitment and investment of resources for the organization, but it considered the time and money well spent, because it gave all managers the same management tools and language. A global evaluation undertaken by the INGO's head office cited the Cambodian initiative with the MDP as the most effective example of capacity development in any of its country programs.

In 1999, VBNK followed up on the MDP with the development of two further modular programs, the WLP, discussed below, and the Proposal Development Program (PDP). The PDP was developed at the request of an in-country donor with a large group of CNGO partners. The country representative told us that they were consistently meeting two difficulties with their Cambodian partners. The first was "Proposals that have six pages of Cambodian history and one paragraph describing the proposed project, whereas what we need is one paragraph of Cambodian history and six pages describing the proposed project." They were also struggling with the shining star syndrome, described in Chapter 2. They asked VBNK to devise a program to address both challenges by training middle managers in all the key stages in project appraisal and design necessary for development of a meaningful proposal. Thus began our first three-way collaboration, in which a donor commissioned customized training for other organizations. The process required the active support of both the CNGO directors and the program team of the donor agency. Although not without its challenges in terms of implementation, the VBNK contribution was deemed to be a success, and with the donor's agreement we adapted the materials developed in this project to create the open access PDP, which was first offered in 2000.

In 2002, after a major review of all training offered in the curriculum, the MDP was changed from one six-module program to two four-module programs, at introductory and advanced levels, the latter including two new courses, Presentation Skills and Management of Change. Registration rates demonstrated the success of VBNK's modular program approach. For example, in 2001 more than 50% of open access training and 40% of customized training was made up of modular programs. Over time, the need for open access training diminished, and VBNK stopped offering these programs as a matter of routine. Nevertheless, in terms of "What works?" the modular concept remains a strong feature of VBNK's approach, and it is used for both training needs and more complex organizational development and learning programs.

The Women's Leadership Program

In the mid- and late 1990s, women managers faced a daunting array of challenges, some of which still exist today, though to a lesser extent. Back then, the notion of a woman working in an organization, as opposed to the government or a family business, was still relatively new. In government and family businesses, there were well-established rules for how a woman should behave and, more particularly, for what she should not do. In the NGO community, however, foreigners had introduced organizational norms that included expectations of women working on equal terms with their male colleagues. My introduction to the impact this had on women was in 1995, during the first course I delivered in Cambodia. For two weeks, a well-dressed woman in her 40s sat in the front row of the participant group, taking copious notes on everything. She spoke only when directly asked a question, and even then her responses were minimal. At the end of the course, she asked to speak to me in private, whereupon she burst into tears and poured out a tale of woe about how no one in her organization would listen to her or do anything she asked them to because she is a woman. I subsequently heard many variations of this story. I recall a discussion in a gender session that went absolutely nowhere. I had presented the scenario of a bright young woman manager having problems with an older man who would not follow her instructions about the work. Expecting that this would prompt a discussion about possible techniques that might enable her to work with him effectively, I was shocked when the unanimous response of all the men in the group was that the female manager should be sacked on the grounds that she shouldn't have been given the job in the first place. None of the women in the group offered a word of disagreement, illustrating the reality that women managers not only meet problems getting male staff to take them seriously but also frequently have the same problem with female staff. As I have written elsewhere, the Western feminists' concept of sisterhood is not one that resonates among Cambodian women (Pearson 2011b).

Women were trying to reconcile strong conflicting pressures when work demands meant they had to do something that went against the usual rules for women's conduct. For example, women were sometimes expected to travel and stay away from home, in the provinces and occasionally abroad, as part of their work duties. No "good" Cambodian woman, especially if young and unmarried, would travel in the company of men without a suitable female chaperone. In addition, women were still expected to carry the primary responsibility for the family and the home, regardless of workload demands and whether husbands were also in employment. It is still very much the case that anyone (female or male) with a regular and reasonable salary can find him- or herself expected to support a large number of extended family members. Many women were suffering intolerable stress as a result of all the heavy demands on them.

In the original proposal for VBNK, there was a commitment to finding ways to work with gender issues. In 1999, the TA conducted a small informal research project to clarify and deepen our understanding about the challenges that women managers were facing so that we could offer something relevant and helpful. Her findings informed the development of the three-module WLP, which was first delivered to a group of 12 women in 1999–2000. The first two modules, Core Management Skills and Organizational Structure and Policy, drew on materials from the MDP in order to equip the women with basic management knowledge and tools. There were, however, some very significant differences in the WLP approach. The first involved facilitated reflection sessions, during which the participants discussed the implications of what they were learning about management in relation to being a Cambodian woman, for example, as in the scenario above, when a female manager needed to assert her authority to get staff to take notice of her. The other major issue that the research highlighted was that women lacked voice in their organizations. This stemmed from the belief, held by both men and women, that women had nothing of value to add to any discussion or process. Because they felt their ideas and contributions were of no value, women rarely dared to offer them; when they did, they were usually ignored or ridiculed. There was a pressing need to change attitudes so that women could contribute as equals with their male colleagues, a need that is yet to be fully met. Presentation and influencing skills were both strands in the first two modules, therefore, and they were the central theme of the final module, Developing Professional Relationships. This last module used methods such as video feedback on role-plays to help build women's confidence to speak and expect to be heard.

Despite very positive feedback from the participants and their organizations, we did not get high registration for subsequent rounds of the program. I was puzzled by this, as many organizations made public declarations about their commitment to women and gender issues. So I made some informal inquiries. It seemed that in many organizations, gender commitments were program oriented, and few gave any thought or resources to gender equality initiatives within their own organization. As part of our commitment to women, VBNK continued to run the WLP regularly, even though some years there were not enough participants to cover costs.

Then a very interesting development occurred in 2003, and the result was that the WLP finally came into its own. The adviser to the Partnership for Gender Equity project, based in the Ministry of Women's Affairs and supported by United Nations Development Programme (UNDP), heard about the WLP. She asked if we could adapt the content to the government context and run the program for some senior women in central ministries. The success of the first delivery resulted in VBNK being asked to run the program 12 more times over the next four years. More than 200 women attended from central ministries, plus all the directors and deputy directors of Provincial Departments of Women's Affairs. An evaluation conducted in 2007 found that the program had been very successful in terms of what the women had learned from the training. The problem, as ever, was what happened when they returned to the workplace armed with new knowledge, tools, and ideas. Some were in positions that enabled them to implement changes, but the majority, in the tightly controlled confines of government departments, needed the permission and support of others to do things differently. For some, neither the permission nor the support was present. Despite these drawbacks, many felt that the program had done a great deal to help the women assert themselves as professional managers within government. The following is an extract from a letter I received from the Minister of Women's Affairs, H.E. Dr Ing Kantha Phavi, at the end of 2005:

I have met the women civil servants who have been participants in this course. . . . I am impressed by their positive comments about the program as well as the change in their attitudes and actions. They now trust themselves and their judgments, which gives them the confidence to advocate for what they believe in. They have a strength of purpose and a new commitment to change for themselves, for other women in the civil service and for the community. . . . Whereas in the past they have been frustrated and passive, they are now feeling empowered and are prepared to organize, to be advocates and to take action.

I have heard that they are also performing better as managers and that some of them have been rewarded with promotions, and increased opportunities to participate in missions and study tours.

They are also rewarded by praise from their superiors and happier relations in their workplaces. (VBNK 2006, 9)

A longitudinal impact assessment study conducted by VBNK in 2009 included five women who had participated in the program in 2006. All five reported having been promoted to senior positions, and they also "talked about becoming braver to speak up, daring to express their needs and say no, with reason, to their hierarchy. They saw themselves as a leader as they helped other women to be brave" (VBNK 2009, 12). It would be inappropriate to claim that the WLP was the only factor contributing to the women's success, because clearly many other factors would also have been influential during those years. Nevertheless, it is a testament to the relevance and helpfulness of the WLP that the women felt that their participation had been instrumental in enabling them to make personal and professional progress.

Creative Innovations for Learning and Change

All of VBNK's courses and facilitation practices are periodically reviewed for relevance of both content and process. As the program teams became more familiar and comfortable with different ways of working and acquired the ability to design and facilitate creative processes, they were able to move away from old training styles that put them center stage as the experts toward training as a process of facilitating experiential learning. Different courses and program modules have progressively been upgraded to incorporate creative activities designed to draw out the wisdom of the group and equip participants with learning and communication methods that they can use in their work. Thus, even core skills training now looks considerably different than it did a decade ago.

What I describe in more detail below are some of the bigger innovations that VBNK developed, all of which had creative practices at the center of their work with individuals and organizations.

The CHART Project

One of the most significant initiatives resulting from my time at CDRA came over time and is, in some senses, still unfolding. This story starts with other people: Moira O'Leary, who had also been on the CDRA program, and a Cambodian friend and colleague, Meas Nee. Together, they developed a research proposal to study the working practices of rural community development workers in four CNGOs. VBNK could not offer funding support, but we were able to offer them office space and support for the duration of the study. I had many interesting discussions with them as they analyzed their data after the fieldwork. Being a sounding board as they considered all the permutations and implications of their findings both helped me understand more about Cambodian culture and context and gave me a sense of the importance of what they had done. They did not have a budget for publishing, having planned to share the report only with the participating CNGOs and the INGOs that had funded the work. Immediately after I read the draft, I knew that *Learning for Transformation: A Study of the Relationship Between Culture, Values, Experience and Development Practice in Cambodia* (O'Leary and Meas 2001) was something that needed to be disseminated as widely as possible. I had some money in an underspent budget line, and my donors agreed that it could be used to publish the report. The impact of the report was immediate and huge. The general and ongoing response from the development community could be summed up as "thank goodness someone has explained what is really going on here so I can now make sense of all the things I didn't understand before." It has rightly come to be considered the seminal work on development practice in Cambodia. I have also had feedback that many people have used the study to helpful purpose elsewhere, because aspects of the findings are relevant for many other countries and contexts.

After *Learning for Transformation* was published, I started to realize that VBNK, although tucked away in Cambodia, a place many consider to be a development backwater, was sitting at the center of some cutting-edge influences. We were working with David Glass on creativity, I was still assimilating different aspects of my learning from CDRA, and now we had the findings of an important study bringing clarity to many challenges that had not previously been understood. A comment in a CDRA report that "development happens not between things, but between people" (CDRA 2001, 6) gave me a moment of insight that started a new train of thinking. I began to envision a project that could draw together the creativity and learning from all of the stimulating influences VBNK was then experiencing to offer development practitioners a new way of working. I wrote a concept paper called "Mending Broken Mirrors," basing the title on a comment made by a colleague who had attended one of David's workshops and been introduced to a mirroring exercise in which pairs hold eye contact while mirroring each other's actions. When trying to use this exercise with a Cambodian group, she ran into difficulties, because the participants were unable to hold eye contact with each other.

The subtitle of my concept paper was "A Creative Approach to Building Relationships for Social Development." I noted that all the approaches then in use, such as community development, village development committees, and self-help groups, together with a range of crosscutting issues, including women's participation and care for the environment, were imported philosophies. Indications were that none of these approaches were achieving sustainable change in the lives of the beneficiaries. Studies repeatedly noted that inequalities and patterns of disempowering dependence in relationships and social structures were being reinforced by the relationships between development agencies, their staff, and their target beneficiaries. I imagine that Cambodia is far from unique in that while most NGO staff are trained on technicalities and tools, very little is done to help them fully understand the intra- and interpersonal aspects of their work. *Learning for Transformation* articulated that practitioners were struggling to be effective in their work because they did not relate their own experiences, learning, development, and change processes to the work they were doing with others. It highlighted the need for practitioners to be aware of how their culture, experience, education, and trauma influence their behavior and attitudes before they intervene in other people's lives.

Since starting work with David Glass in 1999, VBNK had been formulating a person-centered approach to staff development, based on the belief that for people to function to their full capacity as professionals, they first need to overcome any constraints that prevent them from functioning to their full capacity as human beings. This was an important foundation to have in place when we started thinking about how to develop an alternative to the skills and tools training approach then in vogue in the development sector in Cambodia. I proposed an action research project that would focus on helping practitioners come to a mature and conscious understanding of themselves and how they function as workers. The hypothesis was that development practitioners will be more effective in bringing change to their target communities if

- they are first put through a lengthy process of self-development and taught how to apply this developmental process to their work and
- their work is not constrained by the demands of a project cycle with previously identified target outputs but focused on the important task of building relationships.

This concept paper led to the Creative Holistic Action-research for Relationship Transformation (CHART) project, developed by Nigel Goddard, which started its first program in June 2003. After Round 1, the second project manager, Enda Moclair, undertook a major review of all that had been done, which resulted in Round 2 being much shorter. The review process distilled all the experiments and outcomes of Round 1 to focus on the issues of most importance for whole person learning and change, all of which are interrelated. These issues, known in VBNK as the Seven Sisters, are self-awareness, relationships, creativity, critical thinking, power and development, learning, and facilitation. There were further, though less radical, revisions for the third program. Among the key findings identified in various evaluations and follow-up studies are that working with experiential learning methods and alternative literacies improves the quality of learning for all participants, participants had increased self-awareness and personal empowerment, and there was a discernable difference in the way participants worked in villages, resulting in "unusual and very positive" instances of "new depth of ownership, confidence, and hope in villagers."

One of the INGOs that had field project staff participants in Round 1 asked VBNK to develop a Leadership Development Program (LDP) based on the CHART philosophy and approach. This was a challenging request because, at the same time, the organization would sponsor the participant group to participate in a master's-level management program. The organization's idea was to take a two-pronged approach to developing their future leaders—the academic program to develop intellectual and management capacity and the CHART project to address the values and relational aspects of leadership. The LDP achieved its objectives, although from VBNK's perspective it could have been more effective. Factors that we felt detracted from the process were beyond our control. For example, several changes in the participant group over the series of modules meant that few completed the entire program.

The work on the customized LDP produced some rich learning for the CHART team members, which they used to develop an open access LDP. This version, freed from the constraints of harmonizing with an academic program, was much more focused on whole person learning. It continues to run with considerable success. Aspects of the program have also been incorporated into broader organizational development interventions with other organizations.

When I commented to some of my senior colleagues during the first round of CHART that I saw CHART as the future heart of VBNK, it caused a great deal of consternation. Some people chose to interpret the comment as me not valuing what they did and/or giving the CHART project manager a privileged role and position in the organization. Several asked me to specify exactly how and when this would happen, because they thought it would mean redundancies, and they wanted to be prepared. Others suggested that CHART should break away and become a separate organization so as not to threaten

VBNK's stability. The reactions were such that shortly afterward, I felt it wise to retract by saying that it had been a throwaway remark that I had not thought through properly. In some senses this was true, because at that stage I didn't know how or when it might happen. Nevertheless, what we tried to do with CHART is the closest VBNK got to my vision of effective capacity-building practice in Cambodia: not to offer therapy but to work in ways that facilitate individuals, groups, and communities to come to terms with their past, heal, and move on. But even this is not enough, as there are so many factors in contemporary Cambodian society and culture that inhibit the fulfillment of potential. It is only when Cambodians have the ability to analyze and judge these factors for themselves that they will be able to define their own vision of, and path to, positive change. I believe very strongly that vision can be achieved only through practices that nurture creativity and learning, such as those that we introduced with CHART. So, although the path has been tortuous and thrown up many diversions and obstacles, nine years after I first had the idea of offering something different, I am very happy to know that CHART is finally working at the heart of VBNK.

The Center for Creative Development

Through their work with VBNK and street children organizations, David and his colleagues were introduced to other individuals and agencies interested to explore what this approach could offer in relation to their organizational practices. In part, this interest was prompted by a growing awareness in the development sector that the corporate world was using various types of creative practice to help with complex organizational development and change processes. VBNK hosted some open access workshops that David offered for development practitioners. They were well attended and appreciated and led other organizations to request customized workshops. This growing trend of interest prompted us to form the CCD. This was officially launched in 2003 with the then British ambassador, who had sponsored the ensemble to do a performance piece with street children about the dangers inherent in their lives, as patron.

In many ways, the CCD was more an association than a project in the conventional sense of the word. It did not have any dedicated staff, activity plans, or resources, and its home was a simple room in VBNK. The aim of the CCD was

> to be a place where development practitioners and others can explore and share creative processes in order to enhance development

practice and understanding through a holistic exploration of creative methodologies and thinking.

The rationale for establishing the center was written up in a paper produced for the launch, which articulated our thinking about the need to introduce creative practices as widely as possible into development. I believe that what we said then is still relevant now, so I reproduce the most pertinent sections of it:

> The fundamental premise on which the CCD will be based is that development is about relationships, and creative practice is an essential component in establishing the good relationships needed for effective development practice to take place. Many development practitioners are struggling to find effective methodologies for their work and find that the constraints of the logical framework project cycle are not conducive to building relationships with beneficiaries that are based on trust and participation.
>
> The use of creative tools as a method for generating constructive, meaningful, participatory dialogues and activities is full of unexplored potential. Rooted in the primal human cultures of play, ritual, storytelling, music, and dance, these creative activities contain the basis for warm and direct participatory relationships. Creative methodology has recent valued precursors in the work of Augusto Boal, play therapy, music, and dance therapy, a strong tradition of community theater and arts practitioners working on issues of diversity, social inclusion, and conflict resolution.
>
> The recognition of the value of creative techniques in development has been increasing over the years. This has come about through the continuing activities of practitioners but also through a growing awareness in the academic and training fields. Some courses now exist within academic institutions and other organizations. A great deal of activity takes place, largely piecemeal. There does not appear to be any single environment where theory, technique, and actual practice can take place together.
>
> Creative process does not attempt to replace other methodologies and project frameworks but to underpin and supplement them with more effective ways of establishing the fundamental prerequisites for good development practice to take place. Furthermore, the CCD directly responds to the synergy of concerns motivating VBNK's CHART project to address concerns in development

practice in Cambodia and the issues arising from the *Learning for Transformation* report.

In the broader context, the idea of establishing the CCD in Cambodia has another particular and pertinent resonance. In almost no other country has the centrality of culture been so comprehensively attacked and damaged. Few other countries have the level of development input that Cambodia currently receives. This means Cambodia is an almost unique environment because there is not only an imperative to explore new ways of development but also the environment for re-creation exists.

We did some very exciting and substantive projects under the auspices of the CCD. Some were done by mixed VBNK and ensemble teams; some were done by VBNK and local consultants. Of two that stand out, one is the Youth Forum, sponsored by UN agencies as part of the UN60 celebrations in Cambodia. In this project, 60 young people from all over the country came together for three weeks to create their vision for Cambodia in 15 years' time. The young people learned about Cambodia's Millennium Development Goals through inputs from sector experts. Under the guidance of artistic facilitators who introduced them to creative techniques from art, theater, film, music, and dance, they then produced responses in multiple media to articulate their hopes and dreams for the future of their country. The second big project was for an INGO that wanted to do something more than a conventional strategic planning exercise. The organization's leadership felt that it needed to change its culture from a donor orientation to one that held beneficiaries central. The organization realized that this could be achieved only if it was first able to identify and articulate its existing heart and values. It commissioned the CCD to design and deliver a New Visions workshop, for which David led the design process. Over a period of several months, we ran the three-day workshop 12 times, and all of the more than 600 members of the organization's staff attended. A smaller initiative, but nevertheless one that the participants found valuable, was a retreat I ran in 2006 called Time Out: A Creative Space for Expatriate Development Practitioners. This was based on something I had participated in at a CDRA event and adapted to the local context. Three artistic facilitators worked with me to take the participants through a process that prompted them to reflect on, and find creative responses to, the challenges of their practice.

We always intended that the CCD should do more than just deliver projects. As part of the goal of developing a network of practitioners, I started a discussion forum for people working with creative practice. Initially, the forum was welcomed and well attended by an interesting mix of Cambodians and expatriates. Unfortunately, it did not last very long: it ran into two difficulties that I was unable to overcome. First was the perennial problem of busyness and whether or not people could justify time spent on creativity in the face of other work pressures. Many did not consider creativity a priority, and so attendance slipped. The second problem was that one expatriate in the group was seen by others as having abused their goodwill. Those who had shared resources and ideas with her felt she had been unethical when subsequently presenting everything as her own work, without any thanks to or accreditation of her sources. No one was willing to confront her openly about this behavior, but some key people refused to stay in the group if she stayed. Faced with the choice of confronting her with others' complaints or letting the matter go, I decided I was too busy to get into the middle of what could be an unpleasant conflict. I chose to let it go, and so the group did not survive.

There were other ideas that we had hoped to pursue once we got the CCD established. One was for it to be a place where students who were engaged in relevant academic study could come to do an internship or a project. Another was to offer research and further publications about the practice of creativity in development. Unfortunately, because of a set of interrelated and complex reasons to do with funding, theater commitments in the United Kingdom, and health problems, David was unable to return to Cambodia after his last visit in November 2005. The CCD did continue to engage in projects and activities after then, but without the stimulating input of the more experienced creative side of the partnership, it was hard to maintain momentum. With other organizational priorities to manage, I did not actively pursue work for the CCD, and gradually it ceased to function. When I left VBNK in 2008, the CCD project was brought to a formal close by mutual agreement of all parties.

Connecting Through Conversation

In 2004, I attended the Shambhala Institute for Authentic Leadership workshop in Halifax, Canada. My main reason for attending was to join a module with Margaret Wheatley, someone whose work and thinking I admire greatly. Among other sessions I attended was one led by Otto Scharmer and his colleagues on their newly emerging work on "presence"; Peter Senge led another on the environment. Stimulating and informative as both my main module and all the other sessions were, I have no doubt that the most important experience I had at the workshop was about "the art of conversations that matter."

I participated in an intergenerational dialogue led by Juanita Brown, creator of the World Café[3] model for bringing people together in conversation. I had never heard of the World Café before and so was very fortunate that my first experience of it was facilitated by its creator.

I thought that the World Café might be a useful approach for getting around some of the communication challenges that we constantly encountered in our work, both internally and in participant groups. My first idea was to use the model in a discussion forum for practitioners. I decided to call it the Development Café and, in the first instance, to run it once a month for three months. The invitation was distributed to a selected list of people under the auspices of the CCD. It was optional for VBNK staff to attend, and I facilitated an internal café discussion with them first so they would have some familiarity with the idea when external participants were present. I had some anxieties about how it would go, because in many situations expatriates dominate conversations, and Cambodians are confined in a passive listening role. The question for the first discussion was "What could make the most difference to alleviating poverty and injustice in Cambodia?" I observed something that I had never seen before: whenever a Cambodian started to speak, the expatriates leaned in to listen. Sitting at the café tables brought about a dramatic change to the usual intercultural dynamics, and my concerns about expatriates dominating the conversation were dispelled. There was real dialogue in progress, with everyone at the tables showing interest and respect. We ran the Development Café on a monthly basis for two years until the numbers dwindled and it was no longer viable. The questions for discussion were wide-ranging, for example, "Who are the hero and heroine role models for Cambodians who want to change the status quo?" "How well do Cambodia's television, radio, and newspapers serve the population with high-quality information?" and "NGOs and corruption: are we fighting it or contributing to it?" People attended from many different organizations, even some from universities and the private sector when the subject was relevant to their work. I have no way of knowing how many people took the World Café process into their own work, but I do know that even now it is one of the VBNK initiatives that people often comment about.

VBNK's application of the café model did not stop at the Development Café. As the model had worked well for internal learning events, some of the program team felt that it would be useful in their work. One example was in a Commune Council Partnership Strengthening initiative, which was a series of workshops to bring together NGOs, commune councilors, and private sector representatives to explore how they could collaborate on local development initiatives. The team designed part of the program as a Decentralization Café, with great success. Also, when VBNK hosted an international Organizational Learning workshop sponsored by the International NGO Training and Research Centre (INTRAC) Praxis Programme, we designed it in the café format and called it the Learning Café.

Through the same period, we also introduced another method for helping people talk about their experiences as a way of communicating with each other. In its work, CDRA often draws on rich African traditions of story for transgenerational communication of cultural identity and values. This also resonates with Cambodian traditions. I had participated in a very productive storytelling exercise in a CDRA workshop and thought this would be useful for VBNK. First experiences with the method showed that it needed some adaptation to local context. The first problem was that we couldn't get people past thinking that story meant legend or fairy tales, which meant they either got blocked or shared something irrelevant. We solved that by using the term "case stories," which ensured more accurate translation into Khmer. We also found that instructions needed to be very finely tuned so that the purpose and guidance on the process were really clear.

Once participants are clear about the purpose and process, this is an excellent tool that enables small groups to identify learning from their experiences. Many of VBNK's activities now use case story exercises, which are very effective because they resonate with local traditions of using stories to convey messages and meaning. I used the method in an international workshop and found it fascinating that in the evaluation some participants commented that they had gained most from the session when "we just talked to each other." They were surprised when I reminded them that their discussions had in fact been a very carefully constructed experiential learning exercise.

The encouraging outcomes of all our experiences with the café model and case stories prompted us to use them as the basis for the annual conference in 2006. Previously, our conferences had followed a traditional pattern of keynote speaker, followed by workshop discussions, feedback, and synthesis. We decided to try something completely different and designed a process that combined the café model, appreciative inquiry, and case stories. We chose three themes—Participatory Approaches, Gender, and Poverty Alleviation— and brought together representatives of government, NGOs, and communities with specific interests in these topics. Once they understood that this was a different type of conference, the participants engaged the approach very enthusiastically; unlike many other similar events, there was full attendance to the end, including of all the government representatives. Later in the year, some of the participants were interviewed for the annual impact assessment. One, a CNGO director, said,

> I was very interested in the café discussion method. I applied this method in meetings with villagers and local authorities in my work area. I used mats as the table for group discussions, separated villager groups from local authority groups, and let them raise and discuss the issues and concerns they had encountered and share with each other the possible ideas to overcome their issues and concerns. I found that the villagers dared speak/expressed and contributed a lot to the meeting, when compared to my previous meetings on the same theme.

The director's flexibility in using mats for a situation where no tables were available and the successful outcome is a testament to the strength of this method. The feedback on the conference was consistently positive, with many participants commenting that they had gained more from the process than they had from discussion of the subjects. We decided that this would be our default methodology for all future conferences and events.

As 2007 was VBNK's 10th anniversary year, we wanted to do something special for the annual conference. I suggested the subject from my original introduction to the World Café in Halifax, and we decided on A Dialogue Between the Generations. Working with 15 NGOs, we brought together 81 participants aged 17 to 71 years old, organized into three age groups. In different combinations over the two-day process, the participants exchanged their ideas and opinions on two key questions: "What is the most important learning from your experience that you want to share with the other generations?" and "What can all generations do together to contribute to Cambodia's development in the future?" It was interesting to watch as the process changed the feelings between the age groups from initial distance and suspicion, and in some cases blame, to a much closer and warmer understanding of each other's perspectives. The outcomes from the three groups were remarkably similar: all had concerns about morality in society, the quality of education, and how to maintain the integrity of Cambodia's culture. Once again, in the evaluation the majority of participants rated the experience of the process highly.

Building on this success, the 2008 conference was a Community Conversation in one of the northwest provinces. We invited community representatives from across all age groups to join together with representatives of local authorities and NGOs working in the area to have a conversation about

Making a Different Society for Today and Tomorrow. Over three days, the participants contributed to café-style discussions, used the ALC to consider social history and current issues, and then produced creative presentations for group feedback to the plenary. The participants identified many issues of concern to them, such as having the desire for peace and harmony in Cambodian society, wanting gender equality and equal access to quality education and health services, and having enough income to support family needs. They concluded with planning what they could do once back in their own communities to engage others in the discussions on these and other important issues. In their evaluation, the participants commented on the " 'joyful' learning atmosphere" that had enabled them to express their ideas freely.

Coaching

Coaching is a well-established feature of management and professional development in the corporate world. There is a wealth of documentation available about different models and practices that have proven effective in contributing to improved performance and professional development. There are accreditation programs for practitioners. Development sector organizations, however, have been slow on the uptake of this approach to HR development, and it is only now being recognized as useful both within organizations for the professional development of staff and for work with key partners and stakeholders. VBNK was the first organization in Cambodia to offer coaching as a service for its customers.

VBNK staff were first introduced to the idea of coaching in a workshop given by a consultant in 2001, in which he gave basic inputs and then facilitated exercises to practice the method. The consultant used a reflective questioning approach to the subject, in that he did not answer questions directly but referred them back to the group for them to discuss and reach their own conclusions. This was not well received by the VBNK staff, who were not ready for such an open reflective process: they wanted clear and straightforward answers. It was not a success, and the idea of coaching went into abeyance.

Some years later, the CHART team members used the word "coaching" to describe the work they did during follow-up visits to participants between modules. At that time, they were not following any particular model, and what they did was probably not sufficiently systematic to really justify being called coaching. But they were trying to provide the type of support that coaching offers. By 2005, needs in three further projects prompted discussions within VBNK about how to integrate coaching into training programs and other types of intervention. The first was the customized LDP described above, the second was the IPP to develop the organizational capacity of CNGOs, and the third was a large project to develop the capacity of CNGOs to work with commune councils on social development initiatives, in which VBNK was a national partner to the implementing agency. During the design of these projects, coaching had appeared to be the ideal method to achieve desired outcomes for some specific needs, so it had been included in all three: to follow up on specific training or facilitated activities; to give key participants such as CNGO directors individual support; and/or to introduce coaching as a method that participants could consider using in their own work. The ideas were good; the way to implement them was somewhat more challenging, as the Cambodian program staff had no experience of coaching. Although the projects had significant differences and application might vary considerably across different contexts, we felt it was important to have a consistent understanding and practice of coaching. This situation prompted a big discussion in VBNK about what we meant by terms such as "facilitation," "coaching," and "mentoring."

Fortunately, there were two people able to help us move forward, both with clarifying how we defined the different practices and with introducing methodologies and helping staff to acquire the relevant skills. A part-time TA with the CHART team facilitated a lot of the important early discussions. He then designed and supported a peer coaching initiative for selected program staff. It proved extremely difficult for this initiative to gain traction because of the busy schedules that all program team members had. When they did manage to meet, though, they found the process helpful in a number of ways, and this gave them the confidence to introduce coaching activities into project implementation. Rob Hale was also an experienced coach, with a very high-level practice in the corporate sector in the United Kingdom and Europe. Rob did two training workshops for program team members, which contributed a great deal both to the understanding of coaching within VBNK and to the development of individuals' skills. Rob also coached me personally during my last three years at VBNK, and I found his support and guidance invaluable as I identified and dealt with a range of issues related to my upcoming departure from the organization.

A Mixed Palate
The IPP was a good example of how VBNK has developed its practice to work with mixed methodologies, just as an artist has a palette of colors to use as needed. Sometimes methods stand alone; most often they are blended to create a nuanced response to a need. The goal of the IPP was to develop the organizational capacity of a group of CNGOs using a holistic organizational

learning approach. At the start, a process of facilitated participatory assessments concluded with the negotiation of contracts for project participation that focused on learning agreements and learning objectives. During the implementation phase, each organization had a tailored program of facilitated learning activities based on the ALC, facilitated change processes, short training inputs, and regular follow-up coaching visits to support the implementation of learning in the work. These were supplemented twice a year by plenary sessions in which all partners came together to discuss work on issues of mutual concern. The three-pronged approach of facilitation, training, and coaching was, at that time, an innovation in organizational development practice in the NGO community in Cambodia. It proved to be effective, creating long-term impact in those organizations that were ready and able to work with a different approach. But much depended on the attitude and capacity of the CNGO directors, and not all were willing or able to engage. Building on the success of the IPP, VBNK has integrated coaching into other projects and initiatives as a follow-up method, to ground training and learning activities in workplace practices.

Similarly, the 2008 Community Conversation described above was another demonstration of several of VBNK's innovative practices in one event. It built on previous experiences that had each used some of the tools and techniques and merged them into an interesting, stimulating, and empowering process. In his closing speech, the vice governor of the province, who had taken a great interest in what we were doing, made a very telling comment. He said, "Many NGOs bring money to Cambodia, but VBNK brings something more important, they bring new ideas." I was very proud of that observation about my last VBNK conference. The facilitation of Community Conversations is now one of the major new strands in VBNK's program, and impact assessment studies are showing a positive ripple effect as participants take the experiences and methods into their own life and work domains.

Magic or Monster?

While I believe that learning and change are serious and important factors in development processes, I do not believe that a serious approach is necessarily the right way to go about achieving them. Fun, laughter, and creativity can be great facilitators, especially when working on particularly difficult issues. I tried to ensure that VBNK had the means to conduct both internal and external activities in enjoyable and creative ways. Creativity gradually became an important part of VBNK's culture. As the years progressed, program staff came to understand how much creative methodologies could help them support others in their learning processes, and increasingly they designed stimulating and interesting facilitation processes. They used the different exercises and tools that they had experienced themselves, backed up by interesting and attractive visual aids. I watched with great interest how staff took some methods and adapted them for application in the Cambodian context without losing their essential value and purpose. For example, when they use the World Café model, the process is facilitated more closely than it might be elsewhere, and it always leads to a formal output. By doing this, the VBNK facilitators are creatively bridging the gap between the model in its purest form and Cambodian expectations that a good process always results in something concrete at the end. Such adaptations enable the facilitators to preempt much of the potential resistance to doing things differently and are able, step by tiny step, to move people into new dimensions of response.

Despite all the successes, there were times when I wondered if there was, perhaps, a monster in the room. Working effectively with creativity requires holding a balance between providing space and freedom for it to flourish and ensuring that it is purposeful. The purpose can be either professional or personal, so long as there is something to give the practice meaning. There were times, for example, during a learning week exercise, when I could see that groups had become so wrapped up in creating an amusing or exciting presentation that they lost sight of the content of their discussion. It was all show and no substance. While enjoyable, their outputs were not connected to the intended purpose, namely, the articulation of learning.

Another recurring problem is best described as a lack of connection to what already exists. I can still recall the discussion and some of the examples in David's workshops about the fact that, in many contexts, creativity "builds on what has gone before." He used really simple but good examples from everyday life, for example, how we might use a scarf to enhance the appearance of an outfit or a spice to improve the flavor of a dish. Although many staff constantly make small and incremental changes in their work, generally they do not credit these changes as being creative. They hold on to the idea that creativity means "radically new and different," sometimes with problematic results.

I recall one staff member who was engaged in reviewing and upgrading a staff management training course. Having decided that the session plan on delegation needed to be changed, he went on the Internet to see what he could find about the subject. He downloaded some material that had been developed for US corporate training purposes, which he then pasted directly into the module without any adaptation of context or terms. As it did not in any way relate to the rest of the course, he had to be told that the material could not be used in its raw state because it was inappropriate. He did not know how to adapt it, so the original session plan was reinstated. For a long time afterward, that trainer said that he did not dare be creative because management had thwarted his previous attempt. He never understood that initiative and creativity are different things and that both need to be accompanied by analysis and adaptation if they are to be meaningful and helpful.

On the other hand, there were times when the results were pure magic. Experiences like the workshops with Seckon, described above, where Cambodians allowed themselves to put their fears aside and dared to express themselves in creative media, made me both humble and hopeful. There is no doubt that initial engagement with new ideas and behaviors sometimes caused the staff discomfort and anxiety, but once they were through the challenges and experienced the benefits, they never wanted to go back. For example, I saw a perceptible shift in several of VBNK's program team members after we attended a facilitators conference in Singapore. They were really surprised to discover that they already knew and used many of the tools and techniques the program offered. On the way back, one of them commented, "We used to think that all these new ideas were crazy, but now we can see that we are working at the cutting-edge of facilitation skills, and it makes us proud." Thereafter, those staff were all both more confident with the approaches they already knew and much more open to new ideas.

David taught us that there is a creative arc, ranging from least creative *certainties* at one end, through *probabilities* and *potentials*, to *possibilities* at the other (Glass 2003, 17). Each stage in the arc is relevant to circumstance, and the first three are constrained by varying degrees of containment, but this does not mean they are lacking in value or meaning. Certainties give people the confidence that enables them to move forward. Probabilities allow us to function within the bounds of expected outcomes. Potential presents more opportunity for different outcomes but recognizes the parameters of constraint, such as a time frame. Unlike the other stages, possibilities do not need to be connected to what has gone before. However, attempting to work in the realms of potential or possibility without the analytical skills to assess viability creates the danger of detachment from foundations of relevance and meaning. Artists do not need to stay grounded in this way—in fact, many are at their most creative when they free themselves from such constraints—but applied creativity does need to be linked to purpose.

I was fortunate recently to attend a presentation made by the chief designer at Pininfarina S.p.A. in Turin, the company that designs and makes the prototypes for many car manufacturers, including Ferrari and Maserati. Even though my relationship with cars can best be described as functional, I was excited by everything in the presentation. The chief designer described the 15-person design team's working practices and the resulting cutting-edge innovations. When I asked him what he felt was the most important aspect of their creative process, his spontaneous answer was just one word: "curiosity." Given that such a prestigious firm is able to recruit the best of the best for every discipline within the team, I found that answer made complete sense. When the highest-level technical skills of multiple disciplines are accompanied by advanced analytical skills, it is not a problem if curiosity about "What if?" results in ideas with no obvious links to what already exists. In such circumstances, experience, expertise, and experimentation will test the viability of a new idea. The highly skilled and professional design team at Pininfarina is mandated to work with possibilities at the leading edge of the creative arc, and they have all the requisite ability so to do.

That presentation prompted me to reflect on where curiosity and possibilities might sit within creativity as applied in the context of VBNK or Cambodia generally. Intellectual curiosity is a product of many factors, including having an open mind, a good education, and freedom from fear. Few Cambodians are brought up to express their curiosity through asking questions, so it is rarely valued as a feature of Cambodian thinking. I concluded that in current realities, for all the reasons described elsewhere in this book, very few Cambodians yet have the skills, analytical ability, and curiosity that would put them at the leading edge of the creative arc. While this is an ideal to aspire to for the future, for now the more prosaic dimensions of creativity are needed. Organizations like VBNK have to be realistic and understand that their creativity is a means to an end and that they are starting from certainties and probabilities, with tentative steps in the direction of potential. If they are not realistic about this, then the practice is like a runaway train going off track, taking all and sundry with it.

My two key learnings about working with creativity in the VBNK context are, first, that it needs to be grounded in purpose and, second, that for some purposes it has to be combined with analytical skills. For people who are only, and then not always, comfortable in the realm of certainties, it is necessary to work in ways that gently move them further along the arc. There are many ways in which it can help them, for example,

- to recognize and connect with all dimensions of self,
- to develop other skills,

- to understand that the new or the unknown can be fun and enjoyable rather than frightening and dangerous,
- to empower individuals and groups to take risks, and,
- most important, to want to learn and change and thereby facilitate the emergence of capacity.

In small ways, VBNK's work with creativity has achieved these positive outcomes with many people. We know that NGOs that have been involved in various VBNK events have used the ideas and methods in their own work—sometimes for internal processes, sometimes for work with communities. There is still much to be done, and success is dependent on having a culture in which purpose and the ability to assess relevance are held in balance with space, opportunity, and permission to take steps of imagination and risk. When that balance exists, then creative practice can, step by tiny step, allow people to let go of their habitual reactions to stimuli and move into new dimensions of response.

VBNK has demonstrated that creative approaches are effective in helping people let go of the habitual responses created by deeply held feelings of powerlessness and fear of change. The activities involved can range from guided conversation, through storytelling, to different art forms such as poetry and painting and theater techniques such as voice, role-play, and working with masks. The use of such approaches enables creating safe spaces and trustful relationships; examining the values, assumptions, and power dynamics that govern lives and work; connecting participants to their innate creativity; promoting personal growth through emotional and spiritual healing; and building self-confidence to transcend the controls in traditional hierarchies. Linking creativity to development practice through collaborative learning experiences that foster self-awareness and self-expression is now a proven approach to helping individuals unlearn old habits and reconstruct the narratives guiding their personal and professional lives. In keeping with the spirit of creativity and learning, the journey of exploration goes on as VBNK continuously seeks new ideas to deepen understanding and improve practice.

Living systems theory posits that for a system that is in trouble to heal, it needs to be connected to more of itself. Cambodia surely qualifies as a system in trouble because of the complex mixture of inhibiting culture and the damaging and unresolved legacy of war and trauma. If, with these small innovations and events, VBNK is able to introduce practices that facilitate and empower people to connect with each other in meaningful ways, then it is indeed contributing something important to the country's healing and development.

Notes

1. The Lost Child Project was a series of performances based on the folk story "Hansel and Gretel," which was linked to work the ensemble was doing with projects for street children.

2. Rob Hale continues to work with VBNK in a different capacity. He has been instrumental in supporting the development of coaching expertise within the program team.

3. Full information is available at www.theworldcafe.org.

5

Organizational Nuts and Bolts

Funding and Fees

VBNK is a social enterprise in that while working for the benefit of others, it both generates income to support the budget and subsidizes many of the services it provides to other organizations. I often used to reflect that I was running an NGO business—a not-for-profit hybrid with a values- and development-based mission, but one that still needed to follow some business principles and practices in order to generate sufficient income to exist. Maintaining an organization with a staff of 40 to 50 people, plus a large city-center training facility, costs a lot of money, even in a developing country, and the nature of VBNK's work increased the budget in two ways. First, the high level of staff development needed to maintain program viability required resources over and above the norm. Second, the constant need for program innovations required time and resources above those needed for routine program delivery. A proportion of the budget has always been supplemented by core funding, because if VBNK were totally dependent on income from fees, it would likely need to cut costs, and there would inevitably be reductions in staff development and new initiatives. This would almost certainly have a negative impact on both the nature and the quality of the program, which in turn would affect sustainability. There is a very complex relationship between services, quality, costs, marketability, and sustainability that needs constant attention and management.

VBNK was fortunate that two very supportive donors engaged with the process of establishing the organization and remained committed for more than a decade. When the proposal for a new training institute had been finalized, the directors of two INGOs that were helping to get VBNK started facilitated introductions to two of their own donors, EED and ICCO.[1] I met the EED program officer Karl Schoenberg first and found that he was aware of the need for significant capacity development support for the Cambodian staff of NGOs and also that there were no Cambodian training facilities available to provide it. When I met the ICCO representative Henk Bakker, he not only agreed with the need but also suggested that a good way to support the start of a training institute would be for ICCO and EED to form a partnership, which was put into place soon afterward.

I believe this partnership to be one of the critical factors in VBNK's success, and two aspects of it are particularly worthy of note. The first is that the funding covered core organizational needs such as salaries, office expenses, vehicle costs, and support staff. The second was that both donors engaged in partnership with a long-term perspective rather than a short-term project focus. While no one ever made promises about long-term commitments, it was always clear that these two donors had a program approach that recognized local realities. They knew that few problems could be solved in a single funding phase and that it would take decades rather than years to have a sustainable impact on Cambodian capacity. Thus, there was continuity of both personnel and policy from one funding phase to the next, which meant that VBNK knew where it stood in relation to its donors. As I discussed in Chapter 2 on CNGOs, many organizations have struggled to survive because donors would support only project costs, sometimes not even the salaries of project staff, as if an organization could somehow implement projects out of thin air. Organizations that do not have core budget support often spend excessive time and energy working out how to survive and are often able to employ staff only on short-term contracts. The lack of continuity in funding and staffing has a serious detrimental impact on organizations' ability to develop and sustain capacity and to make long-term plans. VBNK was fortunate never to suffer that fate.

Of course, being successful is an important factor in maintaining a good relationship with donors, and VBNK was always able to achieve or exceed its targets and to fulfill all contractual obligations, such as submitting reports on time. In particular, EED and ICCO appreciated that phase by phase VBNK was achieving greater financial independence and that their contribution was a decreasing proportion of the budget. From needing 100% support in the first phase, in 2010 VBNK was able to cover 65% of the budget from its income for services. Both donors always showed a keen interest in VBNK's innovations and the work we were doing to become a creative learning organization. They supported the development of the CHART project and other initiatives, and they never queried the validity of time spent on any learning activities. I understand that we were fortunate and these were not typical donors, but I do find it frustrating that so many people appear to assume that donors will not support learning activities, without even asking. Our experience was that our donors welcomed the fact that we took time to learn: they seemed to find it a refreshing change from those who repetitively do the same things without ever taking time to reflect on their relevance and effectiveness. Another factor in maintaining good donor relationships lies in being honest and open about problems. So many organizations fear donors' responses if problems arise, failing to understand that donor representatives are experienced professionals who know that problems are bound to occur from time to time. When VBNK was having problems with a new initiative, I kept the donors up to date with developments and difficulties. They made no criticism and cast no blame, because they were fully informed and felt that we had done our best. It was a very supportive response.

Having tried hard on several occasions, without success, to expand our funding base and get new donors to join the partnership, I came to appreciate even more how fortunate we were to have EED and ICCO support for so long. It was about so much more than money, because both donors had a deep understanding of Cambodian realities and offered encouragement and other forms of support to help us find effective ways to meet the challenges.

Income from fees is generated either through payments for open access training or through contracts with customers for the provision of specific services, as well as from some other small activities, like book sales. When negotiating contracts, VBNK and the donors agreed how much they would fund and how much VBNK needed to generate as income from fees. Once the contracts were signed, VBNK had to achieve the specified income target, because the donors would not pick up any shortfall. So, if the income target for a funding phase was $500,000 but we earned only $400,000, we had either to make cuts or to raise the money elsewhere. Most NGOs have relatively simple financial systems to account for the disbursement of donor funds. VBNK needs a hybrid system that can both account for donor funds and deal with the sometimes very complex accounting for contracts and then merge the two together to give the whole financial picture. This is where it is important to bring business principles to NGO practices, but it isn't always easy. The need constantly to be monitoring actual and expected income against budget targets calls for a very different type of financial management than is the norm in most NGOs. It is particularly difficult to do accurate planning for a three-year funding phase when you have no idea what requests for services might arise during that period. Accurate prediction of income from activities was virtually impossible:

there were many times when I budgeted for a team to earn X amount from one type of activity, only to find that the requests were for something different. Meeting targets called for considerable flexibility on everyone's part.

A few organizations have very generous budgets for staff and organizational development and understand that organizations like VBNK have costs that need to be covered from fees. Others don't have such big budgets but still recognize that VBNK has to maintain itself as a financially viable entity. Both these groups are usually straightforward to deal with. Others know what they need but don't have the money to pay for it, a challenge that can usually be overcome to everyone's satisfaction somehow. At the other end of the scale, there are agencies and individuals who appear to think that organizations like VBNK should provide them with services at very low, or no, cost, and these can be difficult to negotiate with. At the start, recognizing that some services would need to be subsidized, we worked out a scale of rates for different types of activities and different types of customers. Some costings, such as delivery of a standard one-week course, could be done on a flat-rate basis. Others were much more complex. For example, when we were contracted to work on major projects over periods of years, it might involve many different VBNK staff in multiple activities, such as workshop facilitation, training sessions, and coaching and other follow-up activities. Budgeting all the preparation, delivery, and reporting activities for the different team members on such a project is very time-consuming, but it is a necessary process. While this is, of course, similar to what many organizations do to raise project funds, for a service provider like VBNK, the work can be anything from a one-day workshop to a multiyear project. Program managers are constantly negotiating and managing numerous short-, medium-, and long-term contracts with different customers. Overall, we were fortunate that there were only a few occasions when income dropped. We were, therefore, able to meet our targets for every funding phase.

Growth, Change and Competing Agendas

VBNK inevitably had its share of challenges and heartaches alongside the successes and joys. To tell only of the good times would be an incomplete story. During 2002–2004, VBNK grew too fast, and despite many achievements in those years, a complex set of factors combined to create some substantive problems. In this section, I describe something of what I learned from the growth and change resulting from initiatives to establish new units and projects. We didn't lose our funding or fall apart through major conflicts, and we were fortunate that, for the most part, our troubles never became public knowledge, but at times it seemed that the problems would threaten both our stability and our productivity. For me, 2002–2004 will always be "the difficult years."

While formulating the Strategic Plan 2000–2002, we had recognized the need to develop our capacity to offer organizational development consultancies and to research and publish examples of good NGO management practice in the Cambodian context. We felt there was a pressing need for both initiatives, and we deliberated long and hard about when and how to get them started. Despite initial enthusiasm for starting two new units simultaneously, we eventually agreed to start the Organization Development Unit in 2000 and the Research and Publications Unit in 2001. According to our agreed commitment to localization, we would first recruit expatriate advisers to get each unit up and running and then work toward transferring the unit to Cambodian management. While we were establishing these units, the CHART project and the CCD were added, as well as some smaller initiatives within the core program of open access and customized training being done by the Training Unit. It now seems obvious that this was all too much to take on in such a short time frame, but back then, because we had the support of staff and stakeholders, everything seemed interesting, exciting, and possible.

As there was then only one Cambodian able to take on the most senior level of management responsibilities, we were heavily dependent on expatriates for some aspects of the organization's development. That was not a problem per se, and we probably would have been able to work through the challenges if the group of expatriates leading and supporting the different initiatives had been cohesive and fully competent. Unfortunately, alongside some very good people, there were some who proved to be poorly matched to their responsibilities, and, for a variety of reasons, the group as a whole was far from unified.

Describing what happened chronologically would be confusing, so I discuss each component separately below. However, it should be remembered that most of these initiatives were taking place simultaneously, in addition to a full workload of core program activities. Although each element in the story is an entity in its own right, the initiatives are also woven together like a braid. As with a braid, each strand remains a part of the whole, even when not visible at the front. So it was with the components of VBNK during those years, each sometimes coming to prominence, sometimes staying quietly in the background. All the initiatives started within a two-year period, from late 2000 to mid-2002. From then until mid-2004, they all ran together in a very complex pattern, jostling for place and prominence. Thereafter, the structure began to unravel until it was reformulated in a new design, as some elements were merged and others tapered out.

The Organization Development Unit

It took a while to find an expatriate to get the Organization Development Unit started, but eventually we were successful, and we officially launched the unit on September 1, 2000. One trainer transferred from the Training Unit, and we recruited three more facilitators. Recruiting a suitable woman took time, so initially the team of one expatriate and three Cambodians was all male. The trainer had only the limited experience of organization development consultancy that he had gained at VBNK. The newly recruited staff had no experience at all, but on the basis of their previous work, they appeared to have appropriate potential. We knew that substantive staff development inputs would be needed for the team to be able to fulfill the unit's mandate. Nevertheless, because it was recognized that organizational development consulting called for a higher level of skills than training, Organization Development Unit staff were classified as facilitators and put on a higher salary scale than the trainers, a decision that later caused problems.

As we had already been doing a number of organization development consultancies, creating the unit was in many respects a natural and easy step. The team began by taking a slow and steady approach, limiting the number of contracts it accepted in order to be able to work in a way that maximized opportunities to develop the team's skills. Given the newness of this initiative, I remained fairly actively involved, partly because the TA had no previous experience of negotiating contracts with customers. There were also times when it seemed sensible for me to be the expatriate supporting the team on a consultancy. For example, localization was a subject about which I had significant knowledge and experience by then. I was therefore rather more involved in the work of the Organization Development Unit in the early days than I had expected to be. Initially, all seemed to be on track, and the consultancies ran neatly, but separately, alongside the work of the Training Unit. The team was achieving success in both small and large pieces of work, including some excellent conferences on issues of concern to many NGOs. When attention needed to shift to other initiatives, the unit appeared to be ticking along quietly in the background.

Problems began to surface in 2003. Probably fueled by enthusiasm generated by its successes, the team had started taking on more work than it was able to manage. The team members began to get into difficulties, which showed up in missed deadlines and complaints about the quality of their work. In fact, ultimately, the Organization Development Unit was the cause of more complaints from dissatisfied customers than all the rest of VBNK put together. This came to a head late one Friday afternoon, when I took a call from the country representative of an INGO with which VBNK had previously had an excellent long-term relationship. The team had been doing an organizational assessment exercise with a project that was being considered for localization. The report submitted to the customer was simply unacceptable, and all attempts to get the problems corrected had failed, leaving the customer feeling it had no option but to bring the matter to my notice.

It transpired that there were two big problems. First, contract negotiations had not appropriately addressed the customer's unrealistic expectations about what could be achieved in a relatively short period of time. The team had committed to a far more comprehensive assessment than was realistically possible in the time allowed, and it was then under pressure because of other commitments. Second, the questionnaire used in the assessment had far too many questions on too many topics. This might have been manageable if the team had established a systematic process for analysis of the completed questionnaires. However, no such process had been established, and the team members were overwhelmed because they had gathered a large amount of information and did not know how to analyze it logically and consistently. All was compounded by the fact that the questionnaires were in Khmer but the report was needed in English. The entire team was utterly out of its depth. After various consultations and remedial steps, we were eventually able to work through the data and produce a report that satisfied the customer's requirements, but our relationship with that organization never fully recovered. The organization would have been fully justified in telling others about what had happened, so who knows what damage was done to our reputation.

Meanwhile, a deputy director had taken over supervision of the unit when we restructured management (see below on the Research and Publications Unit). He and a number of external consultants had been involved in various activities to develop the facilitators' capacity, but it was clear that some of them were never going to acquire the level of skills needed to become effective organization development consultants independent of substantial support from outside the unit. At the same time, customer requests increasingly called for a joint response from both the Training Unit and the Organization Development Unit. For example, several organizations wanted us to facilitate their strategy development processes but recognized that their staff and managers first needed training on the basic principles of strategic planning. Trainers were now, therefore, regularly working alongside Organization Development Unit facilitators. The trainers soon saw that the facilitators lacked some essential areas of expertise, sometimes to the point that poor work was damaging VBNK's reputation. The trainers began to protest strongly about the salary differentials.

By early 2004, it was clear that something had to be done about the Organization Development Unit.

The Research and Publications Unit

From the very earliest discussions about creating VBNK, there was an acknowledged need to document and disseminate good management practice examples in the Cambodian context, because many Western management theories are highly countercultural in Cambodia. For example, notions of teams and participatory decision making do not sit comfortably with traditional hierarchies and with senior position holders' expectations of their staff fearing and obeying them, always accompanied by ostentatious shows of respect. So any examples of how people have addressed and overcome such challenges are to be welcomed. Despite our good intentions, ultimately the Research and Publications Unit became, without question, VBNK's biggest failure during my tenure as director, and it caused many people a lot of heartache. I still do not really understand why we were unable to make it work.

Although we decided in the strategic planning process to start the unit in 2001, we were able to take a preparatory step in 1999. This took the form of a small pilot project in response to a recommendation from the 1999 evaluation

> that VBNK undertake a pilot survey using a small sample of course graduates, to explore if and how the management practices VBNK promotes in its training are being used in the field. This initial research is to gain a deeper insight into "what works" in management for Cambodia and should indicate whether a more extensive survey would prove fruitful.

We hired an expatriate researcher, and one of the trainers volunteered to work as her counterpart. Their terms of reference stated that the primary outputs from their inquiries were to be

- identification, documentation, and publication of one example of good participatory Cambodian management (as advocated by VBNK) being practiced by a development agency working in project implementation and
- recommendations about the viability of further research of a similar nature and about the structure, resources, and working practices needed to establish a long-term Research and Publications Unit.

This team of two did an excellent job, producing two very helpful documents by the end of the six-month project. The first was a small but interesting bilingual publication, *Studies in Organisational Structure* (Maclean and Srey 2000), which presented cases studies of three CNGOs that were functioning well within structures other than the traditional hierarchical model with a single director at the top. VBNK had not previously advocated these structures, but we felt that the examples they set were important to share with the community. The second report was a very comprehensive summary of their findings about a range of management issues within Cambodian NGOs, together with recommendations about the viability of future research projects and publications. This was all very constructive, informative, and encouraging—exactly what we had hoped for.

Having such good work from a team of two in a pilot study over six months encouraged us to go ahead with plans to establish a Research and Publications Unit. As with other units, we needed an expatriate TA to get things started, and we had planned to apply for a volunteer for this position. We were approved by a volunteer sending agency, but for various reasons it couldn't offer us anyone who could arrive before July 2002, a year after our target start date. Because of the delays, I agreed to this start date, even though I was due to be away on a long-planned extended absence from the office from July to September 2002. There were a number of straightforward and obvious tasks, like recruiting new staff, that needed to be done, and I reasoned that other colleagues and our strong systems would give the necessary support. I also thought that the timing would be right for me to work on my return with the newly recruited team members to develop their understanding of VBNK, the role we envisioned for the unit, and their first work plans. Subsequently, it proved that I had miscalculated: the timing allowed the team to become established and set on its own path without any guidance from me or anyone else in VBNK.

The Cambodian trainer who had worked on the pilot study transferred to become the first member of the unit, and the volunteer TA arrived just before I went away. By the time I got back, additional staff had been recruited, and the team had already made plans. The team had also begun a series of interviews with NGO managers to identify issues that would be suitable subjects for studies and publications. This inquiry progressed well, and a credible report was finalized, although it was behind schedule. Thus, it seemed initially that everything was going reasonably well.

However, some of the problems that ultimately led to the closure of the unit had already taken root. When I returned to the office, the original VBNK staff member asked to be transferred back to the Training Unit. Another trainer transferred in, but within a few weeks he too was asking for a return to his old position. These proved to be the first of multiple staff changes in the Research and Publications Unit. One lesson was clearly that good trainers and good researchers need significantly different skills and personal characteristics. However, the problem went deeper than that: some of the externally recruited people also left within months, because the TA, who had conducted the recruitment himself, subsequently concluded that they didn't have the right skills or potential for the work. A factor that started to raise questions within VBNK was the fact that all the staff who stayed were young women, whereas all the men left. The TA insisted that this was purely a coincidence, but concerns about this issue were never fully resolved to everyone's satisfaction.

I was not alone in feeling that in terms of its content and the level and quality of analysis, the pilot study publication had been pitched and presented very appropriately to the target audience. The TA, however, was critical of both the publication and the other findings from the pilot study and insisted that the unit's research must conform to the highest international standards of academic rigor. Personally, I did not feel that studies of that nature would be appropriate or helpful for our target audience. I was at the time cochair of the board of Cambodia's leading independent policy research institute, and I knew what challenges even a dedicated research facility had in meeting high-level academic standards. I was in no doubt that achieving those standards was beyond VBNK's reach. Importantly, despite insisting that this was the standard to which we should aspire, the TA, who had been recruited on the basis of other skills and experience, did not have the ability to work at that level. This disagreement about standards and the nature of the unit's work remained an unresolved conflict between the TA and me.

More worrying was the team members' failure to show any real curiosity about VBNK's other units in order to align their work to the organization's mission and program. The TA regularly complained that VBNK had not welcomed the new team and was not interested in research. This was not true, but no one in the team ever seemed to realize that, as newcomers, there was also an onus on them to understand and relate to what already existed. For example, despite repeated invitations and suggestions that attending a VBNK training delivery would be helpful, rarely did anyone from the unit ever sit in to learn about the core program.

The team embarked on its first major research exercise, which was very soon behind schedule, partly because of the high staff turnover. Conflict was beginning to emerge because other staff viewed the researchers, by now all female, as detached, overpaid, and unproductive. Another growing cause for concern was that the TA appeared unwilling or unable to comply fully with VBNK's systems, standards, plans, or timetables. By the middle of 2003, the problems were such that I felt I had no alternative but to put my concerns in writing and ask the TA for a commitment and a plan to address them. The response was astonishing for a number of reasons, most notably because he did not accept any responsibility for any of the problems, preferring to lay all the blame on VBNK and me. Some of his accusations might have been laughable had they not been part of such a worrying situation. For example, the TA posited that the unit was being kept in isolation by means of tactics such as not adding his name to the circulation list for all the journals that VBNK subscribed to and shared among the expatriates. In Cambodia, the post was then so unreliable that it would have been a waste of money to subscribe to any journals: there never was any such list because there was nothing to circulate. Shortly afterward, the board, concerned about the lack of outputs after more than a year, asked that the TA produce a detailed plan for what the unit could achieve in the next three months, including finalizing the first publication. He refused to do so, saying, "Micromanaging me won't solve the problems." I was at a loss about how to proceed.

This impasse coincided with a reorganization of the management structure, in which it was decided that I should step back from direct line management of existing units. The newly appointed Cambodian deputy director was allocated line management responsibility for the Research and Publications Unit. Given the problems I had had with the TA despite my age and years of experience as a manager, I was concerned about this. However, it was agreed by all that my relationship with the TA was probably beyond repair, and so making a fresh start with someone new might be the right way ahead. At first things seemed to be better, but it was not long before the deputy director found himself on the receiving end of the same problems and accusations that I had experienced, and he concluded that he was unable to continue trying to manage the TA. At the December 2003 board meeting, I was unable to report either any finished publications or any progress in resolving the problems. Everyone was in agreement that enough was enough and the TA had to go. Such decisions are never easy to implement, but with the support of the board, I contacted the volunteer sending agency and the TA's contract was brought to early termination.

After 18 months, the Research and Publications Unit had produced an initial report on possible subjects for study and publications, a draft report and a tool kit on boards and governance, and raw data on a further study. It had very poor relationships with the rest of VBNK. On the plus side, it had made a substantive and valuable contribution to the VBNK conference on boards and governance and had been sponsored to present its findings at a regional research conference. The big question was, "Where do we go from here?" We hired an experienced researcher with a lot of Cambodia experience to hold things together while we worked out the best way forward. Her appraisal of the draft report on boards and governance was that it would be unethical to publish it, as the content was not supported by the research findings, a revelation that was particularly troubling given the presentation at the regional conference. Neither was the tool kit publishable, being a rough compilation of resources from multiple sources, none of which had been either properly acknowledged or adapted to Cambodian context. Both the report and tool kit needed to be rewritten. Under the guidance of the experienced researcher, the team set about systematic analysis of data from the second study and eventually produced a credible report, *Management Capacity Building in NGOs: How Advisors in Cambodia Build the Management Capacity of Their Local Counterparts* (Heng et al. 2004), which was published in both English and Khmer.

Meanwhile, VBNK struggled with what to do about the unit as a whole. After consideration of many different options, the management team decided to split the unit's administrative and technical functions between a Cambodian unit manager and an expatriate TA. The recruitment process resulted in an internal appointment to the unit manager position. The expatriate researcher took on the TA position to guide technical matters and to build the research, analytical, and writing capacity of the team. We thought that with these appointments, we would finally be able to make a fresh start and get the unit fully functioning and integrated into VBNK. Sadly, the idea proved a lot better in theory than in practice. It was quickly apparent that, for different reasons, neither the unit manager nor the TA was going to be able to pull the unit through. Matters continued to go from bad to worse. Many factors were at work, some of which were grounded in VBNK's inexperience in research; others resulted from the capacities (or lack of) and personalities of some of the individuals involved. Some people simply didn't know how to do their job, and two of those who did got caught up in a debilitating personality clash. After a few months, the situation was such that there was no alternative but to suspend the unit's operations. The mess that surfaced after that decision meant that no alternative was left but to turn the suspension into closure.

Over time, I came to understand some of the factors that created or contributed to the problems. Some issues stemmed from the fact that the first TA was not fully qualified for the role, and his attitude and approach created schisms and conflicts in the organization. But it would be too easy simply to blame one person, and if any learning is to come from such experiences, they need to be understood systemically. I think one area of difficulty lay in the name we gave to the unit. The word "research" is, for many, value laden, carrying with it expectations of very particular working practices and standards. It was the wrong word for what VBNK wanted to achieve, and we had neither the wish nor the ability to live up to all the demands and expectations of high-level academic research. A different name, perhaps the Good Practice Publications Unit, might have contributed to an entirely different outcome. Another factor was that there was a very limited pool of experienced researchers on which we could draw to staff the unit, and VBNK was not in a position to pay the sort of salaries that would have attracted any of them. As it was, we paid the Research and Publications Unit team very well compared with other program staff, and as with the Organization Development Unit facilitators, this created resentment among the trainers. Furthermore, as with other work, doing studies while simultaneously building the capacity of staff with limited experience created significant challenges. The final factor was that no one in VBNK had any experience of managing research. I firmly believe that it is not necessary to be an expert in every technical field for which one has management responsibility: life in large organizations would be impossible if it were. However, when things go wrong, management's lack of technical experience can be a telling factor. I have no doubt that had we been experienced research managers, all of us might have made our decisions differently. But we weren't, and so we have to face the fact that because of our inexperience, we maybe made mistakes that we couldn't recognize.

The Research and Publications Unit was part of VBNK for two years and three months, during which time it achieved minimal outputs and caused numerous problems for and with others in the organization. I think it is safe to say it was a relief to most people in VBNK when the unit closed, although of course it was a difficult time for the researchers who had worked hard despite all the problems and had certainly done nothing deliberate to contribute to them.

The CHART Project

The next thread in the story line is the CHART project, the genesis of which was described in Chapter 4. What I discuss here is the impact that starting CHART had on VBNK internally. As a time-bounded action-research project, CHART was conceived differently, with no original intention of making it a unit in the VBNK structure. The nature of the project also meant that we expected it to have an expatriate manager throughout rather than follow the usual pattern of working toward Cambodian management. The exploration of options took place through 2002 and resulted in CHART being incorporated into the Strategic Plan 2003–2005 as a four-year action-research project. Thus, CHART was in start-up just ahead of the Research and Publications Unit, which meant two big initiatives were underway at the same time. Compared with other VBNK units and activities, CHART was very expensive—at first we thought it would need to be funded separately. In the event, EED and ICCO both liked the project and agreed that it should be included in the core budget. Nevertheless, some factors and events in the planning and start-up phases of CHART led to many within VBNK, including the CHART project manager, considering it as somehow separate from the rest of the organization, its procedures, and its budgetary considerations.

The first big issue was that the manager and I had significantly different views about the fundamental conception of the project, and it took time for us to reach agreement about a workable approach and framework. I saw it as an opportunity to train development practitioners to work in ways that would be more empowering to their target groups, whoever they might be. The project manager came from a community development background and felt the project could be a vehicle for creating an entirely new approach to community development. His initial dreams and plans, while interesting, were way outside VBNK's mission and mandate, because they would have involved us in direct implementation rather than working with the staff of implementing organizations. Later, there were challenges to resolve about how we approached partnerships with the participating organizations, to which we were offering a substantive staff development initiative for free. This was a large and expensive project for us, but there was a limit to what we could insist on in terms of how the partnering organizations facilitated and supported their staff's participation. It needed long negotiations to resolve some issues, but eventually the project was able to start with 20 participants from three partner organizations.

The challenges and complexity of establishing the project led to a range of problems in terms of CHART's relationships with, and integration into, VBNK. The CHART team became progressively more disengaged from the rest of VBNK as it became increasingly immersed in its own process and the demands of delivering a 19-week curriculum over 18 months. CHART had innovative goals and highly countercultural methods and in this respect was so substantially different from everything else VBNK was doing that it generated anxiety and fear among the other staff, who viewed it with suspicion, sometimes to the point of hostility. It didn't help that the CHART project manager was, on occasion, openly critical of the approach and methods being used in the Training Unit. Staff did not understand what CHART was trying to achieve, and they neither wanted nor made opportunities to learn about it. There was also resentment that CHART was fully funded and therefore was unique in the VBNK program in having no income targets to meet. Another factor was that in addition to the expatriate project manager, CHART also had substantive expatriate consultant input at different times. Finally, there were tensions about the use of resources, including the designated CHART workshop room. In summary, while the CHART innovations were achieving some important successes and attracting a great deal of external interest, internally it was like an isolated bubble of difference, surrounded by all manner of negative responses.

The extent of the schism was highlighted at the end of 2004 in the Strategic Review, which referred to CHART and its approach as a "satellite" to VBNK's core program. I found this disconcerting, because I believed then, and still do, in what CHART was trying to achieve. I felt that we were offering a contribution to help the Cambodian development sector adopt a more effective practice for facilitating sustainable change. In this respect, I felt we should eventually integrate the principles and practices of CHART into all aspects of VBNK's training and consulting activities. This idea consistently met resistance until we were doing the strategic planning for 2006–2009, when there was a general recognition among senior managers that the time had come to stop thinking of CHART as a separate project and to find ways to integrate its practices and philosophy into core program activities. We knew that the transition would not be easy, because some program staff still had negative feelings about CHART, but we also knew that others had the potential to embrace different ways of working. The first step was to make a structural change and locate CHART in the Program Unit under the direct line management of one of the Cambodian program managers. He worked patiently and consistently over the next two years to integrate the team and its work into the main program, and under his supervision, the necessary changes came into place. CHART, as such, no longer exists. The team is now coworking with others, in both open access and customized programs, and achieving exciting and successful cross-fertilization of skills and approaches for leadership development for women and different levels of staff and managers.

Despite a number of remedial steps, it was never possible to fully resolve the problem of separation and the negative feelings that emerged until the project was merged into the Program Unit. It may be stating the obvious to say that innovation, by its very nature, creates tensions, because of the challenges it poses to the status quo. This was not new knowledge for me, but the CHART experience in many ways crystallized the challenges that arose from all the attempts to innovate within VBNK.

The Center for Creative Development
The final thread in the weave of innovations came through our work with David Glass. The relationship had continued to develop, most notably through the important contributions David and his ensemble colleagues had made to VBNK's staff development. They had supported new initiatives by means such as contributions to the development and implementation of the CHART curriculum. David and his closest associate, Matthew Jones, had long been incubating the idea of creating a regional center, both to be a base for their activities and to become a center of learning and resources for those wanting to work with creative practices. I had heard about these ideas from the beginning and was delighted when David and Matthew said they would like to partner with VBNK on this project. We reached initial agreement about the outline of the CCD in early 2000, but there was much to be done before we could establish the center. It was a slow process, because everything was done at long distance, supplemented by meetings when work brought David or Matthew to Cambodia or when I went home to the United Kingdom on holiday. In addition, both David and I needed to get approval from our boards. Eventually, agreement was reached, and the two boards signed a partnership agreement that specified that the center was a joint project between the two organizations, with David and me as codirectors.

Everyone in VBNK valued the work David did with us, and it is no exaggeration to say he was greatly loved. Many therefore welcomed the CCD as a natural extension of the relationship. In the overall scheme of what was happening at the time, starting the CCD was not problematic, except for the additional workload it created in an already busy and demanding time. The only hiccup was that some people were anxious about where the CCD fit into the VBNK structure and hierarchy. I felt it was appropriate to show it on the VBNK organogram as a box outside the main structure, joined by a dotted line (see Figure 5.1). This did not fully assure those who wanted things to be more tightly controlled, but it was never a big problem.

Managing Growth and Change
Change needs careful management, even when it is welcomed and when everyone engages constructively with the challenges and tensions it creates. There proved to be powerful resistance at work within VBNK, as in many other organizations in Cambodia, because of the factors embedded in Cambodian

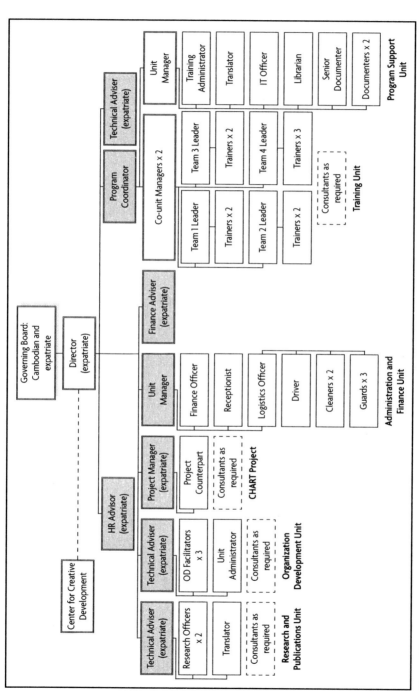

Figure 5.1 Organogram 2003.

culture and experience that I described in previous chapters. Multiple inter-connected factors contributed to making our growth and changes problematic, the most relevant being that we were trying to do too many new things at once and there wasn't enough organizational energy or capacity to work with them all properly. It needed a much more concerted management strategy than any of us realized at the time. I was stretched by trying to support all the new initiatives on top of managing the rest of the organization, external relations, and so on. With the clarity of hindsight, it is now obvious that the strategic planning process for the period 2003–2005 should have incorporated a review of the management structure. But it wasn't obvious then, and so by the middle of 2003, I was directly line managing the Cambodian program coordinator, who managed the Training Unit and Program Support Unit, and his TA; the Cambodian administration and finance manager and his finance adviser; the Organization Development Unit and Research and Publications Unit TAs; the CHART project manager; and the newly appointed HR adviser. In total, this was two Cambodians and six expatriates—as shown in the shaded boxes in the organogram in Figure 5.1. The appointment in a restructuring exercise of two deputy directors solved this problem but had some unintended conse-quences and created new challenges that also needed to be managed.

There were some powerful personalities in the expatriate group, and most had strong views on the importance of what they were doing. This led to com-petition and conflict about organizational priorities and about how the differ-ent initiatives could or should cooperate together. The Cambodian managers were, sensibly and as much as they were able, keeping their heads down and getting on with the work, but eventually even one of them became embroiled in a personality clash with an expatriate that was painful to both of them, re-sulting in accusations of racism and sexism that needed to be addressed. Deal-ing with these problems took a lot of management time, which meant that the core teams, doing the bulk of delivery and consultancies, were not getting the support they needed.

New problems were emerging throughout the organization. With all the new initiatives, people no longer understood what VBNK was about or their role in the scheme of things. Everyone was too busy, too stretched, and increas-ingly confused. Teams responded by retreating into their own concerns and defending their turf, exacerbated by the competition among some of the expa-triates. Quality and coordination suffered badly. Before anyone realized it, the damage was done, and communication and coherence were fragmented to the point where it would clearly take a great deal of work to put things right. This was the last thing that we needed to happen at a time when we were aspiring to be leaders in the sector, inspiring others to do things differently through our example of creative new ways of working.

It was clear that we needed new thinking, new approaches, and a carefully managed process if we were to have a stable future with organizational coherence and harmony. Work began to merge the Training and Organization Development Units, and when that was accomplished in mid-2004, one TA left. The merger was not an easy process because of the vexed issue of salaries. The Cambodian deputy director did an excellent job of leading a working group to revise the salary scale. The result was the creation of a comprehensive structure of staff positions for different work streams, each of which has very detailed analysis of the competencies and criteria for every position and grade in the scale. Staff and managers then did joint assessments for grading against the positions and competencies. This process was difficult for the managers because some staff assessed themselves as more competent than they actually were and were dissatisfied with how they were graded. The closure of the Research and Publications Unit in late 2004 resulted in the Cambodian team members being made redundant and the departure of another expatriate. The HR adviser's position was always planned as a short-term (two-year) contract, so when she left in early 2005, the number of expatriates had been halved.

Gradually, we started to pull through to a new era and began the process of getting things on track—not back on the old track, because VBNK was now a substantially larger and different organization: what we had done before would no longer suffice. The stress began to ease, and we were able once more to look forward rather than constantly be concerned with the tensions of the day. It took a long time to overcome all the problems created during those difficult years, and the years that followed also, of course, had their bad as well as good days.

The 2004 Strategic Review helped us get a balanced view about the impact and implications of the different initiatives. That and the subsequent strategic planning process in 2005 gave us the space and framework to reflect on what had happened and not only to think about how to avoid such problems in future but also to consolidate what had been learned and achieved through the years of difficulty. Briefly, some of the more important learning gained from those years is as follows:

- Too many new initiatives at once create confusion and a loss of identity. We subsequently needed to take time during strategic planning to define a new identity, which helped to restore unity and a sense of shared purpose in the organization.

- In the Cambodian context, it is absolutely essential to ensure that any major new development is fully grounded in both organizational culture and systems before starting another. Trying to do too many new things at once weakens organizational cohesion and purpose. We should have worked on the innovations consecutively, not concurrently.
- Maintaining quality requires constant attention and focus, which gets lost during rapid growth.
- Good communication and coordination between the different components of the organization cannot be assumed or left to chance. We had to put in place appropriate mechanisms to make them happen.
- It is essential to take substantive time to orient and align new initiatives to existing programs. This involves ensuring both that current staff understand what is planned and are kept updated on developments and that newcomers really understand the organization and program they are joining and how their new initiative should link to and build on what already exists.
- Expatriates can and do make important contributions, but they also have the power to cause harm. Small organizations need to limit the number of expatriates in post at any given time and be very sure that those appointed meet selection criteria.

We had learned the hard way that having multiple units with different mandates was not the best way for VBNK to achieve its goal. Putting that learning to practical use, we decided that the main thrust of the Strategic Plan 2006–2009 should be consolidation. We planned to build on what we had in ways that pulled the program together by sharing learning and expertise across all the teams in order to create a unified VBNK approach to facilitating social change. We assumed that senior Cambodians managers were now willing and able to lead the change processes. Happily, that is one assumption that has been proved correct.

Teamwork

As the founding and long-term director of VBNK, clearly I was influential in shaping how the organization functioned and developed over the years, not least because, while others came and went, my long-term tenure was unique among senior managers and advisers. The continuity of my role within VBNK is reflected in much of what I have written here. But, as described in other sections, I was very fortunate to work with, and be supported by, many people who understood what the organization was trying to achieve and who, according to their roles, made invaluable contributions. It requires teamwork to ensure that an enterprise such as VBNK stays on track, and VBNK's success is the result of teamwork at many levels. I described the support VBNK received from its two donors, EED and ICCO, in the "Funding and Fees" section above. In this section, I give a brief summary of the contribution of three other important groups: the board, my senior Cambodian colleagues, and expatriates.

The Board

The first board meeting was held on April 1, 1997, the day of VBNK's official launch. Getting the organization established called for a lot of board-level decisions, so over the next few months, meetings were held monthly. Once everything was in place, the quarterly meetings required by the bylaws were generally sufficient. There were only two occasions during my 11 years as director when we could not achieve a quorum for a meeting, a track record of which to be proud. The bylaws specify that the VBNK board should have seven members, at least four of whom must be Cambodian. There were vacancies on a few occasions, but most of the time there was full membership. The quality of support that VBNK received from its board is in direct relation to the quality of the members we were fortunate to attract. I learned early on that it is not wise to invite any of the stars of the development community onto your board, because they are generally too busy to do the work needed to make a substantive contribution. One of our first members was in that category, and he wasn't really able to engage in the same depth as others. We subsequently found that people with a less prominent profile tended to be more reliable, both in terms of attending meetings and in terms of being well prepared when they got there. Several members served for the full six years allowed under the bylaws, and that level of continuity was invaluable. Many of the Cambodian members said that they learned from the VBNK board how to make a board work effectively, and learning that was useful to them in their own work.

The most helpful source of information I drew on in writing this book was the archive of quarterly reports to the board and the minutes of the meetings. Once every three months for 11 years, I wrote up all that had happened in VBNK, together with a summary of plans for the next quarter, and sent it to the members 10 days in advance of the meeting. The reports also covered issues that needed board decisions and/or guidance, which were then recorded in meeting minutes. Routine meetings were occasionally supplemented by additional activities, for example, workshops to get board input into strategic planning processes. The board took its responsibility for my annual appraisal seriously, usually conducting a 360-degree process. In this and other ways, I was not only supported but also held to account for my management and leadership of the organization. The documentation shows clearly how well the board engaged with VBNK and guided its development. A critical factor in this was having good people willing to give the extra time and contribution as chairperson, and I was always able to call on those individuals for informal inputs and discussions between meetings.

Perhaps the most telling indication of the board's commitment is the way that it dealt with my departure from the organization. I had made it clear for several years that I would retire in 2008, so they had a lot of notice. The board understood that the departure of the long-term founding director would cause some anxiety within VBNK and also that before starting recruitment it was vital to resolve the knotty issue of whether to nationalize the position. The board started working on the issues a full two years before the deadline for my departure, regularly consulting and informing staff and other key stakeholders as the decision-making process progressed. As I describe below in "Localization," the board conducted a very thorough and professional recruitment process and was successful in attracting a superb successor who is taking VBNK forward with new vision and energy.

As I described in Chapter 2, "Serving a Sector," the issue of boards is problematic for many CNGOs, and I have some sympathy for those who are cautious about establishing one, because some instances of board–organization conflicts have been extremely unpleasant. I have had many conversations with directors of CNGOs who talk of the loneliness, stresses, and strains of being responsible for everything in their organization. I find it sad that the situation in Cambodia makes so many people reluctant to have a board, because they fear negative impact rather than positive potential. It leaves them alone and unsupported with their responsibilities. It also leaves organizations vulnerable if their director's behavior becomes inappropriate or damaging in any way. I felt that it was essential for VBNK to be "walking the talk" of good governance and management. Without a fully functioning board of our own, VBNK's work on boards and governance with other organizations would have lacked integrity. My experience, and that of a few CNGO directors, is that if the board is set up and managed appropriately, it is an invaluable source of support and guidance. While there were of course days when I felt stressed and overworked, I never felt I was carrying the burden alone, because I always knew the board was there to support me. I could not have achieved all that I did at VBNK without the board, nor would I have wanted to try going it alone.

Senior Cambodian Colleagues

The word "senior" is here applied to two different groups, one being the staff who hold positions at the top of the organizational structure and the other being those who have achieved a different type of seniority through length of service.

VBNK exists to support Cambodians to develop the capacity of their country. From the start, therefore, it was both integral to our mission and essential for our integrity to build our own Cambodian management capacity. There was always a management team with both expatriate and Cambodian members. In the early days, when the organization was small and had a clear single focus, the management team role was to deal with everyday operational issues. Within that mandate, the Cambodian team members were able to function relatively well, although no one showed signs of being ready to take on significant leadership or decision-making responsibilities. One of the biggest challenges was that we were a management training institute where few of the early managers understood and applied the fundamentals of the management practices in which we were training others. Some operated in an autocratic manner with their staff, ignoring the principles of participatory approaches. Others avoided being responsible for decisions, especially any that might be unpopular. There was one person who liked to take credit for the development of the staff benefits policy until staff complained about anything. Then he professed not to understand that aspect of the policy and would ask me to take over dealing with the problematic issue. Confidentiality is another issue that is viewed and practiced completely differently in Cambodian culture from the way I understand it. There were some worrying incidents when managers shared information that I believed should have been kept private. In summary, VBNK's first managers still had much to learn before they could be considered fully competent and professional as defined within Western management standards.

Although there is still an element of those challenges at the middle levels of management, two factors were influential in bringing positive change among the senior managers. The first was that, with growth, it was possible to attract some people with good skills and experience to fill higher-level positions. A good process for assessment at the end of the probation period ensured that if we had recruited someone who wasn't suited to the job, they would not be confirmed in post. The second factor was that some staff who joined VBNK early on learned and matured in their roles and were able to move into management positions. There was, of course, staff turnover; it would be an exceptional organization where that didn't happen. At times, it was really upsetting to see good people, in whom we had invested many years of time and resources, move on just when they were ready to assume leadership roles. But that's a feature of organizational life everywhere, and we had to live with it.

For years, it was necessary to follow up on everything with all the managers: it can be extremely wearying not to be able to trust that things will get done, or get done on time, unless monitored closely. Gradually that changed, and one day I realized that I was surrounded by a group of senior Cambodians who could be trusted to do what they said they would do on time and to tell me if anything was amiss. It was a huge and important shift in ownership of responsibility, and it was really gratifying to see those managers taking the initiative on important issues like quality and acting preemptively when potential problems loomed. Some of these developments happened when expatriates left and Cambodians showed themselves ready to step into the space. Others were the result of a natural progression, as individuals were able to learn from their experiences and gradually assume more responsibility.

I will never forget the surge of excitement I felt on the day that a program manager came to me and said, "Every call we've had since the start of the year has mentioned facilitation skills. I think there's a new trend developing out there, and we need to be able to respond." This was the first time ever that a Cambodian had offered any strategic analysis of developments in our external environment. Another manager, within a week of taking over line management responsibility for a long-term poor performer, put him on a special performance review and, when that didn't work, later decided he had to go. Previous managers had preferred to work around the problems rather than confront a difficult decision. Such incidents occurred with increasing frequency and eventually became the norm, proving that with time and the right support, Cambodians can, and do, achieve the highest levels of management performance.

The other senior group is those long-term staff who have served VBNK loyally for more than a decade, including several women with whom I worked closely in the women's empowerment process. Some long-term staff are the team leaders and senior trainers who ensure that VBNK services are properly prepared and effectively delivered. Among them are people who have decided they do not want to be managers, preferring a career progression based on increased technical expertise, so we created a two-pronged promotion ladder to accommodate and encourage them in that path. Others, in administration, finance, and support roles, both as middle managers and in staff positions, keep everything working in the background so the program can function smoothly. I value enormously those who strive to do their best to maintain routine functions week in and week out so that the organization is successful. No organization can flourish without such dedicated staff.

Expatriates

Expatriates are a very powerful group of people in the organizations of the developing world. Mostly they come from developed countries in the North, but expatriates can also be from the region or from developing countries in other parts of the world. For example, a large community of Philippine nationals works in development and many other sectors in Cambodia. There are no figures available, but my observation over the years has been that most expatriate development workers come from North America, Australia, and Europe. English tends to be the *lingua franca*, although because of Cambodia's history as a French colony, there is also a large Francophone community.

The time scales of expatriate engagement vary considerably. Innumerable people come for short-term consultancies, sometimes as little as a week. Others come for the duration of a project contract or maybe a volunteer placement, for anything from a few months to three years. Many decide to pick up new contracts or consultancies that enable them to stay on for a few more years. Among them are some who end up staying long term and engaging with the country in a different way. I am one of this group: I arrived on a two-year volunteer placement, I stayed, and Cambodia has become my home. The same is true for many of my friends and most trusted expatriate colleagues. I don't think any of us came with the intention of staying long term, but the work, life, and other events took over, and one day we all found ourselves in the "old Cambodia hands" category. While I have a bias toward long-term stay as the only way to get to the deep understanding of context and culture that is necessary for some work to be effective, I do also know that if all expatriate development workers stayed in one place for the duration of their working lives, it would not be helpful. Newcomers bring new energy, ideas, and experience, which refresh thinking and action in many positive ways. So the combination of the stayers and the movers can work well.

For me, the two key criteria for assessing the contribution expatriates make are skills and personality. With regard to skills, capacity development is essentially what most expatriates are purportedly here to do, yet this ability is often overlooked as a recruitment criterion. Most often, people are hired solely on the basis of their technical ability, with little consideration given to their track record of capacity development, the assumption being that because they can do something, they automatically know how to develop others' capacity in the same area. Capacity development is a significant discipline in its own right, for which personality, attitudes, beliefs, and behavior are equally, sometimes more, important than technical skills. Those who are respectful of local staff and genuinely like the people they work with tend to have patience and an open mind and know instinctively how to work in ways that are helpful and empowering. At the other extreme are people whose behavior and attitudes are far from helpful: no matter how good they may be technically, ultimately they contribute very little to the development of individuals, organizations, or Cambodia. There are also, unfortunately, people who have neither good enough skills nor the right approach for the work they do. They get away with poor performance by moving on regularly from one organization and country to another.

I have worked with and observed many different expatriates during my 15 years in Cambodia. There are, unfortunately, poor performers in every community, and they can do much harm. VBNK was unfortunate to employ more than one such. As I indicated above in "Growth, Change and Competing Agendas," some of VBNK's most challenging problems arose when we employed expatriates who, it later transpired, could not competently fulfill their mandate. As a result, we had situations where expatriates' work needed closer monitoring than should have been necessary, sometimes others had to do their work for them, and sometimes they created big messes that others had to clean up. Such situations take time and energy that should be spent more productively working with Cambodian colleagues. At the other end of the scale are the competent, ethical, and committed people who contribute a great deal in innumerable ways. There are many people at all points in between. It is because of expatriates' importance that I devote this short section to talking about them. As it would not be appropriate to talk about individuals, I describe some general characteristics and behaviors to illustrate the most important points, and of course most people fall into more than one category.

The Missioners

Cambodia and other developing countries attract people motivated by their religious beliefs. I have heard many variations of "I'm here to teach people to read English so they can learn to read the Bible and follow Jesus" from people whose development activities are a mechanism to proselytize and convert people to their faith. Others see service to the poor and disadvantaged of the world as the way to live their faith. They think it is unethical to proselytize, recognizing instead that we all have a great deal to learn from each other, whatever faith we may follow. I have very little time and respect for the former group and a great deal of both for the latter. However, people working in development because of their religious beliefs are only a part of the group who fall under this heading.

Many people come into development because they want to help those less fortunate than themselves. While this is, of course, a laudable motivation, it can become distorted by the individual's own needs. I once had a new expatriate staff member tell me, "I saw my primary role in my last organization as protecting national staff from the other foreigners." Her behavior soon showed that she thought this was her role in VBNK also. Neither I nor other expatriate colleagues felt the staff needed protecting from us, so some of her actions seemed inappropriate, which inevitably led to tensions. From my perspective, such an attitude is patronizing and results in an unhelpful approach to working with national staff. If an expatriate is behaving inappropriately, it is more appropriate to do something about the expatriate and/or help the Cambodians devise ways to deal with her or him themselves.

There are also people on a mission to convert everyone to their way of doing things, whatever their particular area of expertise. A high level of commitment to proven methods is to be admired but not at the expense of building on what already exists. One of the major problems with having a turnover of expatriate personnel in an organization is that national staff find themselves having to adapt to new ideas and working practices on a regular basis. While some incoming expatriates take the time to understand what is already working and why, others simply jump straight into introducing their own favored methods, which can be confusing and sometimes counterproductive for national staff. Cambodians frequently say something like, "new boss, new system," expecting to have to learn a new way to work with every new arrival. A linked issue relates to those expatriates who refuse to make concessions to local realities of what can or can't be done, apparently because they fear what a reduction in standards might mean for their reputation and career. Fortunately, we never had anyone like that in VBNK, but I've seen them elsewhere, disconnected from, and unrealistic about, the context in which they were working and then getting angry when national colleagues couldn't live up to standards they are not yet equipped to achieve.

The Best Friends

It is really helpful when expatriates make the effort to have good relationships with their national colleagues, both those they work with directly and others in the organization. Good relationships facilitate solutions for all manner of work problems and make organizational life much more enjoyable for all. But good relationships should not be allowed to get in the way of good work practices, which might on occasion call for honesty about difficult issues such as poor performance. VBNK had a number of expatriates, coincidentally all men, who repeatedly avoided dealing with difficult issues because they did not want to spoil their relationships with staff. This created a dilemma for me more than once, when performance issues simply had to be dealt with but, despite repeated discussions, the expatriate failed to act. I then had to make a difficult choice between letting the matter go or stepping in and taking action myself. I did not appreciate being cast in the role of disciplinarian who would deal with all staff problems, so on more than one occasion I let matters go.

Another manifestation of the "best friend" scenario is that sometimes expatriates give inappropriate messages to Cambodian staff about how they are seen within the organization. It is the expatriate version of telling the foreigner what she or he wants to hear. We had a huge problem with one Cambodian staff member who had been led by an expatriate to believe it was a given that he would become the unit manager when the position was nationalized. The person's performance in his current role was only adequate, and he was far from being qualified for anything more senior. When the expatriate left and this expectation came to light, we had a difficult time getting the Cambodian to understand why he wasn't going to be promoted and what he needed to do to improve his performance.

The Doers

If Cambodians had the capacity to do everything needed to make VBNK function, then neither I nor any other expatriate would have been needed. But that wasn't the case, so expatriates and their expertise were, and still are, needed for some things. Largely because capacity development is yet to be valued as a practice or profession in its own right, few expatriates really understand what it means either to be an adviser or to build capacity development into all their work and staff management practices. This can result in impatience or the belief that Cambodians don't, and never will, have the ability to do things themselves. I know from experience how frustrating it can be to watch people struggling with a task, knowing how much time you are going to have to spend with them on revisions, a particularly frequent occurrence with writing tasks. Such processes invariably take a lot more time than doing something yourself, but it is the only way people really learn. The annual report was a case in point: after doing it myself for the first few years, I decided it should be a joint effort with contributions from all teams. Invariably, I spent much more time guiding and editing staff contributions than it would have taken me to write it all myself, but the effort was worth it because with multiple contributors, the reports attained greater validity as representative of the organization and its work.

When an expatriate is unwilling to work in ways that support staff learning, it not only fails to build capacity but can, on occasions, also diminish capacity that already exists. This is relevant to both tasks and responsibilities. If a Cambodian has achieved the confidence and capacity to take full ownership and responsibility for her or his work, it is very disheartening when an incoming expatriate takes away hard-earned responsibilities and decision-making authority.

While occasionally task and output might be more important than process, in the larger, capacity development, scheme of things, a process orientation is more effective for helping others acquire knowledge, skills, and confidence. Sometimes a skillful judgment call is needed to decide which orientation should have the priority for any given task, but in most situations it should be part of every expatriate's practice to favor process over task.

Expatriate Behaviors
In "Beliefs and Behaviors" in Chapter 1, I talked about the ways in which some Cambodian attitudes and behaviors create concern. It is important to note here that there are also times when the beliefs and behaviors of expatriates are equally, if not more, disconcerting. As the expatriate community is multicultural, there is no single expatriate culture. There are, nevertheless, some issues on which it is believed that expatriates do, or should, have a common approach. I know that VBNK's Cambodian staff have learned many good things about different beliefs and values from the expatriates with whom they have worked. I could pinpoint the contribution of almost all of the expatriates who worked at VBNK on issues such as learning development principles, treating everyone respectfully, and maintaining our stance on corruption. Yet, even while they were contributing positively in one regard, some of those expatriates were simultaneously undermining their own contribution with their attitude and behavior on other important issues.

Expatriates, especially those in leadership positions, have a particularly important role with regard to what values hold sway within an organization. Any organization operating double standards damages its own integrity, so given the senior positions that expatriates hold in development organizations, it behooves them to set a good example by following the rules. Cambodians watch very closely to see if all rules are equally applied to everyone and justifiably feel aggrieved if it is shown that expatriates are getting preferential treatment, especially as they perceive that most foreigners earn more in a day than they do in a month. I lost count of the number of expatriates who either failed to follow VBNK's rules or expected to have something special put in place to accommodate expectations based on their rights or the working practices in their own country.

Given the struggles that all organizations in Cambodia have with endemic corruption, it has always seemed to me that one of the most helpful ways foreigners can visibly demonstrate ethical practice with regard to money is by following financial policy and procedures. VBNK was not a rich organization, but we had enough money to do what we wanted. Expatriates in staff positions always had a reasonable salary and appropriate benefits such as health insurance. Any consultants we brought were put up in good standard and comfortable accommodation and given enough money to cover their food and transportation costs while they were in country. Even so, on several occasions expatriates seemed to deliberately bypass the rules for expenses and procurement, and it always caused problems. It simply isn't possible to hold the line on issues like corruption if staff see that discrepancies are allowed for some people.

Timekeeping is another perennial problem and always prompts a lot of negative comments from Cambodian staff, not only in VBNK but anywhere that expatriates work. The normal Cambodian working day starts at 7:30 a.m. because the early hours are the coolest and freshest part of the day. A two-hour lunch break allows for a rest when the heat is most oppressive. For some reason, a lot of expatriates think that standard office hours don't apply to them, and some would routinely come in anything up to two hours late, no matter what anyone said. The issue of contract commitments is another illuminating example of unhelpful attitudes and behavior. VBNK had several instances of consultants under contract announcing they had found something more interesting or remunerative and would therefore be moving on before their work at VBNK was completed. We also had a situation where, halfway through a long-term commitment, a consultant announced that he could no longer work for the agreed rate and asked for an increase of about 50%. As what he wanted was far beyond anything we could afford, we had no option but to bring the contract to termination. These examples highlight some questions that could be explored regarding the values that influence expatriate behavior. Contrary to the oft-made assumption that expatriates are working for the good of others, some of them occasionally appear to put self-interest above all other considerations.

The Stars

There are some truly wonderful people working in the development sector. Not only are they skillful and competent, dependable, active learners, and sensitive to culture and context, they are also extremely nice people to have around. On the days when it seems that everything is going wrong, having a trusted colleague in whom you can confide might be the only thing between you and a meltdown. They are few and far between and worth their weight in gold.

Localization

When VBNK was established in 1997, it was with a clear intention to localize the organization's management by the end of the first three-year funding phase. I thought my commitment would be for a maximum of five years, even if I stayed on in an advisory role to support the Cambodian director for perhaps two years after localization. When I left, 11 years later, VBNK had the strongest ever team of senior Cambodian managers, but none of them had applied for my position, and in the absence of any suitable external candidates, I was replaced by another expatriate. The journey between those two points is illuminating on the challenges of trying to localize an organization that is in a constant state of change and adaptation.

Localization describes the process by which either projects or whole organizations change from international to local status, as defined by their registration with the government. Within this movement, the word "nationalizing" is sometimes used to describe the process of Cambodians replacing expatriates, but "localizing" is the more common term for both positions and organizations. Localization is an ongoing trend among the INGOs working in Cambodia. VBNK was founded with the intention of being a Cambodian organization, but given the operational guidelines of the RGC on NGO registration, having an expatriate director necessitated registration with the Ministry of Foreign Affairs as an INGO rather than with the Ministry of Interior as a CNGO. The issues involved in that process were complex, but ultimately this status made little difference to VBNK's routine functioning, although being classed as an INGO was never an ideal scenario.

The hopes and expectations of VBNK becoming a Cambodian-led organization were set out clearly in the first funding proposal, prepared in 1996. This document states the intention to appoint a Cambodian codirector as soon as possible, along with the plan to have expatriate advisers for training and for administration and finance for the first funding phase only. Expatriates were to be appointed with a clear mandate to establish the training program and the organization's support functions, including recruiting the first round of Cambodian staff to all positions. Even before the organization had moved into its first full year of operations, possible processes for appointing Cambodians to management positions were under discussion at board level.

In mid-1998, at the board's request, I produced a localization plan that showed how I would vacate the director position in favor of a Cambodian. The first step would be the appointment of a Cambodian assistant director, essentially an observation and learning position, by the end of the year. Thereafter, a phased process would move the person into a deputy director role with some line management responsibility and from there to the director post by the end of 2000, when I would become an adviser and another Cambodian would be appointed as deputy. The plan also covered the transfer of management responsibility for the program and support elements of the organization from the two advisers to Cambodians. Finally, there were some ideas about how the board could localize itself to model the stated intention for VBNK to become fully Cambodian. The board planned to conduct a consultation process with staff as part of the overall process.

The six original trainers had been split into two teams of three, with one person in each appointed team leader. From the start, the TA and I were monitoring multiple aspects of performance and relationships with a view to identifying a possible candidate for the director position from within this group. At the end of 1998, one of the team leaders was promoted to a newly created training manager position, and the TA relinquished active management of the trainers and program, thereafter focusing on building the training manager's capacity to take over. We felt that this training manager was a very strong candidate for the director position but that it would be essential for him to get some solid experience of managing the program before moving into a director-level role. Thus, the plan to localize VBNK met the first of many setbacks, although at that stage it was thought to be simply a matter of timing.

Meanwhile, just nine months after the board and management had agreed on the proposals in the localization plan, both were rethinking the time frame in view of the unexpectedly high volume of work. As noted elsewhere, client organizations were already asking VBNK to provide a complex mixture of customized training and facilitation services in addition to its open access training curriculum. The board minutes of March 1999 talk about the "range of exciting opportunities and prospects" available to VBNK, but not without "serious implications for organization development, specifically the localization process." However, at this stage, the issue of localization was still viewed as a relatively simple matter, basically finding the right person and taking the time to familiarize her or him with the role before he or she took over responsibility. Coincidentally, VBNK was at that time being asked to facilitate and support some other organizations in their localization processes. Through this work and the discussions within VBNK, I started to gain deeper understanding of Cambodian staff views on the subject. As I subsequently wrote in a short publication about the challenges of localization (Pearson 2002), the prospect of localizing created resistance in many Cambodian staff because they were fearful that it would inevitably lead to multiple losses, most particularly of funding, access to expatriate skills, protection from corruption, and participatory management. This last fear was based on an assumption that a Cambodian director would both be autocratic and fill the organization with her or his relatives. Experiences unfolding in the sector, some of them disastrous, were beginning to show that successful localization processes needed a lot more work than a simple timetable of skills development for the individual destined to become the director.

The evaluation conducted at the end of 1999 paid particular attention to the issue of localizing the organization. While acknowledging VBNK's original good intentions and also subsequent recognition that the planned time frame was too fast, the evaluators also noted that the emerging complexity of program direction and growth for sustainability had to inform decisions about localization. No one had any idea then how much this would be a recurrent theme in VBNK's deliberations. The evaluation team concluded that several aspects of VBNK's program development required skills and experience that the Cambodian staff did not yet have and that "it would be difficult—if not unreasonable—to put a Cambodian with only two to three years of experience into this position." The recommendation was that a program to develop staff in areas such as external representation be put in place at the same time as a substantive dialogue about all the issues between the board and staff.

In the strategic planning exercise that followed the evaluation, two conflicting views emerged. While some ambitious staff were clearly keen for expatriates to move out of management positions, the majority was fearful of the prospect of becoming a local organization under Cambodian management. Most staff were also more interested in growth and diversification, which they saw as the route to the organization's sustainability and for which they believed that expatriate management was essential. The strategic plan noted that with a revised mission and an ambitious program of expansion into new areas of work, it was not feasible to consider localization within the original time frame, and the issue should be revisited after the expansion had been completed. It specified that the process for localizing the management of new units should be the same as that already followed for the Training and Administration and Finance Units.

Shortly afterward, something happened that highlighted the weakness of any strategy that focuses on just one prospective candidate. The unofficial director-designate training manager was one of two people who went to a training program at a university in the region in 1998. The TA and I had both put a great deal of work into supporting the development of his management skills. Early in 2000, the university made contact to offer him a place and scholarship in one of its master's programs. He had not applied for this place, but clearly it would have been foolish to turn down such an opportunity. His impending departure raised a number of problems. The training manager wanted, among other benefits, a guarantee that he could return to the position after his studies, but VBNK was not able to carry a vacancy at that level. VBNK needed a training manager, and I did not feel it would be fair to give someone else the position for a limited time, so we did not agree to his request. Negotiations were rather difficult, until it was agreed that he could have a leave of absence with a guaranteed position on his return, with no promises about what the position would be. (Ultimately, when he returned to Cambodia, he decided he could not return to VBNK in a more junior position.) His departure in mid-2000 coincided exactly with the departure of the TA whose contract period had come to an end. VBNK was therefore back at the start with regard to both developing a training manager and grooming a potential candidate for the director's position. These events showed the vulnerabilities of our approach to selecting a Cambodian director, yet as no other staff in post at that time had demonstrated either the interest or the potential to assume a senior leadership position, there had not been any viable alternative.

In the strategic planning process, it had been decided that there was no further need for advisers for administration and finance and that consultants would support training on an as-needed basis. Meanwhile, we set about recruiting a Cambodian program coordinator and an expatriate to start up the Organization Development Unit in 2000. However, I began to realize that problems were emerging on several fronts. The first was that the finance systems had been set up and localized to Cambodian management at a time when VBNK was a small organization with very simple financial requirements. With the increasing growth in the volume and range of program activities, none of the systems was sufficient, but the Cambodian manager did not have the skills to develop what was needed. On the program side, the issues were even more complex. The newly appointed program coordinator, although very capable, was new to this type of position. He did not yet have all the skills and experience needed to negotiate and manage contracts for customized work. This required me to be directly and simultaneously involved in multiple customer contracts. In addition, I needed to be more actively involved in the start-up activities for the Organization Development Unit than I had envisioned. We pulled in consultant support for some activities, but I soon learned that consultants, depending on their caliber, can create rather than save work. My workload was rapidly becoming untenable, and, of greatest concern, quality was beginning to slip, and I did not have the time to deal with it or with important staff development activities. Recognition of this complex tension between the demands of delivery, the capacity of Cambodian staff to deliver quality services, and VBNK's reputation and sustainability proved to be a crucial point in our learning about being a service provider delivering a constantly changing program.

As the situation clearly called for something to be done, I discussed it with both the board and the staff. The response of the Cambodian staff was that we should recruit more Cambodians, even though everyone knew that previous recruitment rounds had not attracted anyone sufficiently experienced to take on senior positions without substantive expatriate support. Fortunately for me, the board took a different view and pragmatically decided that the organization's policy on expatriates needed rethinking. Shortly afterward, I was able to appoint a part-time administration and finance adviser and a full-time TA, Conor Boyle, as counterpart to the program coordinator, and these appointments solved many of the immediate problems.

The next round of discussions about localization was initiated by the board in mid-2001 in order to fulfill the intention set out in the strategic plan. A lengthy process, including an anonymous staff survey and various meetings between the board and staff, resulted in no clear conclusions. The issue was therefore carried over into the next round of strategic planning in early 2002. The external facilitator who led that process noted in her Reflections Report that the only sensitive issue had been localization. She felt this was understandable because it touched on "personal expectations, ambitions, and fears of individual participants." The discussions during the strategic planning were remarkably similar to those in previous rounds in that a small minority of senior Cambodian men were keen to have expatriates out of management positions, whereas a majority were more concerned with growth and sustainability, which they did not think would be viable under Cambodian management. However, we did at that point reach agreement that being a Cambodian organization involves multiple dimensions of identity, structure, and characteristics, none of which necessarily exclude having expatriate staff. Without exception, the staff agreed that VBNK would need expatriate expertise for the foreseeable future if it was to keep innovating to meet the developing needs of the target community. In the section summarizing the decisions made in the strategic planning process, it was noted,

> The focus and intention to develop a unique Cambodian institute remain intact, and to that end a Cambodian deputy director will be appointed in 2005. However, the current reality is that expatriate expertise will be needed for some years yet to help create and maintain the institute that VBNK wants to become. In order to continue strengthening the capacity of Cambodian staff eventually to take over the management of VBNK, constant attention will be paid to the number and deployment of expatriate staff.

Thus it seemed that consensus had been achieved, and the issue of localization had been resolved for the time being.

In 2003, the period of growth and change described above necessitated another review of my workload, which had once again become overwhelming, and the management team decided that restructuring was necessary. Promoting the Cambodian program coordinator and his counterpart to deputy director positions provided much-needed relief. The appointment of a Cambodian deputy director prompted speculation about whether this was the director-designate. The person in question therefore found himself under a great deal of scrutiny from several directions, as staff and other interested parties assessed whether he seemed to have the requisite leadership qualities. I think that originally the deputy may have had ambitions eventually to lead VBNK; certainly he had always been one of the people arguing passionately for a Cambodian director. He was both very competent and quick to learn in his new role. He frequently sought and absorbed new tasks and responsibilities under an agreed plan to build his management capacity. But there were many instances when other Cambodian staff questioned or ignored his decision-making mandate and inappropriately tried to bypass him and go to an expatriate instead. After approximately two years in post, he was disillusioned with the role and work, mostly because of the high administrative burden it entailed. At first, he requested that we find a way for him to take on more program-based responsibilities while retaining his current status. Shortly afterward, he decided that his priority, even if it required a change of status, was to get back into work where he was learning about organizational development in order to prepare himself for a future career as a consultant. I therefore agreed that he could step down, and in November 2005 he became the manager of the IPP that was just then being developed. He left in 2007 to become an independent consultant, which had, in fact, always been his stated career goal.

VBNK's finances became increasingly complex as the program grew. As noted elsewhere, the organization had an unusual resource base in its mixture of donor funding and income generated from contracts and other sources. A Cambodian manager was nominally in charge, but the post holder did not have the technical skills and experience to fulfill the organization's ever more demanding financial management needs, and the system complexities were far beyond my limited knowledge. This responsibility therefore fell to a series of expatriate part-time advisers, creating a number of tensions about position titles, responsibilities, and authority. Some comments in the auditors' management reports began to raise concerns among the board members about potential problems and vulnerability in VBNK's financial management. As a result, they made, with my agreement, the somewhat politically incorrect decision to delocalize this area of management by creating an expatriate director of administration and finance position. We were lucky to quickly recruit a fully qualified management accountant, Paul Masson, to the position. He rapidly brought about a number of improvements in our financial and management information systems and the quality of support systems generally, all of which considerably lessened my workload and concerns. I am, however, happy to note that since my departure, VBNK has been able to recruit a Cambodian woman with the requisite skills and experience for the position.

Over the next few years, Cambodians were able to assume responsibility for all aspects of program management. A big step forward came in early 2005, when the expatriate deputy director's departure created a gap in the management of some major projects then in delivery. Even as an interim measure, the workload was too much for me to take over and manage effectively, so because the Cambodian program managers knew a great deal more about the projects than I did, they had to take on new levels of responsibility. They showed themselves both willing and able to step into the space created by the expatriate's departure, and as a result we decided we would not replace him. However, we all agreed that the program teams still needed expatriate technical support. We were subsequently fortunate to recruit a very experienced person who actually understood what it meant to be an adviser. As a result of these changes, my last years at VBNK were extremely happy, as I worked alongside Cambodians who had successfully taken over responsibility for increasingly large and complex areas of the program. It was a pleasure to watch them grow and develop, and I believed that finally we were on the right road to having a Cambodian director.

I observed rather than participated in the last of VBNK's localization discussions during my tenure, those about recruiting my replacement. The board took its responsibilities on this issue very seriously and started some two years before on a process of consultation with staff and stakeholders about the transition and recruitment. Once again, there was a survey to elicit staff views on the subject of localization, and the responses were mixed along the same lines as previously, with the majority favoring an expatriate replacement because none of the fears previously cited had yet gone away. Ultimately, the board decided that its priority was to recruit against criteria for the position rather than make a decision in advance about nationality. This was despite the urging of one of VBNK's donors, which expressed the view that the organization should localize come what may, and if that resulted in the loss of capacity and quality, which might be damaging to long-term sustainability, then so be it. There were Cambodians I felt that, given the right support, had the capacity for the job. When I asked the former deputy director if he was going to apply, his response was, "No, this organization isn't ready for a Cambodian director yet." Another manager said he did not personally feel ready yet, and I concluded it would not be helpful to push either of them against their instincts.

So, despite VBNK's early intentions to localize quickly, when the founding director left after more than a decade, VBNK remained an expatriate-led organization. Rob Hale, who was coaching me through this period, once observed that he thought the role of director of VBNK was the most complex he had ever encountered. I started and led the organization in the last part of my formal professional life, drawing on decades of work experience in the United Kingdom and the benefits of an excellent education and professional study opportunities. There were many days when the challenges and workload stretched me to the limits, and I often used to wonder, if I was feeling stretched, what it would be like for a Cambodian who did not have the background advantages that I was able to bring to the job.

Even though it did not happen during my tenure, I believe strongly in VBNK becoming a fully Cambodian organization and hope that aim will be achieved in the next director transition. Then VBNK will finally be able to register with the Ministry of Interior as the CNGO it should be in every respect. I have no doubt that had we localized in the early days, as originally planned, VBNK ultimately would have become a very different organization than the one it is now. Some Cambodian-led training NGOs did not thrive and, in some cases, did not even survive because their leaders were unable to develop their programs to keep pace with emerging needs. That might also have been VBNK's fate, but equally it might not.

The challenges of localization are by no means unique to VBNK, and for all organizations they are linked to many of the other issues discussed in this book, most notably those of staff and organizational development. My early assumption was that all it needed was to put the right candidate through a good development plan. I know now that the overall process is a great deal more complex than simply training one person to take over, because it is about many different aspects of organizational functioning. When national staff take over leadership from expatriates, they need to inherit an organization that is strong in every aspect, because if the expatriate's departure creates a significant vacuum, then problems are almost certain to follow. Most especially, there needs to be clarity about values, so that all relationships, daily functioning, and decision-making processes are based on honest, transparent, and fair rules that serve the organization's purpose. All necessary policies, systems, and procedures must be in place and operating effectively. A strong board is needed to provide both support and oversight. A new national director would not survive long as a loner carrying all the responsibility; she or he needs the support and cooperation of a cadre of strong managers who know how to work together as a team. Managers must also have the skills to support the development of all national staff if the organization is to stay relevant and vibrant. Thus the road to localization must be about building multiple aspects of organizational capacity.

I came to realize that a localization process also requires that critical choices be made at various crossroads and turning points in an organization's life. For VBNK, the choices always sat in the tension between localization and growth and innovation. For a variety of reasons, VBNK and its key stakeholders chose the latter rather than to localize. However, in line with the growing capacity throughout the country in general, and in the development sector in particular, a new and exciting generation of leadership is beginning to emerge, and that was true of VBNK when I left. I believe that this generation will be much better placed to take VBNK forward with commitment and vision than those of the past, and while we can never know for sure what would have resulted from the other choices, I think that ultimately it will be proved that we were right to wait for them.

Note

1. *Evangelische Entwicklungsdienst* (Church Development Service), then known as *Evangelische Zentralstelle für Entwicklungshilfe* (EZE) (Church Center for Development Aid).

Learning From the Long Haul: Some Conclusions

In several of the preceding sections, I set out some of my key learning points relevant to the subject at hand. Below, I provide a brief consolidation of the important understanding about capacity development, learning, and creativity that I have gained from my experiences working in a postconflict society.

The Essential Starting Point for Effective Capacity Development Is Culture, Culture, Culture!

Culture is the means through which people understand the world and thus is how they conceptualize, interpret, and respond to everything, including the learning and change essential to sustainable capacity development. Culture is the medium through which beliefs, values, and attitudes about the world and any individual's place in it are formed and constantly reinforced through relationships and daily social interactions. Those beliefs, values, and attitudes, especially those about social structures and power, are powerful forces maintaining the status quo, and they lead people to behave as if they are irrefutably true. Culture also defines how a nation and its citizens will deal with the experience and aftermath of extreme trauma. For these reasons, and because it is now understood that capacity is about a great deal more than technical skills, it is impossible to overemphasize the importance of culture to all aspects of capacity development.

Using the lens of culture promotes understanding about those challenges to capacity development that are rooted in belief systems, but many superficial appearances can mask what people hold as their real truths, and there is no simple and systematic way to uncover the different beliefs at work. Values are at the heart of many development change processes, which means that development practitioners must understand not only the culture in which they are working but also the values that underpin their own behavior and influence their decision making. This can create considerable challenges for both national and expatriate development practitioners to find ways to hold the balance between being respectful of, and sensitive to, local culture and working to bring about change where aspects of that culture contribute to poverty and injustice. Asking people to let go of their deeply held beliefs in order to change can create great stress, especially if the people around them are not involved in the same change process. Nothing highlights this more clearly than women's empowerment processes that do not simultaneously work with all the significant others in their lives.

The Psychosocial Legacy of Complex Trauma Creates Significant Challenges for Effective Capacity Development

Although relatively new, the concept of complex trauma is the best option I have found so far for understanding the psychosocial legacy of extended trauma, because it documents the damage that can be done to physiological functioning as well as cognitive, emotional, and spiritual health. Studies have shown that extended experience of trauma can, literally, change how the brain and body work. Other studies have shown that the impact of complex trauma is more significant at societal levels than with individuals. As culture is a major influence on how health and ill health are conceptualized, it also affects how people respond to traumatic experiences. The extremely complex relationships between culture, context, and psychosocial functioning create deep-seated blocks to change initiatives. Resistance and risk-averse behavior are usually deeply rooted in fear and other emotions produced by both culture and experience. For the actions and expectations of development practitioners in postconflict societies to be appropriate, they need to approach their work in light of this understanding, because without it their interventions will be at best irrelevant and at worst damaging.

Capacity Development Is a Discipline in Its Own Right, and It Is Values Based

Effective capacity development practice requires the application of specific knowledge and skills over and above the technical expertise required for any given sector or theme. Values are largely unacknowledged aspects of capacity development, but it is essential for development practitioners to have self-awareness not only about their technical expertise but also about their motivations and agenda and how these concur with or differ from those with whom they are working. What people understand or want as capacity and effective ways to develop it can vary significantly from one culture to another.

Quick wins can contribute to sustainable capacity development for both individuals and organizations, but only if they are part of careful and consistent long-term processes that take account of relevant environmental and systemic factors. Staff in any position are so much more than their technical skills, and support for their development must acknowledge multiple facets of their cultural socialization and ongoing life experiences. VBNK's experience shows that developing capacity for a support organization is a very particular task, but it has strong resonance with the challenges for all development organizations, because capacity, learning, and change are all intricately linked to program quality and effectiveness, whatever an organization's core business may be.

One of the conclusions arising from placing culture central to an understanding of capacity development is that first steps often have to be about "unlearning" in order to make space for new ideas. While this can be relatively easy for technical skills, it is much harder and takes much longer for other aspects of capacity: no single intervention can undo powerful beliefs and attitudes. Too many simultaneous initiatives can result in loss of focus and confusion, negating any positive outcomes: success is more likely if fewer initiatives are implemented with patience, perseverance, and repetition.

Learning Is a Skill That Needs to Be Learned and Practiced

Learning and analytical skills that can be acquired with ease during childhood can be almost impossible to learn later in life. Those whose education failed to develop these skills need both time and tools if they are to acquire them as adults. This again requires repetition and perseverance to unlock rigid thinking patterns that prevent the welcoming, understanding, and assimilating of new ideas. Learning processes are a journey, not an event. It isn't possible for development practitioners to support others in acquiring a learning practice unless they visibly demonstrate that they are also learners. As Gandhi said, "You must be the change you want to see in the world."

Individual and Organizational Learning Are Inextricably Linked

Neither individual nor organizational learning can happen in isolation from each other, so it is necessary to address the issues strategically in order to simultaneously coordinate and integrate learning practices at all levels of the organization. Leadership is also important for many reasons, and when senior national staff start to take ownership and lead learning practices in ways that are relevant to their own culture, the pace of progress can increase considerably.

Creativity Builds Safe Space for Change and Has Proven Benefits

VBNK's experimentation has proved that using creative practices can have multiple benefits for both individuals and organizations. But there is a paradox in that while creative processes can be the best way to build safe space for change, they are often journeys into the unknown that require risk taking, which for some is a major hurdle because they do not initially feel safe enough to try something new.

Creative practices can give people who are stuck in patterns of rigid left-brain thinking a substantive nudge toward releasing their innate right-brain creativity and ability to innovate, but effective use of creative practices calls for them to be grounded in purpose and linked to analytical skills. It is important to know what you are trying to achieve within any given culture and context. In my Cambodian working environment, the need was to find ways to help people let go of repressive self-control and blocks so they could be open to new learning. In another culture and context, creative processes might be needed for entirely different reasons, but the purpose would still be to find new dimensions of response.

Very simple activities can have the greatest impact, such as when people find a new and meaningful way to talk to each other or get release by being able to tell their story in safety or to express feelings without words. As with other approaches to capacity development, it is rare that any one creative method is sufficient: significant contributions to individual and organizational growth usually come through a combination of methods. The development practitioner's skill lies in knowing how to mix methods for any given need. Often, only those who participated can fully understand a creative experience and its benefits. One of the challenges of trying to convince others of the benefits of creativity is that it doesn't fit neatly into a LogFrame and can be extremely hard to quantify or document in a way that has meaning for others. For example, VBNK found it very difficult to fully articulate the impact of the "artist in residence" project, but all those who participated are unanimous that they found it beneficial.

Creativity and Learning Support
Relevance and Sustainability

It is a paradox that while the root causes of poverty and social injustice remain intractable, much in the development sector everywhere is in a state of constant and rapid change. Within any given context, complex combinations of social, economic, legal, and environmental factors will be in constant flux, creating new influences on the sector and new issues requiring a response. Both stuck systems and dynamically evolving environments call for creative responses. Organizations that are not open to learning and creative adaptation are unlikely to thrive and possibly may not survive, yet new ideas are often rejected because of inherent resistance to change that works to maintain the status quo. For a support organization like VBNK, sustainability depends on keeping ahead, but not so far ahead that the new ideas offered seem irrelevant to others. Being at the leading creative edge of a community is a very exciting place to be, but it can also be uncomfortable. Allies can appear in the most unexpected places, but so can resistance and rejection. It is the role of organizations like VBNK to model a finely tuned balance between, on the one hand, systems, structures, and procedures that provide safety through effectiveness, transparency, and predictability and, on the other, the freedom and flexibility to risk experimentation and innovation.

Some Simple Ideas That Anyone Can Try

I know that VBNK's story represents a unique journey in a particular set of circumstances. Our organizational mandate required us to look for new solutions to long-standing problems. We were fortunate to be working in a time and place that did not put restrictions on what we did, so we were able to experiment and innovate as we saw fit. We were particularly lucky to have the support of understanding and committed donors. Few organizations are able to work in such circumstances, but that does not mean that they cannot experiment with introducing learning and creativity into their working practices. A few ideas that are easy to implement anywhere without too much time and expense are as follows:

- Use different formats for important communication needs, for example, the World Café and/or storytelling processes in meetings.
- Start meetings with a few moments of meditation or fast writing about the subjects to be discussed.
- Use different formats for presentations, shifting people away from left-brain thinking by asking them to make their contributions creative in some way.
- Don't take learning or its integration for granted: keep revisiting, refreshing, and revising, getting one initiative fully grounded before moving on to the next.
- Continuously ask, "What can we learn from this?" and "How can we apply that learning to improve the way we work?"
- Take time to understand how people really feel about change and how they view learning.
- Be aware that behaviors that look like passivity and resistance are possibly the manifestations of much deeper and more complex blocks to learning and change. Try to explore what they are and what creative processes might help overcome them.
- Most important of all, regularly ask yourself if you are working with the right questions or if you have perhaps jumped straight through the questions to some assumption-based answers.

I came to Cambodia with a set of ideas and expectations that very soon proved to be inappropriate and unhelpful. Since then, I have traveled a long road of personal learning and change on which I have, of course, gained far more from my Cambodian experiences than I have given. In this book, I have sought to demonstrate that the risks of doing things differently pay off, because new and creative ideas, when appropriately applied, can achieve a great deal for everyone. My life and work in Cambodia have been many things—interesting, exciting, challenging, frustrating, invigorating, bewildering, fun, demanding, and much, much more—but never dull and always rewarding. And I know that there is no final destination on my learning journey: there will always be new horizons to explore.

Appendix:
Post Trauma Stress Disorder and Its Relevance in Postconflict Societies

The definition of "post trauma stress disorder" (PTSD) was first incorporated into the *Diagnostic and Statistical Manual of Mental Disorders* of the American Psychiatric Association in 1980. It was the successor to related syndromes such as shell shock and concentration camp syndrome and followed extensive work with Holocaust survivors and veterans of the American–Vietnamese war. PTSD was deemed to fill an important gap in psychiatric theory and practice, most notably because it firmly located the causes of disorder as outside rather than inside the individual.

Since it has been conceptualized as an illness, PTSD can now be diagnosed by the presence of a range of physical and emotional symptoms, which may occur following a traumatic event. The symptoms, which an individual may display singly, multiply, or in changing combinations at any given time, fall into four categories:

- *Emotional:* depression, extreme fear, survivor guilt, flashbacks, anxiety, and loss of meaning
- *Cognitive:* problems with memory, concentration, discrimination, and decision making
- *Behavioral:* insomnia, substance abuse, hypervigilance (an extension of a valid survivor behavior), aggressiveness, and irritability
- *Physical:* headaches, general malaise and fatigue, and a range of psychosomatic complaints

Onset can be delayed, and the symptoms may continue over a prolonged period, as anyone who knows veterans of either World War or the American–Vietnamese war may have observed.

There are, however, dangers in blanket application of labels across all cultures. For example, a nightmare may be viewed as a PTSD flashback in one diagnosis, a symptom of a physical illness in some cultures, or a message from ancestors in other cultures. The pitfalls of diagnosing and treating across cultures, without local knowledge of how symptoms are interpreted, are obvious. Melissa Parker questioned the generalization of PTSD studies to something that can transcend cultural context, because the body of evidence that defines it was drawn mostly from self-selecting patients in Western countries. She cited an example of research in Uganda that found that while many people display symptoms of trauma, instances of survivor guilt are rare, raising questions about the applicability of this aspect of the PTSD syndrome in non-Western cultures (Parker 1996, 81). While noting that a few responses to major trauma appear to be common to all cultures (Summerfield 1991, 160),[1] Summerfield cautioned,

> It is simplistic to regard victims as mere passive receptacles of negative psychological effects which can be judged "present" or "absent." A checklist of mental state features applied in a war context does not offer a rigorous distinction between subjective distress and objective disorder. (Summerfield 1996, 16)

Summerfield also questioned the validity of applying PTSD criteria in some circumstances, because some symptoms may be healthy, adaptive, and coping responses to a traumatic experience after which it would be abnormal to behave normally. He reminded us that victims are ordinary people, often of huge resilience, and victimhood is not a helpful concept because it triggers an array of negative consequences for people who are, in fact, survivors. The tendency to label people victims can result in their being viewed through an inappropriate and negative lens, with a corresponding push toward diagnosis as ill under the medical classification of PTSD.

In postconflict situations, an additional complexity is that some survivors are victims, some are perpetrators, and some are both. Such complications inevitably affect how individuals process their past and adapt to postwar circumstances. For example, in Bosnia, Maria Kett observed that ex-combatant male survivors had a complex array of reactions, including having survivor guilt and being demoralized and depressed. These feelings, combined with other factors, led to high rates of problems like alcoholism and domestic violence in their family lives (Kett 2005, 209).

One of the shortfalls of the PTSD concept is that it applies only to individuals and not to groups or whole societies, thereby containing responses within the medical treatment model. While this may help individuals, it does not contribute to wider relational and social healing or to the construction of the shared meaning necessary for understanding and healing to take place. Summerfield noted that while the characteristics of individuals obviously have an effect on how they respond to trauma, when trauma happens to whole communities, there is a blurring between the individual and the collective (Summerfield 1996, 19). Judith Zur made a similar observation in a study of the psychological impacts of impunity in Guatemala (Zur 1994, 12–16). She identified the impact of extreme trauma at both group and societal levels and concluded that if a society is to heal and move forward constructively without the risk of conflict erupting again in the future, attention is needed at these levels as much as for individuals, and arguably more so. Summerfield also asserted that war and trauma have very significant repercussions at the level of society: "War is a collective experience and perhaps its primary impact on victims is through their witnessing the destruction of a social world embodying their history, identity and living values" (Summerfield 1996, 19). This, he stated, is particularly devastating in developing countries, where society has neither the resources nor the structures to support recovery of individuals or the entire population.

David Becker, a practitioner at the Latin American Institute on Mental Health and Human Rights in Chile, set out a powerful analysis of why the PTSD concept is insufficient in some contexts (Becker 1995). His first challenge to the concept relates to its dependence on the visibility of symptoms to define illness in individuals, when the reality of what happens to, and between, individuals is much more complex. Second, he takes issue with the word "post" and its implications of an event that was limited to a point in time in the past. As with many other societies, some parts of Chilean society experienced long-term repression under a military regime, during which many people suffered extreme and ongoing trauma. His next issue is with the labeling of victims of genocide, torture, or political repression as disordered. Like others, he holds the view that abnormal reactions are the right response to extreme experiences such as being forced to witness the murder of loved ones and that to maintain normal behaviors in such cases would be symptomatic of dysfunction. Becker's argument is that treatment processes should not assume individual pathology but instead focus on the consequences of a disturbed society.

Becker and his colleagues drew on studies that had deepened understanding of the effects of the extended and cumulative trauma of prolonged suffering, such as in concentration camps or from living under violent, repressive regimes. As a result, they adopted the concept of "extreme traumatization" (Becker 1995, 107) to encompass trauma of intensity and lengthy duration, as well as its effects on individuals, the collective, and the relationship between social and individual processes. They found this to be the most appropriate concept for the institute's patients and of particular benefit in bringing insight to their work, not only with people who present with classic PTSD symptoms but also with people or their family members who presented with other dysfunctions and illnesses, sometimes many years later and sometimes in family members who did not directly experience any trauma.

Martha Cabrera and her colleagues documented an example of multiple factors affecting the psychosocial functioning of individuals and groups beyond the definitions of PTSD when they started their work in the postconflict but pre-Hurricane Mitch period in Nicaragua. She said that even though they were psychologists and social workers and had named their work "affective and spiritual reconstruction," they came to realize the "profound ignorance" with which they embarked on their project (Cabrera n.d.). When she and her colleagues started reflecting on why the millions of dollars that had been spent on workshops and training in the postconflict period had had so little effect and why the population seemed so passive and unable to mobilize to rebuild society, they realized the depth of the unresolved pain and trauma that individuals had kept locked inside them, because circumstances had not allowed the population any opportunity to process reactions to traumatic events. Over time, once they began to create safe spaces in which people could talk about their losses and pain, Cabrera and her colleagues came to define Nicaragua as "a multiply wounded, multiply traumatized, multiply mourning country." Much of what Cabrera identified could equally apply to Cambodia, as illustrated by the findings of a study of Cambodian land mine victims, which documented the psychosocial impacts seen in the sample group (Somasundaram and Kea 1996). All the study respondents had many symptoms and problems that were impairing the victims' ability to relate to others and function within society.

Another interesting example is a study of the effect of the violent Janatha Vimukthi Peramuna conflict in Sri Lanka. Jonathan Watkins explored the difficulties of understanding fully the relationship between the experience of violence and mental illness (Watkins 2005). He noted that both individual predispositions and cultural factors will influence how violence is experienced and the effect it will have. The degree of control that people feel they have during the violence is relevant, in that incidents of loved ones or self being totally helpless and vulnerable to violence will create stronger negative effects than those in which the individual feels able to exert some control. Other factors, such as the extent and randomness of the violence, will be important, but if circumstances can offer a rational explanation for the violence, it has less negative impact than when it appears to be irrational. Watkins also found that when violence creates adverse conditions in society and the local economy, it becomes an indirect trigger for individual problems. In summary, he noted,

> The disrupting effect that conflict has on social relationships leads to reason being replaced by aggression, a loss of a common frame of reference across social groups and a lack of institutional and individual truthfulness as the key forces in this social disruption. The effect of these forces is to undermine relationships of work and love, and senses of personal identity and history. (Watkins 2005, 225)

His conclusion is that while violence may trigger mental ill health in some circumstances, the norm is that extreme and extended violence will lead to anxiety and stress disorders rather than psychosis and that these extend across large sectors of the population, inhibiting full and effective social and economic functioning. He made links between the detrimental effect that violence has on social relations and the ability of the group to maintain a shared sense of meaning.

Note

1. Summerfield listed this repertoire as sleep disturbance, lability of mood (including sadness and irritability), undue fatigue, poor concentration, and diminished powers of memory.

References

Becker, David. 1995. The deficiency of the concept of posttraumatic stress disorder when dealing with victims of human rights violations. In *Beyond trauma: Cultural and societal dynamics*, ed. Rolf J. Kleber, Charles R. Figley, and Berthold B.R. Gersons. New York: Plenum.

Bennett, Jon, and Charlotte Benson. 1995. Cambodia: NGO cooperation in a changing aid context, 1979–94. In *Meeting needs: NGO coordination in practice*, ed. Jon Bennett. London: Earthscan.

Blatner, Adam. 2007. *Aggregate experiences*. www.blatner.com/adam/psyntbk/aggregatexperiences .html.

Cabrera, Martha. n.d. *Living and surviving in a multiply wounded country*. Managua, Nicaragua: Centro Antonio Valdivieso.

Community Development Resource Association. 2001. *Measuring development: Holding infinity*. Annual report 2000–2001. Cape Town, South Africa: CDRA.

CNGO Support Network. 1996a. Summary: Impressions on the NGO movement in Cambodia. Background reading for Partnership Workshop, Phnom Penh, June. Original report: Michiel Van der Drift. 1993. *Impressions on the NGO movement in Cambodia*. Phnom Penh: SAWA Consultants for Development.

CNGO Support Network. 1996b. Summary: Strategic planning process, field validation report for 1997–1999. Background reading for Partnership Workshop, Phnom Penh, June. Original report: Coopération Internationale pour le Développement et la Solidarité (International Cooperation for Development and Solidarity). 1996. *Strategic planning process, field validation report for 1997–1999*. Phnom Penh: CIDSE Cambodia.

CNGO Support Network. 1996c. Summary: Feasibility study for ACR's program development in Cambodia. Background reading for Partnership Workshop, Phnom Penh, June. Original report: Australian Catholic Relief. 1996. *Feasibility study for ACR's program development in Cambodia*. Phnom Penh: ACR.

CNGO Support Network. 1996d. Summary: Cambodian NGOs. Background reading for Partnership Workshop, Phnom Penh, June. Original report: Steeman, Anne-Marieke. 1995. *Cambodian NGOs*. The Netherlands: Novib.

Criddle, Joan D., and Teeda Butt Mam. 1987. *To destroy you is no loss: The odyssey of a Cambodian family*. Boston, MA: Grove/Atlantic.

Dixit, Shikha. 2005. Meaning and explanations of mental illness: A social representations approach. *Psychology and Developing Societies* 17 (1): 1–18.

Fadiman, Anne. 1997. *The spirit catches you and you fall down: A Hmong child, her American doctors, and the collision of two cultures.* New York: Noonday Press; Farrar, Straus and Giroux.

Freire, Paulo. 1970. *Pedagogy of the oppressed.* Trans. Myra Bergman Ramos. New York: Herder & Herder.

Glass, David. 2003. *Creative practice: A guide to creativity in development.* Phnom Penh: VBNK.

Godfrey, Martin, Toshiyasu Kato, Chan Sophal, Long Vou Piseth, Pon Dorina, Tep Saravy, Tia Savora, and So Sovannarith. 2000. Technical assistance and capacity development in an aid-dependent economy: The experience of Cambodia. Working Paper 15. Phnom Penh: Cambodia Development Resource Institute.

Harmer, Anne. 1995. *Rebuilding war-torn societies: Psycho-social vulnerability and coping mechanisms in Cambodia.* Social research feasibility study funded by the International Development Research Centre with support from the UN Children's Fund.

Heng Molyaneth, Kak Viraktheary, and Tou Tony. 2004. *Management capacity building in NGOs: How advisors in Cambodia build the management capacity of their local counterparts.* Phnom Penh: VBNK.

Hinton, Alexander. 2005. *Why did they kill? Cambodia in the shadow of genocide.* Berkeley: University of California Press.

Kett, Maria. 2005. Internally displaced peoples in Bosnia-Herzegovina: Impacts of long-term displacement on health and well-being. *Medicine, Conflict and Survival* 21 (3): 199–215.

Kumar, Krishna, Hannah Baldwin, and Judy Benjamin. 2000. Aftermath: Women and women's organizations in postconflict Cambodia. Working Paper 307. Washington, DC: Center for Development Information and Evaluation, US Agency for International Development.

Land, Anthony, and Peter Morgan. 2008. *Technical cooperation for capacity development in Cambodia: Making the system work better.* Phnom Penh: Cambodian Rehabilitation and Development Board of the Council for the Development of Cambodia.

Leng Chhay, and Jenny Pearson. 2006. *Working in Cambodia: Perspectives on the complexities of Cambodians and expatriates working together.* Phnom Penh: VBNK.

Locard, Henri. 2004. *Pol Pot's little red book: The sayings of Angkar.* Chiang Mai: Silkworm Books.

Maclean, Alexandra, and Srey Vanthorn. 2000. *Management Tools Series: 1. Studies in organisational structure.* Phnom Penh: VBNK.

Meas Nee. 2006. Challenges of human development in the contemporary social process and change (a Cambodian perspective). Working paper presented at the Cambodia Launch of the World Development Report 2006: Equity and Development, Phnom Penh, June 13.

Mueller, Felicia. n.d. *Complex trauma.* www.counselingseattle.com/content/complex-trauma.htm.

Nichanian, Marc. 2002. Catastrophic mourning. In *Loss, the politics of mourning,* ed. David Eng and David Kazanjian. Berkeley: University of California Press.

O'Leary, Moira. 2006. The influence of values on development practice: A study of Cambodian development practitioners in non-government organisations in Cambodia. PhD thesis, La Trobe University, Melbourne.

O'Leary, Moira, and Meas Nee. 2001. *Learning for transformation: A study of the relationship between culture, values, experience and development practice in Cambodia.* Phnom Penh: VBNK.

Ou Sivhouch, Lun Pide, and Kim Sedara. 2010. Searching for an improved path to civil society–parliamentarian interactions in Cambodia. In *Annual development review 2009–2010,* ed. Cambodia Development Resource Institute. Phnom Penh: CDRI.

Parker, Melissa. 1996. The mental health of war damaged populations. *IDS Bulletin* 27 (3): 77–85.

Pearson, Jenny. 2002. Localisation. Issue paper. Phnom Penh: VBNK.

Pearson, Jenny. 2010. *Beyond the budget: The linkages between long-term donor–NGO relations and capacity development in Cambodia. A summary of the partnership between VBNK and EED.* www.vbnk.org.

Pearson, Jenny. 2011a. Integrating learning into organisational capacity development of Cambodian NGOs. *Development in Practice* 21 (6).

Pearson, Jenny. 2011b. No visible difference: A women's empowerment process in a Cambodian NGO. *Development in Practice* 21 (3).

Richardson, Megan. 2001. *NGO support sector review.* Phnom Penh: CNGO Support Network.

Senge, Peter M. 2006. *The fifth discipline: The art and practice of the learning organization.* Rev. ed. London: Random House.

Schein, Edgar. 1956. The Chinese indoctrination program for prisoners of war: A study of attempted brainwashing. *Psychiatry* 19 (2): 149–72.

Schein, Edgar. 1985. *Organizational culture and leadership.* San Francisco, CA: Jossey-Bass.

Sinclair, John. 2001. *Collins cobuild English dictionary for advanced learners.* Third ed. Ottawa, OT: HarperCollins Canada.

Somasundaram, Daya, and Kea Kiri Renol. 1996. The psychosocial effects of landmines in Cambodia. *Medicine, Conflict and Survival* 14 (3): 219–36.

Summerfield, Derek. 1991. The psychosocial effects of conflict in the Third World. *Development in Practice* 1 (3): 159–73.

Summerfield, Derek. 1996. The impact of war and atrocity on civilian populations: Basic principles for NGO interventions and a critique of psychosocial trauma projects. Network Paper 14. London: Relief and Rehabilitation Network, Overseas Development Institute.

Taylor, Maurice. 1997. *Transfer of learning: Planning effective workplace education programs.* Ottawa, OT: National Literacy Secretariat, Human Resources Development Canada.

VBNK. 2005. *Annual report 2004.* www.vbnk.org/uploads/VBNKdocs/VBNK annual report 2004.pdf.

VBNK. 2006. *Annual report 2005: Making a difference.* www.vbnk.org/uploads/VBNKdocs/VBNK_REPORT_2005.pdf.

VBNK. 2009. *Impact assessment report October 2009: Learners celebrating success.* www.vbnk.org/uploads/VBNKdocs/VBNK%20Impact%20Assessment%20%202009%20FINAL.pdf.

Volkan, Vamik. 1998. Transgenerational transmissions and chosen traumas. Opening address, XIII International Congress of the International Association of Group Psychotherapy, London, August 24–28.

Volkan, Vamik. 2006. The next chapter: Consequences of societal trauma. Keynote address, conference on Memory, Narrative, and Forgiveness: Reflecting on Ten Years of South Africa's Truth and Reconciliation Commission, Cape Town, November 22–25.

Watkins, Jonathan. 2005. The state, conflict and the individual: The effect of the Janatha Vimukthi Peramuna (JVP) insurrections in Sri Lanka on the mental welfare of a population. *Medicine, Conflict and Survival* 21 (3): 216–29.

Zur, Judith. 1994. The psychological impact of impunity. *Anthropology Today* 10 (3): 12–16.

Index

accountability, 93, 94
Accra Agenda for Action, 48, 66
Action Learning Cycle (ALC), 88, 90–91, 92–93, 94, 106n3
Action-Reflection-Learning-Planning (ARLP) cycle, 106
ADB. *See* Asian Development Bank
age, 16–17, 24
ALC. *See* Action Learning Cycle
alcoholism, 186–87
ambiguity, 15
American-Vietnamese War, 10, 45n1
analytical skills, 94, 96
Analyzing Development Issues, 104
angkar (organization), 33
antisocial behavior, 33
ANZ Royal Bank of Cambodia, 75n4
ARLP. *See* Action-Reflection-Learning-Planning cycle
Armenia, 40
art, 110–11
ASEAN. *See* Association of Southeast Asian Nations
The Asia Foundation, 54
Asian Development Bank (ADB), 76
assessment
    of competencies, 98
    of creativity, 182–83
    of expatriates, 163
    of training, 18
Association of Southeast Asian Nations (ASEAN), 11

Australian Agency for International Development (AusAID), 75n4
autocracy, 14, 61, 101, 161

Bakker, Henk, 140
Becker, David, 187–88
behavior. *See also* post trauma stress disorder; resistance
    antisocial, 33
    coping, 33, 40
Better Factories Cambodia (BFC), 71
blame, 100
Blatner, Adam, 39, 42
boards, 159–61
Bosnia, 28, 46n12, 186–87
Boyle, Conor, 173
brainwashing, 33
Brooks, Sally, 15
Brown, Juanita, 127
budgeting, 141–42
Butt Mann, Teeda, 39–40

Cabrera, Martha, 188
Cambodia. *See also* ANZ Royal Bank of Cambodia; expatriates; Royal Government of Cambodia
    art in, 110–11
    change in, 41, 44, 102
    communication in, 13–14, 91–92, 99–100, 130, 135
    complex trauma in, 5–6, 25–26, 33–34, 41, 43–44

corruption in, 21, 22
culture of, 13–16, 80–82, 121, 133
education in, 17, 24, 45n2, 104–5
gender in, 16–17, 24, 84, 116–19
history of, 9–12
HIV/AIDS in, 55, 60, 66
human rights in, 61, 64
industry of, 70–71
INGOs in, 48–51
isolation in, 17–18
land mine victims in, 188
learning in, 102–3, 104
management from, 18, 161–62, 170–71,
     172, 173, 174, 175, 176
mental heath care in, 32
Ministry of Foreign Affairs, 50, 169
Ministry of Interior, 58, 75n3, 169
Ministry of Rural Development, 64, 73
mistrust in, 34, 37–38, 42
NGO law, 75n3
NGOs in, 4, 48, 50
passivity in, 42, 100
questions in, 13–14, 91–92, 130, 135
refugees from, 49
resistance in, 19, 41–42, 43, 94, 102–3,
     154, 156
somatization in, 27–29
training in, 4, 5–6, 77, 78, 99–101
UN in, 11, 125
youth in, 17, 24
Cambodia Labor Law, 61
Cambodian NGOs (CNGOs), 12
  boards, 160
  corruption, 63
  criticism of, 55–56
  funding for, 57, 62–63, 140
  governance of, 62–63
  history of, 58–59
  INGOs and, 51, 53–55, 57–59
  law, 75n3
  leadership, 56, 60–61
  personnel, 55, 60
  RGC and, 63–64
  start of, 53–54
  strategy by, 60
  support for, 57

training of, 59
VBNK with, 59–60, 63, 71–72
Cambodian NGO Support Network
     (CNSN), 55
Cambodian People's Party (CPP), 11
capacity
  development of, 163–64, 166, 180–81
  for learning, 105
case story exercises, 128
the Catastrophe, 40
CCC. *See* Cooperation Committee for Cam-
     bodia
CCD. *See* Center for Creative Development
CDRA. *See* Community Development Re-
     source Association
Center for Creative Development (CCD),
     73, 123–26, 154
certainties, 134
change, 42
  in Cambodia, 41, 44, 102
  creativity for, 106, 107, 136, 183
  management of, 154, 156, 158
  values and, 179–80
  at VBNK, 156–58
chaperone, 117
CHART. *See* Creative Holistic Action-re-
     search for Relationship Transformation
Chile, 187
chkoo-ut (crazy), 29
Christians, 50, 51, 164–65
Church Development Service, 139–40
Church World Service (CWS), 52–53
civil society organizations, 54
CNGOs. *See* Cambodian NGOs
CNSN. *See* Cambodian NGO Support Network
coaching, 130–31, 137n2
Commune Council Partnership Strengthen-
     ing initiative, 127–28
commune councils, 52, 65, 72
communication, 81
  in Cambodia, 13–14, 91–92, 99–100,
     130, 135
  of expatriates, 127
  eye contact, 120
communism, 9
Communist Party of Kampuchea, 10

Community Conversation, 129–30, 132
Community Development Resource Association (CDRA), 86–90, 128
competencies, assessment of, 98
complex trauma. *See* trauma, complex
concentration, 189n1
conferences, 53, 128–30
confidentiality, 161
contract commitments, 168
control, 81, 82, 188–89
Cooperation Committee for Cambodia (CCC), 50, 104
coping behavior, 33, 40
corpses, 35, 46n12
corruption, 21–22, 63, 168
costing, 3–4
courses, designing, 94, 96
CPP. *See* Cambodian People's Party
creative arc, 134
Creative Holistic Action-research for Relationship Transformation (CHART), 46n7, 73
  results of, 151–54
  start of, 121–23
Creative Practice: A Guide to Creativity in Development (Glass), 109
creativity
  assessment, 182–83
  for change, 106, 107, 136, 183
  definition, 107
  Glass's work with, 82, 85, 108–9, 126, 133, 134, 154
  as incremental, 133–34
  purpose and, 134
  for relationships, 124
  as risk taking, 182
  training, 108–10, 111, 123, 125–26, 132–33, 135–36
critical thinking, 81
criticism, 16, 55–56, 100
cross-organization learning, 103
cross-unit learning, 91
culture. *See also* norms, cultural
  Cambodian, 13–16, 80–82, 121, 133
  complex trauma interaction with, 25–26, 29–30, 32, 34, 180, 187, 189n1

definition of, 179
  of expatriate, 167
  leadership and, 182
  management and, 146
  as obstacle, 6
  PTSD and, 185–86
  resistance and, 180
curiosity, 92, 135
curriculum, 14, 94, 96
CWS. *See* Church World Service

DanChurchAid (DCA), 59
David Glass Ensemble, 108
DCA. *See* DanChurchAid
Decentralization Café, 128
decentralization projects, 52, 65
defensive routines, 19
Delvecchio, Arthur, 104
Development Café, 53, 127
development supervision, 98–99
diagnosis, 29
Diagnostic and Statistical Manual of Mental Disorders, 185
A Dialogue Between the Generations, 129
didactic teaching, 13–14
disagreement, 47
discrimination, 24–25. *See also* gender
dishonesty, 21–23
dissociation, 40
Dixit, Shikha, 29
Documentation Center of Cambodia, 35, 46n11
domestic violence, 186–87
donors, 66–67, 139–41, 152, 175

echo training session, 79
education, 17, 24, 45n2, 84, 104–5, 181
EED (*Evangelische Entwicklungdienst*), 139–40
Einstein, Albert, 2
ELC. *See* experiential learning cycle
empowerment, 25, 42–43
English language, 79–80, 84–85, 163
epilepsy, 46n10
equality, 167–68
Erd, Wendy, 112

expatriates
    assessment of, 163
    communication of, 127
    culture of, 167
    duration of, 163
    failures of, 164, 165
    learning for, 102
    as management, 51, 143, 158, 166–68,
        169–70, 171, 172, 173, 174, 175,
        176
    in Phnom Penh, 49
    relationships of, 165–66
    visas, 50
expectations, 145
expenses, 21, 168
experiential learning cycle (ELC), 78–79,
    93–94
extreme traumatization, 188
eye contact, 120

facilitation. *See also* VBNK
    skills for, 104
    of training, 12–13
Facilitating Development From the Inside
    Out, 86
factories, 70–71
family, 38
fatalism, 42
fatigue, 189n1
favoritism, 98
fear, 62, 81
feedback, 98, 100
fees, 142
feminism, 116
flashbacks, 186
follow-up, longitudinal, 3
foreign aid, 11, 48, 54, 62
formula, security of, 81
foundations, 54, 66
fragmentation, 40
Freire, Paulo, 42
French Indochina, 9
French language, 163
FUNCINPEC party (*Front Uni National
    pour un Cambodge Indépendant, Neutre,
    Pacifique, et Coopératif*), 11

funding
    for CNGOs, 57, 62–63, 140
    for INGOs, 66
    long-term, 140
    by USAID, 54
    for VBNK, 139–41, 142, 152, 175

garment sector, 70–71
Gates Foundation, 66
gender, 16–17, 24, 84, 116–19. *See also*
    women; Women's Leadership Program
General Introduction to Management course,
    78
Gide, André, 2
Glass, David, 80
    background of, 108
    creativity work of, 82, 85, 108–9, 126,
        133, 134, 154
Goddard, Nigel, 121
Good Manufacturing Practice standards, 69
gossip, 81
governance
    CNGOs, 62–63
    commune councils, 65
    key elements, 76n5
government. *See also* Royal Government of
    Cambodia
    corruption, 21–22
    Ministry of Foreign Affairs, 50, 169
    Ministry of Interior, 58, 75n3, 169
    Ministry of Rural Development, 64, 73
    personnel, 22, 23
    resistance in, 64–65
    training of, 64–66
    women in, 118–19
grief, 35–36
grounding, of ideas, 94
Guatemala, 187
guilt, 37, 186

Hale, Rob, 110, 131, 137n1, 176
Handicap International (HI), 68
Hansel and Gretel, 137n1
Harmer, Anne, 27, 30
harmony, 27
healing, 5–6, 26–27, 30, 31–32

health, 27–30
Heng Molyaneth, 150
HI. *See* Handicap International
hierarchy. *See* status
history
 of Cambodia, 9–12
 CNGOs, 58–59
HIV/AIDS, 55, 60, 66
Hmong, 46n10
honesty, 21–23, 100, 101
human resources (HR) development, 97–98,
 101
human rights, 61, 64
Hun Sen, 11

ICCO. *See* Interchurch Organisation for Development Cooperation
ICCO Partners Project (IPP), 59, 61, 130–32
identity, 112–13, 157
ILO. *See* International labor Organization
implementation, 4–5. *See also* Learning
 Implementation Plan
individuals, 30–31
industry, 70–71
Ing Kantha Phavi, 118–19
INGOs. *See* international NGOs
initiative, 53, 162
inner voice role-play, 112
innovation, 112–13
insecurity, 31
inspiration, 4–5
Institute to Serve Facilitators of Development. *See* VBNK
Interchurch Organisation for Development
 Cooperation (ICCO), 59, 139–40
Intergenerational Dialogue Conference, 53
International Labor Organization (ILO), 71
international NGOs (INGOs), 3
 in Cambodia, 48–51
 Christian, 50, 51
 classification as, 169
 CNGOs and, 51, 53–55, 57–59
 funding for, 66
 personnel of, 57–58
 specializations of, 50–51
 VBNK use by, 52–53, 67, 71, 72

International NGO Training and Research
 Centre (INTRAC) Praxis Programme,
 128
international organizations (IOs), 18, 66
INTRAC. *See* International NGO Training
 and Research Centre Praxis Programme
IOs. *See* international organizations
IPP. *See* ICCO Partners Project

Janatha Vimukthi Peramuna, 188
Jones, Matthew, 110, 154
journaling, 87
*Journal of American Society of Training Direc-
 tors*, 46n4

Kak Viraktheary, 150
karma, 42
Kett, Maria, 28, 46n12, 186–87
Khmer Rouge, 9, 10, 11
 art about, 111
 brainwashing by, 33
 effect of, 39
 loss during, 34–36
 making meaning of, 40
 mistrust with, 38
Kirkpatrick, Donald, 46n4
kru khmer, 30

land mines, victims of, 188
language, 79–80, 84–85, 163
 translation, 68, 69, 128
Laos, 9
laws, 61, 75n3
LDP. *See* Leadership Development Program
leadership. *See also* Women's Leadership
 Program
 of CNGOs, 56, 60–61
 culture and, 182
 resistance, 61
Leadership Development Program (LDP),
 53, 122
learning
 articulation of, 133
 blocks, 95, 101–2, 104, 105–6, 114, 181,
 182
 in Cambodia, 102–3, 104

capacity for, 105
coordination of, 182
cross-organization, 103
cross-unit, 91
definition of, 102
with didactic teaching, 13–14
by doing, 166–67
versus earning, 105
for expatriates, 102
learning weeks, 92–93
organizational, 105
unlearning, 181
whole person, 87
Learning Café, 128
Learning for Transformation (O'Leary and
    Meas), 13, 15, 31, 37
    culture in, 121
    development of, 119–20
    reflective practices in, 43
Learning Implementation Plan (ILP),
    113–14
Learning to Learn, Continued, 101–2
learning *versus* earning, 105
Leng Chhay, 34, 41, 44
Levick, Nicol, 97
Lia, 46n10
LIP. *See* Learning Implementation Plan
living systems theory, 87, 136
local initiative groups, 53
localization, 143, 144, 145, 169–77
Lon Nol, 10
loss, 34–36
Lost Child Project, 108, 137n1

Maclean, Alexandra, 147
Making a Different Society for Today and
    Tomorrow, 129–30
management. *See also* leadership
    from Cambodia, 18, 161–62, 170–71,
        172, 173, 174, 175, 176
    of change, 154, 156, 158
    commitment of, 105
    culture and, 146
    expatriates as, 51, 143, 158, 166–68,
        169–70, 171, 172, 173, 174, 175,
        176

localization of, 143, 144, 145, 169–77
middle, 51–52, 99–101
senior, 105
time, 145, 168
training in, 4, 17, 51, 99
of VBNK, 169–71, 172, 173, 174–76
*Management Capacity Building in NGOs:
    How Advisors in Cambodia Build the
    Management Capacity of Their Local
    Counterparts* (Heng, Kak, and Tou),
    150
Managers Development Program (MDP), 68
    mentors in, 113–14
    success of, 115–16
Marais, Dirk, 90
mass graves, 34
Masson, Paul, 175
MDP. *See* Managers Development Program
meaning, 38–40
Meas Nee, 13, 15, 31, 37, 38, 42, 43, 119–
    20, 121
Memorandum of Understanding (MOU),
    50, 64, 75n3
memory, 189n1
    meaning from, 38–39, 40
    suppression of, 33–34
"Mending Broken Mirrors" (Pearson), 131
mental illness, 32, 188–89
mentors, 113–14
microfinance, 71
Millennium Development Goals, 125
Ministry of Foreign Affairs, 50, 169
Ministry of Interior, 58, 75n3, 169
Ministry of Rural Development, 64, 73
Ministry of Women's Affairs, 118
missionaries, 164–65
mission drift, 73
mission statement, 72–74
mistrust, 34, 37–38, 42
Moclair, Enda, 121–22
money, 21–22, 141, 142, 158, 168. *See also*
    funding; salaries
monitoring, 4
moods, 189n1
MOU. *See* Memorandum of Understanding
mourning, perennial, 35

Mueller, Felicia, 31

names, 151
nationalizing, 169
negotiation, 81
New Visions workshop, 125
NGO Forum on Kampuchea, 49
NGOs. *See* non-governmental organizations
Nicaragua, 188
Nichanian, Marc, 40
saying no, 81
non-governmental organizations (NGOs), 1.
 See also Cambodian NGOs
 budgeting of, 141–42
 in Cambodia, 4, 48, 50
 registration, 169
norms
 cultural, 27–28, 34, 41
 organizational, 21
Novib, 56

O'Leary, Moira, 13, 15, 20, 31, 37, 43,
 119–20, 121
Organization Development Unit, VBNK,
 143, 144–45, 172, 173
organogram, 155
other, 32–33
Oxfam United Kingdom, 49

Pact, 51, 59, 62
painting, 110
Paris Declaration, 48
Paris Peace Accords, 11, 43
Parker, Melissa, 186
participation, 42
 power and, 81–82
 in WLP, 117–18
Partnership for Gender Equity project, 118
passivity, 42, 100
PDP. *See* Proposal Development Program
Pearson, Jenny, 34, 41, 44, 120, 131
People's Republic of Kampuchea, 10–11
People's Socialist Community, 9–10
perennial mourning, 35
personnel, 3. *See also* management; recruitment; training

at CNGOs, 55, 60
 government, 22, 23
 of INGOs, 57–58
 of support agencies, 57–58
 turnover, 74, 148, 162, 165
 VBNK, 77–85, 86, 87, 89–94, 96–99,
 103–4, 105, 108–12, 121, 161–63
persuasion, coercive, 33
Phnom Penh, 10–11, 49
Phnom Penh Water Supply Authority, 71
Pininfarina S.p.A., 134–35
planning, strategic, 145. *See also* VBNK
Ponleu Khmer, 62
possibilities, 134
post trauma stress disorder (PTSD), 31–32,
 185–86, 189n1
Potala Palace, 70
potential, 2, 134
poverty, 32
power, 81–82, 112
praise, 100
probabilities, 134
problem solving, 81
professionalism, 18
Proposal Development Program (PDP), 115
psychoanalysis, 29, 30
psychosocial functioning, 30–31
PTSD. *See* post trauma stress disorder
purpose, 134

qualifications, 3, 17, 18, 148, 163, 173, 178
questions, 13–14, 91–92, 130, 135

reading, 18
recruitment
 qualifications with, 3, 18, 148, 163, 173,
 176
 retention after, 22
 training after, 82
 of women, 77, 84, 144
reflection weeks, 92
reflective practices, 43, 130
refugees, 49
relationships
 creativity for, 124
 of expatriates, 165–66

of women, 180
relevance, 16
religion, 50, 51, 164–65
remediation, 71
repression, 33, 82
reputation, 3, 112–13
research, 18
Research and Publications Unit, VBNK,
    146–51, 157
resistance, 45
    in Cambodia, 19, 41–42, 43, 94, 102–3,
        154, 156
    culture and, 180
    in government, 64–65
    leadership, 61
    in VBNK, 91, 101–2, 154, 156
respect, 23
    self-, 25
responsibility, 162, 167
RGC. *See* Royal Government of Cambodia
risk taking, 81, 182
role-play, 112
Rosenboom, Jan Willem, 80
Royal Government of Cambodia (RGC), 32
    CNGOs and, 63–64
    with VBNK, 64–66

salaries, 51, 63–64, 117, 144, 157, 168
Sangkum Reastr Niyum (People's Socialist
    Community), 9–10
satisfaction, 18
Scharmer, Otto, 126
schedule, 168
Schein, Edgar, 20, 33
schizophrenia, 32
Schoenberg, Karl, 140
Scholarship Fund, 59, 75n4
Seckon Leang, 110–11, 112
self-awareness, 181
self-censorship, 112
self-confidence, 58
self-control, 82
self-criticism, 43
self-development, 121
self-evaluation, 19, 87, 89
self-expression, 87, 110, 111–12, 134

self-portraits, 111
self-respect, 25
Senge, Peter, 14, 15, 16, 126
Seven Sisters, 122
shades of gray, 15
Shambhala Institute for Authentic Leader-
    ship, 126
shining star syndrome, 60–61
Sihanouk (king), 9–10, 11
sisterhood, 116
skilled incompetence, 19
sleep, disturbance of, 28, 189n1
social development organizations, 73
somatization, 27–29
Srey, Vanthorn, 147
Sri Lanka, 188
Staff Development Policy, VBNK, 97
standards, 69, 148
starvation, 10
stasis, 34, 41
status
    alternative, 147
    as obstacle, 13–14, 15–16, 19
    participation and, 81–82
    with training, 15–17
storytelling, 128, 182
Strategic Life Management program, 90
Strategic Plan, VBNK, 73, 90, 103, 143,
    157–58
Strengths, Weaknesses, Opportunities, and
    Threats (SWOT), 12
stress, 30, 109. *See also* post trauma stress
    disorder
Studies in Organisational Structure (Maclean
    and Srey), 147
Summerfield, Derek, 27, 32, 186, 187,
    189n1
supervision, 98–99
support agencies, 2–3, 57–58
survival, 39–40
survivor guilt, 186
SWOT. *See* Strengths, Weaknesses, Opportu-
    nities, and Threats

taxation, 17–18
teachers, 13–14

teamwork, 158–59
theory-in-use, 14–15, 19, 61
three-pronged approach, 132
Tibet, 68–70
time management, 145, 168
Time Out: A Creative Space for Expatriate
    Development Practitioners, 126
torture, 32
Tou Tony, 150
traditional Tibetan medicine (TTM), 69
training
    after recruitment, 82
    assessment of, 18
    in Cambodia, 4, 5–6, 77, 78, 99–101
    of CNGOs, 59
    contradiction in, 14–15
    creativity, 108–10, 111, 123, 125–26,
        132–33, 135–36
    customization of, 96, 115
    echo, 79
    facilitation of, 12–13
    gender awareness, 84
    of government, 64–66
    in management, 4, 17, 51, 99
    mentor with, 113–14
    open access to, 115–16
    self-development, 121
    status with, 15–17
    in strategic planning, 145
    transfer of, 14, 45n3, 113
    VBNK personnel, 77–85, 86, 87, 89–94,
        96–99, 103–4, 105, 108–12, 121,
        162
Training Unit, VBNK, 144, 145, 148
transfer of training, 14, 45n3, 113
transgenerational transmission, 33, 39
translation, 68, 69, 128
transparency, 62
trauma, complex
    in Cambodia, 5–6, 25–26, 33–34, 41,
        43–44
    culture and, 25–26, 29–30, 32, 34, 180,
        187, 189n1
    extreme traumatization, 188
    healing from, 5–6, 26–27, 30, 31–32
    PTSD from, 31–32, 185–86, 189n1

societal, 32–33, 187
Truth and Reconciliation Commission,
    46n12
TTM. *See* traditional Tibetan medicine

UN. *See* United Nations
UN60, 125
UNDP. *See* United Nations Development
    Programme
United Nations (UN), 11, 118, 125
United Nations Development Programme
    (UNDP), 118
UN Transitional Authority in Cambodia
    (UNTAC), 11
US Agency for International Development
    (USAID), 38, 51, 54

validation, 15
values
    in capacity development, 180–81
    change and, 179–80
    discrimination and, 24–25
    money and, 21–22
    practiced, 14–15, 19, 61–62
    at VBNK, 20–24
VBNK (Institute to Serve Facilitators of De-
    velopment), 2
    ALC at, 88, 90–91, 92–93, 94
    art at, 111
    board of, 159–61
    budgeting at, 141–42
    CDRA program and, 86–90
    change at, 156–58
    CHART, 46n7, 73, 121–23, 151–54
    with CNGOs, 59–60, 63, 71–72
    coaching by, 130–31, 137n2
    conferences by, 128–30
    creativity training at, 108–10, 111, 123,
        125–26, 132–33, 135–36
    criticism of, 16
    Development Café, 53, 127
    discrimination in, 24
    donors and, 66–67, 139–41, 152, 175
    funding for, 139–41, 142, 152, 175
    growth of, 142–43
    HR development strategy of, 97–98, 101

ideas from, 183–84
identity of, 112–13, 157
ILO projects, 71
influence, 75
INGO use of, 52–53, 67, 71, 72
localization, 169–77
management of, 169–71, 172, 173,
    174–76
mission statement of, 72–74
Organization Development Unit of, 143,
    144–45, 172, 173
personnel of, 77–85, 86, 87, 89–94,
    96–99, 103–4, 105, 108–12, 121,
    161–63
qualifications, 17
regional work by, 67–68
reputation, 112–13
Research and Publications Unit of, 146–
    51, 157
resistance in, 91, 101–2, 154, 156
RGC and, 64–66
Staff Development Policy of, 97
start of, 4
Strategic Plan of, 73, 90, 103, 143,
    157–58
structure of, 155, 156
sustainability of, 104, 183
teamwork at, 158–59
theory-in-use at, 14–15
in Tibet, 68–70
Training Unit, 144, 145, 148
values at, 20–24
victims, 39–40, 188
Vietnam, 9, 10
violence. *See also* trauma, complex
    domestic, 186–87
    mental illness and, 188–89

visas, 50
Volkan, Vamik, 32–33, 35
Voluntary Service Overseas (VSO), 5
voters, 53
VSO. *See* Voluntary Service Overseas

wall, of learning blocks, 95, 114
war, 9, 10, 45n1, 186, 187
Watkins, Jonathan, 188
whole person learning, 87
win-win, 81
WLP. *See* Women's Leadership Program
women, 16–17, 24
    in factories, 70–71
    in government, 118–19
    recruitment of, 77, 84, 144
    relationships of, 180
    rules for, 116–17
Women's Leadership Program (WLP),
    65–66, 113
    participation in, 117–18
    start of, 116
    success of, 118–19
workshops, 82, 125
World Bank's Water and Sanitation Program
    (WSP), 71
World Café, 127, 133
World Trade Organization (WTO), 69
writing, for self-expression, 87, 112
WSP. *See* World Bank's Water and Sanitation
    Program
WTO. *See* World Trade Organization

Youth Forum, 125

Zur, Judith, 187

About the Author

Jenny Pearson has lived and worked in Cambodia since 1995. She has qualifications in social work and management and worked in the public sector in England before coming to Cambodia. She arrived in Cambodia as a volunteer and went on to found and direct VBNK, Cambodia's leading capacity-building institution. She has played a leading role in developing the capacity of the not-for-profit sector in Cambodia, introducing creative approaches to capacity development and serving on the boards of several prominent development organizations. In 2007 she was a visiting fellow at the Institute of Development Studies in the United Kingdom. Since her retirement from VBNK in 2008, Jenny spends her time consulting and writing about capacity development, drawing on her years of experience to contribute the voice of practice to the international discourse on capacity development. She holds dual British and Cambodian citizenship and lives in a village outside Phnom Penh with her adopted Cambodian family.

Also From Kumarian Press . . .

Managing Development:

The Change Imperative:
Creating the Next Generation NGO
Paul Ronalds

Coping With Facts:
A Skeptic's Guide to the Problem of Development
Adam Fforde

Everywhere/Nowhere:
Gender Mainstreaming in Development Agencies
Rebecca Tiessen

Development Methods and Approaches:
Critical Reflections
Edited by Deborah Eade

New and Forthcoming:

Inside the Everyday Lives of Development Workers:
The Challenges and Futures of Aidland
Edited by Anne-Meike Fechter and Heather Hindman

The Politics of Collective Advocacy in India:
Tools and Traps
Nandini Deo and Duncan McDuie-Ra

Dual Disasters:
Humanitarian Aid After the 2004 Tsunami
Jennifer Hyndman

Advancing Nonprofit Stewardship Through Self-Regulation:
Translating Principles Into Practice
Christopher Corbett

Visit Kumarian Press at www.kpbooks.com or call toll-free
800.232.0223 for a complete catalog.

 Kumarian Press, located in Sterling, Virginia, is a forward-looking, scholarly press that promotes active international engagement and an awareness of global connectedness.